Fairleigh Dickinson University Library
Teaneck, New Jersey

Unruly Corporatism

UNRULY CORPORATISM

Associational Life
in Twentieth-Century Egypt

ROBERT BIANCHI

New York   Oxford
OXFORD UNIVERSITY PRESS
1989

Oxford University Press

Oxford   New York   Toronto
Delhi   Bombay   Calcutta   Madras   Karachi
Petaling Jaya   Singapore   Hong Kong   Tokyo
Nairobi   Dar es Salaam   Cape Town
Melbourne   Auckland

and associated companies in
Berlin   Ibadan

Copyright © 1989 by Oxford University Press, Inc.

Published by Oxford University Press, Inc.,
200 Madison Avenue, New York, New York 10016

Oxford is a registered trademark of Oxford University Press

Library of Congress Cataloging-in-Publication Data
Bianchi, Robert Richard, 1945–
Unruly corporatism : associational life
in twentieth-century Egypt / Robert Bianchi.
p.   cm.   Bibliography: p.   Includes index.
ISBN 0-19-506031-8
1. Corporate state—Egypt.
2. Egypt—Politics and government—1919–1952.
3. Egypt—Politics and government—1952–
I. Title.   HD3616.E32B53   1989   338.962—dc19   89-2862   CIP

9 8 7 6 5 4 3 2 1

Printed in the United States of America
on acid-free paper

For Layla

Preface

While writing this book I have incurred many debts and formed many friendships, both in Egypt and in the United States. From 1980 to 1984 I had the good fortune to live and travel in Egypt as a faculty member of the American University in Cairo. Hence, my field work coincided with a fateful period in modern Egyptian history during which many of that country's leading social scientists became not only my valued colleagues but my patient teachers as well. While many scholars helped to shape my understanding of Egypt's political, cultural, and socioeconomic development, none was more influential than Galal Amin, Heba Handoussa, ʿAli al-Din Hilal, and Saʿd al-Din Ibrahim. As the main lines of this study began to gel in Cairo, each of these Egyptian social scientists added a special dimension that confirmed my growing dissatisfaction with the manner in which American scholars were applying the notions of dependency, corporatism, and authoritarianism to the experiences of Egypt and the rest of the Third World. My critique and attempted revision of what I term "the syndrome of the semiperiphery" gradually evolved from four years of interchange and debate with my Egyptian counterparts at A.U.C.

Although my Egyptian colleagues helped me conceptualize the project, it was my students who were most important in carrying it out. At one time or another we all have research assistants. But how many of us have a voluntary and self-recruited team of multilingual students who collect documentation, arrange interviews, teach their native dialect, create and analyze data sets, see through the cultural and ideological biases that pervade Western studies of the Middle East, and turn seminars on political economy and interest group politics into wide-ranging debates over their country's future? To my frequent amazement and utter delight, this is precisely what emerged around my office and classrooms at A.U.C.

Some of the most energetic assistance came from Manal ʿAbd al-Majid, Hoda ʿAwad, Iman Bibars, Maha Dajani, Nahed Dajani, Aliya Dauda, Mushira al-Gaziri, Tariq al-Gohari, Maha al-Gharbawi, Layla al-Hajin, Bahi Ibrashi, Shahira Idris, Amani al-Khatib, Ashraf Muhsin, Nevine Qadri, Ruwaida Saʿd al-Din, ʿUmar Saʿd al-Din, Nihal al-Shimmi, Nevine Yussuf, and Nihal Yussuf.

The Center for Strategic Studies at al-Ahram offered several opportunities for informal meetings with Egyptian intellectuals and journalists who shared my interest in associational life. I am grateful to al-Sayyid Yassin and Ahmad Bahaʾ al-Din for encouraging me to revive the question of Nasserism and its complex legacy for contemporary group politics. In the past few years the center has become an important sponsor of original research on occupational associations and religious groups, including the work of Amani Qandil and Mustafa Kamal al-Saʿid.

A number of government agencies cooperated in providing detailed enumerations of association membership, including breakdowns by year, by province, and by social or occupational category. Many officials in the Ministries of Agriculture, Awqaf, Manpower and Vocational Training, and Social Affairs expended considerable effort to provide data that was both comprehensive and up-to-date.

The generosity of official agencies was more than equaled by leaders, administrators, and members of syndicates and chambers, unions and cooperatives, associations and societies who supplied documentation, who invited me to their meetings, and who candidly shared their personal views and experiences. Although some of them would be gratified to be thanked in print, I believe they would be even more pleased to know that my pledges of confidentiality were entirely sincere.

Among the many foreigners who inundated Egypt during the early 1980s, a small group of friends and fellow field workers stood out. Hamied Ansari, Kirk Beattie, Chris Eccel, Everett Rowson, Susan al-Shammy, and John Stewart were good neighbors and great companions.

At each stage of the research and writing there were a number of more experienced "Egyptologists" who gave timely encouragement, knowing full well that many of my conclusions and interpretations would differ from their own. As a student of co-optation, it seems at least a bit ironic that I should have been the beneficiary of so much kindness from my predecessors in the field, particularly Raymond Baker, Leonard Binder, Louis Cantori, John Esposito, Iliya Harik, Michael Hudson, the late Malcom Kerr, Clement Henry Moore, John Voll, and John Waterbury.

After returning to the United States, I had several opportunities to attend conferences where I presented early drafts of certain chapters. Three international meetings were especially important forums for discussing the broader theoretical implications of the work with scholars from Europe and the Middle East. I would like to thank the National Science Foundation for supporting my participation in the World Congress of the International Political Science Association in Paris during July of 1985. The Social Science Research Council and the American Council of Learned Societies sponsored some exciting if inconclusive debates during their conference "Retreating States and Expanding Societies: The State Autonomy/Informal Civil Society Dialectic in the Middle East and North Africa" held in Aix-en-Provence in March 1988. The following month Georgetown University's Center for Contemporary Arab Studies brought together an impressive group of Egyptian and American scholars in Washington, D.C., to discuss "Egypt 1988: Critical Choices."

Parts of two chapters were published previously. Portions of chapter 5 appeared in "The Corporatization of the Egyptian Labor Movement," *Middle East Journal* 40 (Summer 1986), and portions of chapter 7 were published in "Interest Group Politics in the Third World," *Third World Quarterly* 8 (April 1986). Revised versions of both pieces have been included in the current study with permission.

I would also like to thank David Laitin, Lloyd Rudolph, Susanne Rudolph, and Bernard Silberman, my friends at the University of Chicago who commented on early drafts and chapters of the manuscript, as well as Jefferson Gray who gave cheerful and timely aid during the hectic months of rewriting.

Finally, I am most grateful to Valerie Aubry and her colleagues at Oxford University Press for their extraordinary combination of competence and good humor in guiding me through each phase of publication.

Chicago   R.B.
May 1989

Contents

Unruly Corporatism

1

Dependent Development, Corporatism, and Authoritarianism

Egypt is not a country that deals kindly with stereotypes and conventional wisdom. Egyptians do not mirror the generally dualistic images that dominate our commonsense thinking and social scientific discourse. Foreign visitors frequently discover that classic distinctions between "traditional" and "modern," "urban" and "rural," "religious" and "secular" can blur or evaporate before their bags are unpacked. A week or two of exploring the markets, visiting neighbors, and working in virtually any complex organization is sufficient to challenge our most basic assumptions about the dichotomous nature of "capitalist" and "socialist," "public" and "private," "civilian" and "military," "state" and "society."

Viewed through the polarizing prism of familiar categories and expectations, Egypt is bound to appear as a land of anomalies. Even by the cosmopolitan standards of Mediterranean cultures, Egyptian society tolerates and at times actively encourages what might be considered the most improbable mélange of contradictory elements. Indeed, in many areas of Egyptian life, it seems that the anomaly is the norm.

Egypt possesses a highly segmented mixed economy in which production and distribution are (dis)organized around a multitude of sectors:

3

public, private, foreign, cooperative, syndical, military, Islamic, informal, and illegal. Firms in each sector operate under different rules and often pursue divergent goals. Different types of enterprises may collaborate in joint ventures or they may compete for resources and markets. Mostly, however, they are content to ignore one another and go their separate ways as long as a tacit division of labor preserves their niches from the threat of outside encroachment.

One of the most notorious examples of the coexistence of what are presumed to be hostile economic sectors is visible in the operations of the black market. For many years the government tolerated a brisk illegal traffic in foreign exchange that thrived on the chronic shortage of hard currency among local importers, the desire to repatriate the earnings of Egyptian workers abroad, and the rapidly growing communities of resident foreigners. Gradually, an extensive underground network of currency smugglers emerged, linking Egypt's villages and provincial towns with banks in Europe and the Gulf.

By 1984 many of President Mubarak's economic advisers were insisting that the government had to regain control over the supply of money in order to curb inflation and to redirect investment away from the overstimulated trade and banking sectors in favor of more productive industrial and agricultural ventures. They prepared sweeping reforms of the banking and foreign trade regimes, including a vigorous crackdown on many of the largest money changers. When state prosecutors insisted on pursuing penalties of confiscation and imprisonment, the government found itself pulled into a bitter tug-of-war with the black marketeers that lasted more that a year.

The currency smugglers presented the government with a clear ultimatum. They vowed to increase the price of foreign exchange every week until the government released their arrested comrades, rescinded the new regulations, and fired the minister who had sponsored them. As the cost of money soared, ex-ministers who held high posts in the ruling party asserted that some of the leading clients of the black market were state enterprises that had been unable to find adequate financing through the banking system.

Responding to businessmen's intense dissatisfaction with the economic dislocation that accompanied this confrontation, the prime minister himself took the lead in killing the new regulations only two months after they were promulgated. Almost simultaneously the minister of economy, the leading target of the black marketeers' opposition, was forced to resign when his own family was implicated in currency smuggling. What had begun as a rather naive, technocratic effort to reassert a modicum of state control over monetary policy ended with a sudden government retreat and an embarrassing admission of the state's routine reliance on well organized, criminal activity.[1]

Just as Egypt's leading economic actors violate our notions of "public" versus "private" and "legal" versus "illegal," the behavior of its defense and security forces contradicts expectations about the relations between "civilian" and "military," "state" and "society." The army's high visibility in and around the major cities sometimes creates the aura of a garrison state, yet many of these soldiers are not carrying arms and some who are do not have permission to load live ammunition. The strong military presence signifies not merely the regime's nervousness over internal security but the steady expansion of the army into activities that generally are the responsibility of civilians: laying new telephone cables and repairing broken water mains, operating high-tech bakeries and running gigantic chicken farms.

Military commanders try to justify their growing role as managers and entrepreneurs by arguing that whenever the army can fulfill its needs through its own production, a major burden is removed from the rest of the economy. However, the nature of peacetime military production has been shifting more and more from foodstuffs and uniforms to arms and munitions and, more recently, to consumer durables such as washing machines and refrigerators. As the army pursues greater self-sufficiency by expanding and diversifying production, it is advancing greater claims to scarce investment capital alongside the claims of the conventional economic sectors.[2]

The entrepreneurial army remains a key pillar of the regime, prepared to guarantee public order when the regular police forces cannot. Recently, however, the most spectacular popular disturbance requiring military intervention originated not in civil society but among another contingent of the state apparatus whose isolated and impoverished condition continued unrelieved while the army was receiving greater attention and a larger share of public resources. The Central Security Forces are peasant conscripts trained as a kind of auxiliary police force to help maintain public order in the cities, but they are never allowed to settle their families among the other "urban villagers" who constitute the bulk of Cairo's working-class neighborhoods. Instead, they were confined to an encampment near the Great Pyramids where the casual opulence of nearby tourist hotels seemed to mock the hardship of the women and children who lined up outside the barracks for weekend visits.

Learning that the government intended to extend their tours of duty by a full year, the security police touched off the longest and most violent street riots in a decade. The revolt quickly spread to other barracks in the city and its southern suburbs, but in each case there was a clear pattern to the destruction that deliberately focused on the newer hotels and office buildings that most clearly symbolized the marriage of Egypt's *nouveaux riches* businessmen with foreign investors.

The spectacle of a street riot organized by the riot police is certainly a contradiction in terms, but it is hardly more anomalous than private businesses masquerading as government agencies, than public enterprises enlisting the aid of admitted felons, or than army units manufacturing washing machines. The policemen's revolt highlighted one of the most paradoxical features of the Egyptian political system: the remarkable degree to which the authoritarian regime fears its own people (including state employees) and its surprising responsiveness to demonstrations of discontent by the poor and the powerless.

The power of the street has induced swift policy "corrections" on a number of occasions. The "bread riots" of January 1977 led to a cancellation of cuts in food subsidies. The assassination of Anwar Sadat pushed the regime to seek a rapprochement with the opposition parties and with the rest of the Arab world. After the bitter protests caused by the interception of an Egyptian airliner by the United States in the autumn of 1985, Mubarak tried to distance himself from Washington. He also allowed the government press to publish scathing criticisms of Egypt's pro-U.S. foreign policy, including attacks on the Camp David accords that just a few weeks earlier would have been inconceivable even in the opposition parties' newspapers. The policemen's revolt in February 1986 was followed almost immediately by yet another postponement of planned reductions in consumer-goods subsidies despite the insistent demands of Egypt's foreign creditors. The plasticity of Egyptian authoritarianism is evident not only in its strategic retreats after such eruptions of mass fury and desperation but in its willingness to be worn down by protracted struggles arising from the daily defiance of unpopular and unenforceable laws.

Similarly, in the spheres of culture and religion one finds a diversity of opinion and styles of piety at odds with the common assumption that the renewed attachment to Islam and Islamic law represents a regressive or monolithic yearning for theocracy. The "Islamic revival" and "Islamic dress" enjoy their most enthusiastic support not in the most backward regions and social strata but in the bustling provincial capitals of the Delta and Upper Egypt, especially among university students enrolled in the most competitive and technologically oriented faculties and professional schools.

The growing preference of well-educated Muslim women for modest dress in no way suggests their rejection of modern roles; more often it is a statement of their determination to preserve their privacy and independence as they assume new prominence and visibility in the work force and in public life. Single women in the universities and the professions have taken the lead in creating a new trend in fashion by adopting a variety of often stylish head coverings and loose fitting garments that symbolize not only their devoutness but also their demand to be treated seriously and respectfully as they pursue modern careers.[3]

Egypt's Islamic movement is commonly identified with the most extreme and violent underground organizations, yet these secret societies are painfully aware of their isolation from and rejection by virtually all of the legitimate branches of the movement. ʿAbd al-Salam Faraj, the spiritual leader of the Jihad organization that planned the assassination of Anwar Sadat, provided vivid testimony of his contempt for the gradualist and accommodationist strategies of the various groups competing for preeminence among Egyptian Muslims. His tract on the necessity of armed struggle against Egypt's "apostate regime," *al-Farida al-Gha'iba* (The neglected duty), explicitly denounced every major Islamic organization in the country, including al-Azhar, the Sufi orders, the Islamic benevolent societies, the Muslim Brotherhood, antigovernment *shuyukh,* the Islamic associations, and even previously unsuccessful revolutionary groups. One could hardly imagine a more poignant expression of the extremists' despair in finding reliable allies among organized Muslims.[4]

Ironically, even Faraj seemed to understand that the principal demand of the Islamic movement, the adoption of the *shariʿa* as the law of the land, can be substantially advanced in Egypt by incrementalism, bargaining, and pressure group activity. In a rare display of realism, he observed that contemporary Egypt does not conform to either of the ideal types most frequently invoked by advocates of the *shariʿa.* It is not an iniquitous "Meccan society" in which a minority of Muslims are persecuted by unbelievers nor a virtuous "Medinan community" in which life is organized according to the Qur'an and the example of the Prophet. Rather, Egypt exemplifies a third and mixed type of community in which Meccan and Medinan themes coexist and struggle for preeminence. It is a society of Muslims, but not a Muslim society. The majority are true Muslims, but their laws are a confused blend of foreign codes imposed by the imperialists, of local customs that have survived the conversion to Islam, and of particular elements of God's law—all combined in changing proportions depending on the whim of the ruler.

Nevertheless, according to Faraj, this corrupt condition is less sinful than states in which law is altogether unrelated to and unaffected by the *shari'a*. In this uncharacteristic passage the author of *al-Farida al-Gha'iba* himself conveys some appreciation of the room for negotiation and improvement that is perceived by most Egyptian proponents of the *shari'a* who are increasingly confident that peaceful missionary activity and patient politicking can produce a closer approximation of their vision of a just society. Thus, Faraj's radicalism highlights the inherent conservatism of the Islamic movement as a whole. It is, after all, a movement whose principal demand is not revolution but the implementation of a system of law—a system that has been distinguished by its traditional support of private property, social hierarchy, and political compromise.

Egyptians are well aware of the pervasive eclecticism and inconsistencies that characterize their economic, political, and cultural life. Indeed, much of their public discourse and personal humor is inspired by such concerns. Often, however, they are divided or ambivalent as to whether these tendencies represent vices or virtues. On one hand, eclecticism is regarded as evidence of corruption and hypocrisy, of deadlock and random motion, of the chaos of millions of isolated quests for survival based on improvised adaptations (sometimes ingenious, sometimes pathetic) with no overall design or direction. In the stilted, technocratic language that Mubarak adopted during his early days in office, these characteristics were described as "laxness" *(tasayub)*. For several weeks, television ads featured a valiant cartoon figure, wielding a sledgehammer and chipping away at a gigantic representation of the word *ma'lish*—the popular expression of complacency and reassurance that the government tried to portray as an indomitable public enemy.

On the other hand, the same characteristics are also viewed as signs of tolerance and flexibility, of resourcefulness and adaptiveness, of self-control and equanimity. This does not suggest passive resignation or "fatalism" so much as a sober recognition of inherent limitations on the power to change one's conditions or one's countrymen, as well as an understanding that, beyond a certain point, insistence on greater control and uniformity is likely to be futile and self-defeating. Much of the tragedy of Anwar Sadat stemmed from his reckless indifference to these inherent limitations as he trampled upon vested interests and popular sensibilities that were offended by his increasingly autocratic rule. Although his successor has been described as timid and indecisive by comparison, one of the key strengths of the Mubarak regime has been its willingness to acknowledge the limits of power and its readiness to bargain with organized groups and oppositions instead of trying to crush them.

Especially since Sadat's assassination, Egypt's rulers have begun to realize more than ever that eclecticism in economy, polity, and culture can serve some very useful purposes and that this may be precisely why it is so prevalent and persistent. Despite its self-evident irrationality in economic terms, the incoherence of institutions and policies has a strong appeal to leaders of a crisis-ridden authoritarian regime who desperately wish to avoid clear-cut choices between "purer" models of capitalism versus socialism, democracy versus despotism, secularism versus an Islamic state. Fearful of the social unrest and political opposition that such choices would inevitably provoke, Egypt's rulers have tried to promote a live-and-let-live attitude among antagonistic interests and ideologies without relinquishing power to any of them.

Consequently, a compartmentalized economy, a state bureaucracy riddled with special interests, and a thriving Islamic counterculture have had to serve as crude substitutes for a more inclusive system of interest representation. Taken together, they reflect the underlying diversity and vitality of competing social groups that are still inadequately integrated into the nation's political process despite two decades of repeated assurances from the ruling elite that it is committed to a transition to democracy. The increasing incoherence of policy and institutions amounts to a kind of "strategic compromise" (although by no means a full-scale retreat) by the state in the face of long-term advances by several well-organized special interests.

The beleaguered authoritarian elite evidently regards such arrangements as a useful defense mechanism that will buy it time by discouraging the emergence of strong interest group coalitions and opposition movements. But relying on such defense mechanisms as an alternative to genuine political reform is also a great gamble—and a very risky one at that because Egypt's increasingly desperate economic situation virtually rules out the possibility that demands for the wider sharing of power can be bought off with greater material rewards.

For the social scientist, these "discoveries" about Egypt's economic, political, and cultural incoherence are both vexing and rewarding—vexing because they come only after a period of culture shock and inelegant adjustment to what a fellow foreign resident aptly described as a "constant assault upon the senses"; rewarding because they breed a healthy and invaluable skepticism toward many of the concepts and assumptions that we bring to "the field."

The social scientist's task is to enlist this on-the-ground realism in refining and refashioning theory, not in demolishing it. This is particularly important for those of us working in the Middle East, but it is often more difficult than we realize. On one hand, many of us are eager to move beyond the traditional confines of area studies by placing our work in broader comparative perspective and providing it with clearer theoretical import. The desire to "mainstream" our research naturally leads us to import paradigms from other regions where scholarship has been more innovative, hoping that their breakthroughs can spill over and inspire similar advances in our own thinking. In recent years this expectation has led many Middle Eastern specialists (me included) to a growing interest in adapting concepts that have enjoyed great popularity in Latin American studies and that are becoming more widely diffused in other areas of the Third World.

On the other hand, even the most enthusiastic and shameless poachers among us understand that such borrowing is most fruitful when it is selective, critical, and reinterpretive. The goal is not to recycle theory but to reformulate it. As we extend new paradigms to additional cases where they have obvious relevance, it is important to highlight aspects of the new cases that most seriously confound or contradict the expectations of those paradigms. Often it is precisely such apparent anomalies and unanticipated findings that prove to be indispensable in reshaping prevailing theory, especially when they are observable in a number of other cases as well. Hence, students of the Middle East are by no means bound to be theoretical "free riders" relying on innovations in other regions; they can also look forward to playing a more vigorous role in the interdisciplinary and interregional debates that are generating and transforming social science theory.

Egypt's experience is particularly pertinent to ongoing debates over three "Latin American" concepts that are being applied with increasing frequency to countries in other regions, including the Middle East: "dependent development," "corporatism," and the distinction between "populist authoritarianism" and "bureaucratic authoritarianism." All of these terms have become fairly common elements in the lexicon used by analysts of Egypt's political economy. This applies not only to Western social scientists but also to many Egyptian intellectuals, especially the most outspoken critics of policy changes in the post-Nasser era.

Indeed, within Egypt the debate over the legacy of Nasserism has never stopped. Its open revival under the Mubarak regime has served to frame ideological and policy alternatives in terms that are strikingly similar to notions of dependency versus self-sufficiency, corporatism versus pluralism, triple alliances versus populist alliances. It is either the genius or the fatal flaw of the Mubarak regime (depending on one's point of view) that it has tried to represent and placate all of these contradictory tendencies at the same time.

How can this convergence of interest and vocabulary among foreign social scientists and native Egyptian critics contribute to the revision of prevailing assumptions about dependent development, corporatism, and authoritarianism? Does Egypt's experience provide examples of these phenomena that may be more relevant to other countries in the Middle East and elsewhere in the Third World than the Latin American models that are so often used as points of reference for comparative analysis?

Students of political economy in the non-Western world commonly view dependency, corporatism, and authoritarianism as mutually reinforcing processes that combine in shaping what might be termed a "syndrome of the semiperiphery." Analysts may differ as to which of these subprocesses is antecedent to the others—which is the driving force or linchpin and which is the eventual by-product or ineluctable concomitant. Nevertheless, there is remarkable agreement that "late developers" are particularly susceptible to the "elective affinity" between the denationalization of economic decision making, the emergence of contrived, state-manipulated systems of interest representation, and the appearance of authoritarian regimes that employ rising levels of coercion to advance the interests of increasingly narrow social coalitions.

Throughout the 1970s it seemed that Anwar Sadat was pulling Egypt deeper and deeper into precisely this sort of "semiperipheral syndrome." Yet each step in that direction also promoted powerful countertendencies that made additional steps far more difficult. While Sadat's murder did not "rescue" Egypt from this syndrome, it certainly demonstrated that Egyptian society possessed a number of potent antibodies capable of mounting a sustained and, at times, coordinated resistance.

If Sadat fatally misjudged his own society's vulnerability to the combined effects of dependency, corporatism, and authoritarianism, he was by no means out of step with the views of his counterparts in many other Third World countries or with the assumptions of social scientists who have inspired so much of their recent thinking. Sadat's setbacks should not be understood in terms of an idiosyncratic "Egyptian exceptionalism" but as an invitation to reassess the prevailing (and perhaps overly pessimistic) paradigms of political and economic "underdevelopment" in late-industrializing societies. There are three areas in which Egypt's experience contradicts the expectations of Latin American observers who have elaborated the "semiperipheral syndrome" and urged its application in other regions.

First, it has been extremely difficult to shape harmonious alliances between state, multinational, and local private capital. The effort to promote dependent development under the aegis of a weak and unstable triple alliance has stimulated widespread demands for a renewal of economic nationalism—demands that have been embraced by the Mubarak government itself as it acknowledges and attempts to correct earlier errors in economic policy.

Second, a differentiated and flexible network of corporatist groups has helped to buttress authoritarian rule as long as it has left a degree of maneuver for weak and isolated opponents. But attempts to squeeze interest representation into a tighter corporatist straightjacket have provoked political disorder and aided the rise of a more powerful opposition demanding the transition to pluralist democracy.

Third, an earlier experiment with "populist authoritarianism" during the Nasser era left a lasting and troublesome legacy that is frequently described as an impediment to further industrialization. This has encouraged a new coalition of army officers, technocrats, and businessmen, including some who might be tempted to advance dependent development by imposing a more repressive "bureaucratic authoritarianism." Nevertheless, the enduring strength of many syndical organizations inherited from the Nasser era, coupled with a newly invigorated Islamic movement, has removed any illusion that such a regime could be installed without great bloodshed and economic dislocation. Thus Egypt's previous experience with populist authoritarianism has served more as a long-term deterrent against bureaucratic authoritarianism than as its unwitting forerunner.

Dependent Development

In many ways Egypt is a preeminent candidate for the type of dependent economic development described by Henrique Cardoso, Enzo Faletto, and Peter Evans.[5] Along with Turkey and Iran it is a leading Middle Eastern member of the industrializing "semiperiphery." It has passed through an extended period of prior industrialization, endowing it with a substantial and diversified manufacturing base that is outmoded and inefficient, requiring large infusions of foreign capital and technology if it is to achieve a measure of competitiveness in the international marketplace. It possesses a large and attractive domestic market, including a cosmopolitan middle class with a strong demand for consumer goods that was pent up by years of revolutionary egalitarianism and wartime austerity.

Moreover, its economic planners, businessmen, and intellectuals widely agree that the resumption of industrialization is an inescapable imperative in the face of expanding population and diminishing returns from agriculture. It possesses an "autonomous state" ruled by an authoritarian elite that has demonstrated the ability to shift its social bases of support while implementing radical changes in economic policy. It has accomplished a decisive reorientation of international alliances from the socialist to the capitalist bloc, involving an economic as well as diplomatic opening to the "core countries" of the "world system."

Nevertheless, Egyptian efforts to promote dependent development have produced conspicuously modest results. Evans, in particular, portrays dependent development as a harmonious and self-sustaining network of transnational alliances. But Egypt's experience demonstrates that it might more realistically be viewed as a protracted and highly conflictual process that is likely to become stalled or reversed at any stage unless a number of disparate actors periodically redefine their division of labor and renegotiate their balance of power. Whereas Evans suggests that dependent development promotes the suspension or suppression of politics in the pursuit of common economic interests, the Egyptian example highlights the degree to which dependent development can be initiated, shaped, and limited by continuous political competition.

The fitful and tentative nature of Egypt's experiment with dependent development is attributable to three factors that are seldom cited by Latin American writers: the great powers' continuing perception of Egypt as a key actor in international relations; the difficulty of forging stable and mutually beneficial "triple alliances" between state, multinational, and local private capital; and widespread ideological and cultural resistance to large-scale foreign participation in the economy from the mutually reinforcing traditions of nationalism, socialism, and Islam.

Dependent development in Egypt has been both aided and hindered by the country's pivotal role in world affairs. The eagerness of the United States to pry Egypt out of the Soviet orbit and to reward its nonbelligerency with Israel inspired one of the most huge commitments of foreign economic assistance since the Marshall Plan. In the short term government-to-government aid was intended to underwrite Sadat's pledge to the Egyptian people that peace would be accompanied by a new era of prosperity. In the long term it also was intended to pave the way for direct investment by foreign firms, who were encouraged to participate in a private sector renaissance by entering into joint ventures with local entrepreneurs.[6]

In fact, multinational investors have been extremely reluctant to replace donor states as the major providers of foreign capital and technology. Generous concessions and legal assurances against nationalization have not dispelled apprehensions about investing in a country where war and revolution remain constant threats no matter how firmly the regime and its foreign backers proclaim their commitment to peace and stability. The same unpredictability that induced Western governments to invest so heavily in Egypt has deterred foreign businesses from assuming more than modest risks. Consequently, the driving force behind dependent development continues to be intergovernmental relations rather than direct collaboration between local and multinational businessmen.

Furthermore, the highly politicized nature of U.S. assistance has engendered so much resentment among its recipients that even its original diplomatic objectives are in jeopardy. It is widely believed in Egypt that the generosity of the aid is exceeded only by the strings that Congress has attached to its volume and utilization. The total amount of assistance is always set well below the level received by Israel, and the methods of disbursement are considerably more restrictive. Much of the aid finances a growing national debt and vital food imports rather than productive enterprises. This, in turn, provides Egypt's creditors with increasing leverage for reshaping national economic policy in many fields, such as investment, public sector management, consumer subsidies, foreign trade, banking, and exchange rates.[7]

Egyptian leaders are understandably perplexed and embittered by relentless pressure from their allies to impose unpopular austerity measures, even when they agree in principle to their desirability. The Mubarak government feels that it is caught up in an odd type of U.S. brinkmanship in which its major Western backer vacillates between an insistence on "opening" Egypt more and more to the pressures of foreign competition and a fear of pushing so hard that it "loses" Egypt altogether. Instead of priming the pump for a new flow of foreign private investment, the aid program has gone a long way toward poisoning the well of bilateral relations. In response, Egypt's leaders are trying to reassert a modicum of control over their own economy through a modest revival of economic nationalism that might somehow reconcile what are now thought to be the excesses of both Nasserism and Sadatism.

Intergovernmental conflicts are by no means the most serious obstacle to dependent development in Egypt. Although Evans skillfully elaborates the operation of mature triple alliances in various economic sectors, he seriously underestimates the difficulties in fashioning and maintaining such alliances. The multiplicity and competitiveness of actors in the Egyptian economy point to the need to disaggregate conventional categories such as the "state sector," "foreign capital," and the "private sector" so that attention can be focused on divisions and rivalries within these groups instead of assuming a tendency toward greater collaboration between them.

Egypt's vast government bureaucracy is itself deeply divided over the proper strategy of economic development. These conflicts are reflected in numerous disputes between cabinet ministers representing different constituencies, in the high turnover of officials in the key economic ministries, and in recurrent revisions and reversals of economic policy. Two lines of interagency cleavage are particularly persistent sources of bureaucratic infighting. Ministries concerned with coordinating policies that affect the economy as a whole (Finance, Planning, Economy and Foreign Trade, and Interior) are frequently aligned against virtually all other ministries that are responsible for regulating particular economic sectors and social groups. In addition, regulatory agencies that are heavily penetrated by special business interests (Investment, Supply, Construction, Industry, Transportation, Energy, and Agriculture) are often opposed by welfare ministries that distribute benefits to much larger and poorer constituencies (Manpower and Technical Training, Social Affairs and Insurance, Health, Education, Youth, Pious Foundations, and Cooperatives).

As these interagency rivalries become entangled in a growing number of hotly contested policy disputes, embattled ministers have greater incentives to seek support for their positions outside the government—and often outside the country. This provides multiple points of access and influence for businessmen's associations that frequently are able to amend or annul unfavorable government initiatives despite their own weaknesses and disagreements. The widening interface of a more divided state bureaucracy and a more densely organized private sector helps to explain much of the tentativeness and drift of Egypt's recent economic policy.

As Egypt's private businessmen have become more organized and more assertive politically, they also have become more keenly aware of their differences with one another and with their foreign partners and competitors. The Mubarak government has responded to the pleas of local capitalists by providing them with most of the privileges and incentives previously reserved for foreign or joint venture firms and by encouraging foreign investors to enter into more partnerships with Egyptian entrepreneurs. By strengthening the bargaining position of local businessmen vis-à-vis foreign capital, Mubarak has tried to moderate some of the tensions that have been accumulating in the nascent private sector alliance that Sadat created but could not consolidate. The state remains committed to foreign investment as a key instrument for the reindustrialization of Egypt, but it is under enormous pressure to carve out a larger piece of the action for its clients in the local business community, especially those who are well connected with the ruling National Democratic Party.[8]

The National Democratic Party has tried to operate as the principal steering committee of Egypt's private sector, aggregating its demands, arbitrating its internal conflicts, and serving as its conduit for state largess. However, with the proliferation of specialized businessmen's associations during the past decade, the party is encountering more and more difficulty in performing its harmonizing role between business and government. It has been forced to defend policies that clearly discriminate in favor of certain business interests and against others. It has been directly implicated in a string of spectacular business scandals. And its preferred candidates are regularly challenged by dissident factions in the elections of business chambers and professional syndicates.

Divisions within the private sector have been sharpened considerably by the Mubarak government's attempt to reorient the strategy of dependent development from a "consumptive opening" (infitah istihlaki), allowing quick profits from importing, construction, and banking, toward a "productive opening" (infitah intaji), encouraging long-term investment in manufacturing and agriculture. All of the major businessmen's groups quickly lined up with their own responses to this shift in policy— some offering their help in implementing it, others trying to bend it to their advantage, and still others hoping to subvert it. The government's ability to salvage the main outlines of its new developmental strategy has stemmed less from its own commitment and coherence than from the growing pluralism and fragmentation of organized business.

As with the other two components in Evans's conception of the triple alliance, foreign capital must also be disaggregated when examining the Egyptian pattern of dependent development. Egypt's external investors include an impressive assortment of donor states, international organizations, financial consortia, multinational corporations, Islamic banks, family firms, and individual entrepreneurs. Foreign governments and banks have valued Egypt's political support enough to renegotiate loans and soften demands for economic reform on a routine basis. Private investors eager to obtain a privileged foothold in the Egyptian market have been willing to accept a number of costly conditions for doing business, such as shifting from importing to local production, forming partnerships with local firms, and supporting a dense network of consultants, middlemen, and political fixers.

The role of Arab capital, primarily from the Gulf countries, is so different from other types of foreign capital that in the case of Egypt it might be more appropriate to speak of quadruple alliances instead of triple alliances. The modest and irregular flow of direct investment from other Arab countries has been one of the greatest disappointments of the infitah era. During the oil boom of the 1970s it was assumed that a combination of Arab capital and Western technology would provide the driving force for the rebirth of the private sector and the renewal of industrialization. The Arab League boycott of Egypt after the Camp David accords cut the flow of Arab investment drastically, and it resumed only when Mubarak sought a rapprochement with Sadat's old adversaries in the Arab world by reasserting a degree of political independence from the United States.

Even after Egypt's "return" to the Arab world, however, the resumption of Arab investment is viewed as a mixed blessing because it does not appear to serve either the regime's economic strategy or its domestic political allies. Arab investors have shown little regard for the new emphasis on productive enterprises. The bulk of their financing is still directed toward the safe but overstimulated sectors of luxury housing, tourism, and banking, which Egyptian planners now regard as major sources of inflation.[9]

Egypt's leaders also have reason to fear that the growth of Arab investment may have undesirable political consequences. Arab businessmen do not generally enter into joint ventures with local partners and supporters of the ruling party. If there is a segment of the local business community that benefits directly from Arab investment, it is probably the old members of the Muslim Brotherhood who took up residence in the Gulf during their exile from Egypt and who once again have become a leading force in the Islamic opposition to the current regime. Given the modest developmental gains and the potentially high political costs of Arab investment, it is not surprising that Egypt has remained content with a more indirect form of economic linkage to the Gulf via remittances from overseas Egyptian workers and revenues from oil transport through the Suez Canal.

The most serious obstacles to dependent development in Egypt lie not in the unpredictability of the international system or the lack of coordination among different types of capitalists but in particularly tenacious ideological and cultural opposition from the country's strong socialist and religious traditions. From the very beginning of the open door period, both leftist and Islamic critics have been vigilant in exposing evidence of "neoimperialism" and in resisting its threats to the "historic gains" of the Nasserist revolution or to the "authenticity" of Egyptian culture. The gradual convergence of these forces has inspired an important revival of economic nationalism that has been embraced by the Mubarak regime itself even as it attempts to strengthen its ties with foreign capital and local private enterprise.

Over the past decade Egypt's economists, social scientists, and journalists have produced a rich literature in Arabic on dependency *(taba'iya)* that resonates many of the themes of their Latin American counterparts in a distinctively Egyptian idiom. Their work combines a wide range of intellectual traditions and styles, including scholarly research, techno-cratic analysis, political satire, muckraking reportage, and partisan po-lemics. Their indictments of the *infitah* period cluster around a number of common issues that have become the core domain of public debate about economic policy in the opposition parties, in the syndical move-ment, and in the cabinet.[10]

Egyptian critics of dependent development have focused their attacks on what they regard as the detrimental consequences of the increasing privatization of the economy and its heightened vulnerability to fluctua-tions in international markets. The thrust of their assault has been directed against the state's retreat from central economic planning; the diversion of public resources for private enrichment; disinvestment in public sector industry; the abandonment of wage earners and consumers to the anarchy of the market; mounting trade deficits and foreign indebtedness; uncon-trolled inflation and increases in the cost of living; growing inequalities in income distribution; the neglect of low-cost public housing in favor of luxury apartments, office buildings, and resort hotels; inadequate govern-ment regulation of importing, banking, and construction; and the wide-spread corruption of businessmen with political connections in the ruling party.

In contrast to conventional theorists of dependency such as Paul Baran, André Gundar Frank, and Samir Amin, Egyptian critics of post-Nasserist economic policy do not contend that the "core" countries of world cap-italism are trying to confine Egypt to a permanent state of economic stag-nation and underdevelopment.[11] Instead, they argue that Egypt has em-barked upon a distorted and externally controlled pattern of growth that has created a false sense of prosperity among the privileged while ignor-ing the basic needs of the masses. Egyptian critics are closer to theorists of dependent development such as Cardoso, Faletto, and Evans in por-traying foreign economic penetration as the result of overtures from local political and business elites seeking to fashion collaborative transnational alliances. They see dependency as invited from within rather than im-posed from abroad, as overstimulating the service sectors of the economy rather than locking it into monoculture and unequal exchange.

Compared to Latin American observers, Egyptian writers are far less optimistic that foreign capital will stimulate any serious renewal of in-dustrial growth, to say nothing of a Brazilian-style "economic miracle." Their fear is not so much that greater foreign investment will lead to the

denationalization of industry but that it will fail to promote industrialization at all. However, they are much more confident than their counterparts in Latin America that the Egyptian state can redefine the role of foreign capital to advance a type of industrialization that will be more compatible with their concerns for national independence and social equity. These Egyptian intellectuals give surprisingly little credence to the notion that the price of modern industry is the surrender of economic decision making. They view dependent development not as a prepackaged, take-it-or-leave-it formula imposed by imperialist hegemons but as a bad bargain that can be renegotiated if Egypt's rulers are prodded toward a more assertive defense of the national interest.

These critics believe that Egypt's leaders have become complacent about industrialization because of excessive reliance on external sources of hard currency, such as foreign aid, petroleum exports, Suez Canal revenues, and remittances from overseas workers. Egyptian writers often describe dependent development as a false sense of security that has been generated by unreliable flows of foreign exchange, flows that are constantly threatened by fluctuations in the international demand for oil and by strains in diplomatic relations with the United States. They characterize these resources as windfall earnings to which Egypt has become dangerously addicted, and accuse the architects of the *infitah* of squandering these revenues instead of devoting them to projects that might enhance the long-term prospects for self-sufficiency by strengthening the industrial and agricultural base of the economy. Their criticisms have been instrumental in persuading the Mubarak government to renegotiate the conditions under which foreigners can do business in Egypt, giving priority to investment in manufacturing and food production and requiring the greater use of local labor and raw materials.

Many of these writers have broadened their conception of dependent development to include an important cultural dimension. Although most of them are economists and social scientists, they portray the *infitah* policies not only as undermining economic independence and social equality but as threatening the integrity and authenticity of national culture as well. For a time their criticism focused on the rapid increase in foreign residents, especially Americans connected with the enormous U.S. aid mission. Egyptian social scientists took the lead in demanding greater supervision of foreign consultants and researchers, asserting that they were blocking the employment of qualified university graduates and gathering sensitive information that could compromise national security.[12]

But many of these writers quickly moved beyond such narrow professional concerns, decrying the damaging impact of foreign culture on the educational system, the cinema and television, fashion, popular music and literature, morality and interpersonal relations, the use of leisure time, and even on the Arabic language.[13] On most of these points the protests of Egypt's Western-trained intellectuals converge with those of religiously motivated critics who identify the new capitalist order with casinos and discotheques, boutiques and exclusive hotels, pornography and prostitution. When English-language television ads for Charlie perfume focus on Shelley Hack's legs as she slinks out of a long black limousine and into her favorite nightclub, there is remarkably little difference in the pained expressions of neo-Nasserist and Muslim viewers. As secular critics become more protective of cultural authenticity and religious critics become more attentive to social justice, the socialist and Islamic strands of Egyptian nationalism blend into an increasingly potent countercoalition against the continued disarray of the "triple alliance."

Corporatism

At first glance Egypt's associational life appears deceptively simple and uniform because of the clear prevalence of corporatist over pluralist organizations in virtually every interest sector.[14] However, looking beyond the formal facade of common structures, it becomes clear that Egypt's authoritarian regime is based on an unusually flexible and incoherent variety of corporatism that promotes great diversity in group power and that allows considerable leeway for dissident group leaders.

For nearly a century Egypt's rulers have regarded corporatist associations as valuable instruments of social control, but they generally have avoided the high levels of repression that would be necessary to eliminate the vestiges of pluralism and to impose a cohesive corporatist design. Instead, they have opted for strategies of corporatization that are far more tentative, partial, and inconsistent than the "state corporatist" systems of Latin America or the "societal corporatist" systems of Western Europe. Hence, Egypt is a leading example of a persistently heterogeneous system of interest representation in which both pluralist and corporatist structures have played enduring roles, but in which neither mode of representation has attained anything approaching universal or permanent hegemony.[15]

The continued diversity and vitality of Egypt's associational life reflects wide variations in the process of corporatization during successive historical epochs and across different social and economic sectors. In each interest sector corporatization has occurred at different times, to different degrees, and for different reasons. The periodic mixing and remixing of pluralist and corporatist elements has resulted in three types of sectoral organization, each of which is the product of a distinctive historical pattern of associational evolution. Important variations in group activity and influence are observable not only between these three categories but within them as well.

First, there are the ''corporatist sectors'' in which corporatism always has been the predominant and often the exclusive mode of representation. These include virtually all of the middle-class professional syndicates. Second, there are the ''corporatized sectors'' in which originally spontaneous and voluntary social movements came under more and more state regulation until they were eventually transformed into or supplanted by corporatist organizations. The primary examples of this pattern are the labor movement and the agricultural cooperatives. Third, there are the ''hybrid sectors'' in which both pluralist and corporatist structures continue to coexist and compete for predominance, sometimes producing a highly conflictual chain reaction of group organization and counterorganization. These include the business community, where groups have passed through a series of pluralist and corporatist reincarnations, as well as religious associations, which remain the last major preserve of pluralism in Egyptian society.

A brief but important exception to this historical pattern of associational eclecticism occurred during the rule of Anwar Sadat. Sadat never came to terms with the extensive network of corporatist occupational groups that he inherited from the Nasser regime. At first he regarded them as dangerous vestiges of authoritarian socialism that were incompatible with his supposed desire to redirect Egypt toward capitalism and democracy. Then, as Sadat became disenchanted with pluralist strategies of reform based on multiparty competition, he tried to purge and co-opt the major corporatist groups, hoping that they would allow him to retain control over a more cautious and halfhearted policy of political liberalization. Finally, Sadat abandoned both pluralist and corporatist strategies of democratization and prepared for the coercive imposition of a more comprehensive and centralized system of authoritarian corporatism.

Egypt's loose and alterable set of corporatist structures were indispensable to Sadat's efforts to keep his enemies off balance while carrying out far-reaching changes in the social bases of the authoritarian regime and in its economic and foreign policies. He found numerous ways of manipulating and modifying corporatism, the most effective of which included admixtures and trappings of pluralism. However, when Sadat became intolerant of the openness of corporatist channels to manipulation by his opponents as well, he began to threaten the very flexibility and heterogeneity that had made Egypt's associational life so useful to his shifting strategies of authoritarian rule. His intention to remold Egyptian corporatism into a more cohesive and repressive system of control backfired dramatically, resulting in a countermobilization of both pluralist and corporatist groups that jolted his regime and seriously limited the decisional autonomy of his successor.[16]

By the end of 1980 Sadat had become highly irritated with his opponents' ability to build alliances that crisscrossed Egypt's mélange of pluralist and corporatist associations. Over the next several months he confronted one group after another with the threat of reorganization and tighter state controls. By the summer of 1981 Sadat was engaged in open struggles with all of the opposition parties (legal and illegal), several occupational groups (pluralist and corporatist), and a host of religious organizations (Muslim and Christian).

Sadat was surprised and alarmed to see that the generally effective barriers of organizational, ideological, and communal divisions were no longer adequate to prevent the coalescence of a heterogeneous opposition movement around a common set of powerful grievances: growing restrictions on political freedom; unchecked economic corruption and inequality; the failure of the Camp David "peace process"; and the government party's exploitation of religious disputes. When Sadat responded to this challenge by imprisoning his critics and attacking the few remaining vestiges of associational liberty, he provoked an even greater political crisis that culminated in his murder and that abated only when his successor took clear steps to free opposition leaders and to seek their cooperation.

As long as Sadat tolerated and manipulated Egypt's traditional mixture of contrived pluralism and incoherent corporatism he was remarkably successful in almost single-handedly reversing his country's economic and foreign policies despite mounting protests from a wide variety of aggrieved groups. But as it became increasingly clear that he had opted for a more ambitious authoritarian design, Sadat triggered simultaneous confrontations with several groups that temporarily overcame their deep divisions to form an unusually broad and unified opposition movement.

The traumatic results of these confrontations, culminating in the assassination of Anwar Sadat, have made Egypt's current rulers more reluctant than ever to risk antagonizing powerful and well-organized interests. Thus, Sadat's efforts to bolster the authoritarian regime with tougher corporatist policies severely weakened its ability to formulate any decisive strategy of reform. The result has been a new period of drift and procrastination in which the country's economic stagnation continues and its social conflicts intensify.

Egypt's experience illustrates that the concepts of pluralism and corporatism are most useful when not regarded as diametrically opposed ideal types or as coherent molds shaping whole political systems. Rather, it is theoretically more elegant and empirically more accurate to conceptualize them as alternative patterns of representation that can emerge and develop simultaneously in the same political system, trading positions of relative predominance in successive historical periods, across various socioeconomic sectors, and even in different issue areas or geographic regions.[17]

An eclectic and alterable mixture of corporatist, pluralist, and hybrid structures may be attractive to authoritarian modernizers for several reasons. It alleviates the need for sustained and widespread campaigns of coercion involved in more ambitious efforts to recast entire associational systems from a common mold. It promotes a shared sense of weakness and disorganization among groups isolated in differentially structured compartments that can be reshuffled at the whim of the ruling elite.

A mixed system of representation can help to preserve the autonomy of the authoritarian state not only vis-à-vis potential opponents but also vis-à-vis ambitious allies aspiring to become full coalition partners or to maneuver the state into guaranteeing a particular imbalance of power between contending social classes. Finally, such a system can provide authoritarian modernizers an important measure of flexibility and adaptiveness in reordering their relations with dominant and subordinate social groups. This can enhance a regime's chances of implementing and surviving abrupt changes and even complete reversals in its economic policies, its social bases of support, and its international alliances.

The coexistence of pluralist and corporatist structures can produce many paradoxical results. Indeed, there is a frequent and ironic inversion of roles between groups that challenges our conventional expectations that pluralism will promote pressure for more genuine democracy while corporatism will buttress ever more invincible forms of authoritarianism. Instead, pluralist policies can operate not as catalysts for disruptive participation and demand-making but as valuable instruments of social control. Similarly, corporatist policies of co-optation, "concertation," and coercion can unwittingly provoke precisely the kinds of political opposition they seek to prevent and even provide them with ready-made channels for countermobilization.

Pluralism can help to support stable authoritarianism in several ways. It can maintain a facade of voluntarism and respect for freedom of association that is sufficient to satisfy the very modest expectations of international lenders and donor democracies for evidence that noncommunist authoritarians are behaving in a tolerant, "tutelary," or even quasi-democratic manner. It can serve as a powerful tactic of disorganization and fragmentation by delaying the emergence of unified representatives in sensitive sectors and by promoting the proliferation of weak, financially dependent, and squabbling leaders who can be manipulated and discarded by government patrons.

Pluralism can also allow state security and intelligence agencies to acquire otherwise unobtainable information about the strength and intentions of interest group leaders and to amass copious files of their "subversive" statements and activities for later use in criminal proceedings. Finally, pluralism can serve as a form of punishment for group leaders who refuse to collaborate in state-controlled corporatist arrangements and as a vivid reminder of the marginal, precarious, and impotent roles awaiting current collaborators who might try to exploit the privileges of corporatism in an independent manner.

Alternatively, corporatist policies can seriously destabilize and even help to undermine authoritarian regimes. In some sectors corporatism can become too co-optive and inclusionary. This can result in a partial surrender of policy-making to veto groups whose political support is indispensable to the authoritarian coalition, but whose privileges nevertheless must be curtailed if the regime is to adapt and survive. In other sectors co-optation of particular leaders and factions can result in the alienation of a general constituency and its recurrent explosion in rank-and-file revolts against the isolation and betrayal of its own representatives.

Corporatist policies have an uncanny propensity for dividing those they seek to unite and uniting those they seek to divide. On one hand, the clearly discriminatory and asymmetrical nature of most corporatist arrangements can intensify rivalry and disarray within and between the very sectors the state wishes to rationalize and coordinate. On the other hand, all sorts of aggrieved groups that are excluded from or unsuccessful in the corporatist arena may be able to suspend their mutual differences long enough to collaborate in fashioning a parallel and competing pluralist arena as the preserve of a mounting political opposition.

No authoritarian regime relies exclusively or even primarily on corporatism. The unreliability of corporatist means of social control and the vulnerability of authoritarian regimes that employ them are evident from the long list of alternative control techniques that invariably are required to reinforce and sustain the edifice of corporatist occupational associations. This list includes cosmetic islands of associational pluralism; contrived party-electoral systems and recurrent promises of "political openings"; incessant ideological campaigns, production drives, and neotraditionalist revivals; the launching, atrophy, and reincarnation of successive ruling party organizations; multiple and overlapping domestic intelligence services; the exaggeration or fabrication of external threats to national security; and when all else fails, coercion, terror, and exile.

The persistent heterogeneity of Egypt's system of interest representation requires a rethinking of conventional assumptions, derived primarily from Latin American and Western European experiences, about the historical and causal connections between pluralism and corporatism. Most analysts of interest group politics in these regions regard corporatist arrangements as constituting a new system of representation that arises in response to and ultimately *replaces* a more "unruly" pluralist system.[18] However, many authoritarian modernizers in the Middle East and Asia have tried to use corporatism as a *supplement* to pluralism rather than as a replacement for it. They intentionally have avoided trying to impose ambitious and cohesive corporatist systems, preferring instead to combine supposedly incompatible elements of both pluralism and corporatism.

Moreover, in many countries where authoritarian elites have attempted to force associational life into a tighter state corporatist mold their regimes have been deeply shaken or overturned by unanticipatedly powerful oppositions. In these cases it may be more accurate to argue that corporatism itself has been a source of new political instability and the unintended *cause* of a more vigorous pluralism.

Observers of state corporatism in Latin America and societal corporatism in Western Europe commonly argue that these systems are more stable or "governable" to the degree that corporatist structures and processes have eclipsed pluralist ones. Regarding the Middle East and Asia, however, there is substantial evidence that corporatism is most effective when combined and diluted with pluralist elements in a heterogeneous system of representation, especially when the coexistence of isolated and differentially organized groups serves to fragment civil society and prevent the emergence of autonomous centers of power.

Alternatively, corporatism is most troublesome and destabilizing when authoritarian elites abandon such flexible and pragmatic arrangements and try to reshape associational life into a more cohesive instrument of political domination and economic mobilization. When authoritarian modernizers with diminishing political tolerance and rising economic ambitions seek to impose a "purer" brand of corporatism, they may unwittingly pave the way for the coalescence of previously divided or mutually hostile groups into a new opposition movement that can threaten the very existence of the regime or greatly reduce its autonomy from the demands of specific social and economic sectors.

Far from enhancing the "governability" of authoritarian regimes, the abrupt shift to repressive corporatist policies may merely provide a new recipe for revolution. The misadventures of Anwar Sadat coincided with setbacks to other corporatist experiments in Iran, India, and South Korea. Even as observers of Latin America debated corporatism's contribution to the rise of a "new authoritarianism," it was already clear that such regimes could not be easily exported to the Middle East and Asia. If these regions were cultivating a "new authoritarianism," it was a brand not previously envisioned by corporatist theory—a highly explosive and self-defeating variety that (parodying Schmitter) might aptly be called "unruly corporatism."

"Populist Authoritarianism" versus "Bureaucratic Authoritarianism"

Egypt provides an intriguing test case for evaluating contending arguments concerning the historical and causal relationship between what Guillermo O'Donnell has described as "populist authoritarianism" and "bureaucratic authoritarianism." [19] O'Donnell's elaboration of these concepts has been adapted and criticized by a number of Latin American observers, particularly Alfred Stepan and David Collier. [20] Understanding the similarities and differences between their views provides an indispensable starting point for examining the evolution of authoritarian rule in Egypt as well.

The crux of O'Donnell's argument is that populist authoritarianism and bureaucratic authoritarianism are distinct responses to different kinds of crises that emerge at different stages of delayed, dependent development. Populist authoritarianism relies upon an "inclusionary," co-optive form of corporatism, promoting a broad multiclass alliance in favor of import substitution. Bureaucratic authoritarianism relies upon an "exclusionary," repressive form of corporatism, promoting a narrower transnational bourgeois alliance in favor of the "deepening" of industrialization through more capital-intensive production. Populist authoritarianism mobilizes and strengthens working-class organizations in order to break the power of the traditional landed oligarchy. Bureaucratic authoritarianism deactivates and "conquers" working-class organizations to insure the political "predictability" that is necessary to consolidate alliances with foreign capital. [21]

O'Donnell sees a clear causal connection between these two authoritarian episodes. In his view, populist authoritarianism sows the seeds of bureaucratic authoritarianism by unleashing political forces that encourage industrialization at an early phase of development but that then become an obstacle to industrialization at a more advanced stage. It is this deterministic interpretation of populism as a transitory interlude paving the way for increasingly repressive forms of authoritarian rule that sets O'Donnell apart from the analyses of Stepan and Collier.

For Stepan and Collier populism is a highly differentiated historical phenomenon that has taken several forms and that has had varying consequences for subsequent periods of political and economic development. Whereas O'Donnell portrays late developing societies as being at the mercy of common economic imperatives that drastically restrict their political options, Stepan and Collier note that the legacy of populism renders civil society more or less amenable to bureaucratic authoritarianism because populist rulers themselves may have endowed organized interests with sufficient power and resources to prevent or defeat later efforts to install a more repressive regime. Accordingly, Stepan and Collier try to explain why attempts to establish bureaucratic authoritarianism have succeeded in some countries and failed in others, and why, even when successful, they have required vastly different levels of coercion. Both writers seek the answer in historical and political variables rather than in the supposedly irresistible imperatives of late (or late, late) industrialization. In each case they ask how the corporatist policies of populist authoritarian regimes altered the balance of power between organized interests, paying particular attention to changes in the structure and strength of the labor movement.

Where corporatism kept associational life closely tied to the state or a semiofficial party, the transition to bureaucratic authoritarianism was swift, as in Brazil, or imperceptible, as in Mexico. But where interest groups enjoyed greater autonomy and strong alliances with radical party organizations, the imposition of rigid corporatist controls was accomplished only with extreme bloodshed, as in Chile, or was ultimately defeated, as in Argentina. Stepan argues that in revolutionary Peru corporatist experiments devolved so much power to lower-class groups that the populist authoritarian regime eventually lost control over the very mass organizations it had created.

The corporatist and socialist experiments of the Nasser era were undoubtedly the leading Middle Eastern example of populist authoritarianism. Nasserism was, initially, a fascinating and often intentional Egyptian counterpart to Peronism, and later, a prototype for some of the more innovative and "democratizing" corporatist projects of Velasco's revolutionary regime in Peru.[22] Like Peron, Nasser relied on corporatist associations to create a mass movement whose core has survived its leader's demise. Like the Peronists, Nasserists have tenaciously clung to their strongholds in several working-class and professional syndicates despite the repeated efforts of subsequent governments to dislodge them.

Like Peronism, Nasserism has continued to exert a paradoxical influence on the political system. Its irritating defense of associational autonomy invites recurrent retaliation from ruling elites who would prefer a more centralized and controllable brand of corporatism, but its ability to form tactical alliances with rival opposition groups deters more ambitious authoritarian projects and creates constant pressures for greater political freedom. Hence, the continuing debate over the nature and legacy of Nasserism is relevant not only to understanding Egypt's current malaise and future options but also to a more general reassessment of the political and economic conditions that are most conducive to the emergence and success of bureaucratic authoritarian strategies for advancing dependent development.[23]

In many ways Egypt's experience appears to confirm O'Donnell's observation that radical, "inclusionary" corporatist regimes make an indirect, long-term contribution to the later rise of reactionary, "exclusionary" corporatist regimes. In Nasserist Egypt, as in several Latin American countries, a revolutionary elite used corporatism to strengthen working-class organizations as junior partners in a multiclass ruling coalition that benefited briefly from ambitious efforts to combine redistributive reforms with import substitution. Moreover, post-Nasserist governments have sought to refashion inherited corporatist structures into more effective instruments for controlling a powerful working-class movement that now is perceived as a major obstacle to a more advanced stage of industrialization, requiring greater reliance on imported capital and technology.

Noting Egypt's gradual shift from socialism to capitalism, as well as the eclipse of the Nasserist "alliance of popular working forces" by a renascent bourgeoisie with growing ties to foreign capital, more and more Middle Eastern analysts have begun to refer to Egypt's political system as an example of bureaucratic authoritarianism.[24] The characterization is premature and misleading.

Post-Nasserist governments have not smashed the power of the centralized organizations that the labor movement inherited from the 1952 revolution nor have they divested the state industrial enterprises that make up the unions' core constituencies and economic strongholds. Organized labor may have lost its privileged status within the ruling coalition, but demotion is by no means the same as suppression and forcible expulsion. In fact, Sadat was and Mubarak has been unwilling to employ the costly and sustained repression of working-class organizations that has been the hallmark of "exclusionary" bureaucratic authoritarian regimes.

Government spokesmen frequently declare that the economic privileges granted to workers during the socialist revolution are extravagant for a developing country and that they must be curtailed or repealed for the sake of greater productivity. Nevertheless, the government has tried to persuade union leaders to relinquish these economic gains voluntarily and in a piecemeal fashion rather than launching a full-blown counterrevolutionary assault against the labor movement. Sadat made it clear that he was willing to grant still greater authority and resources to workers' organizations in exchange for a gradual relaxation of guaranteed employment and of the many legal protections required by individual work contracts, and Mubarak has done the same. Even while post-Nasserist governments have pressured union leaders to give up some of the gains of socialism, they have increased the power of the Egyptian Confederation of Labor by negotiating broader union participation in the management of public sector enterprises and by allowing the confederation to establish a new investment bank.[25]

Similarly, despite repeated government threats to abolish or drastically reorganize many of the middle-class professional syndicates, these groups have retained a good deal of autonomy and continue to harbor stubborn opponents of the ruling party. The government has generally preferred to manipulate factional disputes within these associations by packing them with what it hopes will be more loyal members, especially civil servants and public sector employees. In many cases the state has substantially increased the economic power of these groups by endowing them with new entrepreneurial activities and promoting a novel type of associational capitalism. The electoral campaigns of the syndicates have become important battlegrounds in which progovernment forces are regularly challenged and often defeated by candidates representing virtually all of the opposition parties, both legal and illegal. Consequently, the diverse and competitive professional syndicates often appear to be more representative of partisan and ideological cleavages than the contrived system of political parties.[26]

Furthermore, by encouraging a "capitalist renaissance" and an "Islamic awakening," post-Nasserist governments also have contributed to a partial revival of associational pluralism. Private businessmen and organized Muslims have shown a remarkable ability to bypass older corporatist structures and to create a wide assortment of independent, voluntary groups. Both the new bourgeoisie and the Islamic movement have acquired a vitality and diversity that can no longer be adequately represented by unitary and semiofficial bodies. In these sectors associational life has become more heterogeneous than ever, moving Egypt even further away from conventional notions of state corporatism.

Contrary to O'Donnell's expectations, Egypt's experience with populist authoritarianism has hindered rather than facilitated the rise of a bureaucratic authoritarian regime. No such regime has yet emerged in Egypt and its installation in the future is by no means inevitable. The obstructionist and disruptive powers bequeathed to many corporatist interest groups by the Nasserist era have provided Egyptian society with a healthy defense against, if not a lasting immunity from, bureaucratic authoritarianism. The very group insolence and independence that seem to make Egypt a likely candidate for (or victim of) a more ruthless variety of authoritarian rule have helped to deter overly ambitious attempts to accelerate dependent development by replacing Egypt's pliable and co-optive brand of corporatism with a more rigid and repressive variety.

It is difficult to believe that the "bloodless purge" and "economic miracle" that accompanied the installation of bureaucratic authoritarianism in Brazil are attainable goals in Egypt. The far more likely outcomes of any attempt to replicate such a regime in Egypt would be the economic disappointments and political tragedies of Argentina and Chile: recurrent cycles of mass resistance and state repression, leading to an aggravation of the developmental blockages and social turmoil that bureaucratic authoritarianism supposedly was intended to break in the first place.

Alternatively, it is possible that deepening political and economic crises will weaken Egypt's authoritarian rulers to the point that they will become more eager to experiment with novel forms of power sharing. But they are far more likely to opt for corporatist formulas of power sharing than pluralist formulas. Sadat showed and Mubarak has shown a strong preference for experiments in political liberalization that envisage greater bargaining with interest group leaders over more risky and unpredictable ventures in unfettered party competition. When Sadat became disenchanted with his original project to create a more open multiparty system, he tried to induce interest group leaders to accept functional representation as an alternative strategy of reform. At the same time that he froze the creation of new parties and corrupted the electoral process, he established a new "upper house" of the legislature, the Majlis al-Shura (Consultative Assembly), in which one-half of the membership was appointed from a wide cross-section of occupational associations.

Similarly, while Mubarak complains with increasing frequency that the "irresponsible" behavior of the opposition parties is jeopardizing his supposed plans for a transition to democracy, his government is becoming more open to and more divided by the pleading of special interests, particularly business and labor. After several years of trial and error with various projects of reform it is clear that Egypt's rulers are much more attracted to the prospect of actively fashioning a "corporatist democracy" based on some type of functional representation than to standing back and allowing the emergence of a "pluralist democracy" based on a genuine multiparty system.

The Egyptian state still retains the initiative vis-à-vis differentially organized sectors whose major preoccupations are the defense and expansion of their turfs rather than the subjugation or elimination of their rivals. Mubarak is by no means a prisoner of foreign capital or of rigidified domestic coalitions. He is neither the policeman of a newly hegemonic bourgeoisie nor the immobilized victim of a society on the brink of class warfare. Instead, he is gradually becoming the reluctant arbiter of fragmented but well-entrenched groups who have their backs to the wall, knowing that they all will have to give up something voluntarily or risk an upheaval that could strip them of a great deal more.

In this context the devolution of authority to associations could be viewed as an evolution of the existing regime rather than a sudden reversal of power relations. Political liberalization need not appear to authoritarian elites as a risky and radical departure from the past. Instead, they might come to view "corporatist democracy" as a new compromise with civil society in which the state reallocates authority from one set of publicly accountable organs to another while retaining clear responsibility for overall coordination and concertation.[27]

Egypt's desperate economic situation precludes not only the promise of an expanding pie that can be shared by all but even more modest expectations that the lot of particular groups can be improved by threatening the already precarious positions of others. What the regime has to offer is a virtually inevitable austerity that can be made palatable only if its burdens appear to be apportioned more or less evenly across all social sectors. Egyptian notions of social justice no longer demand discrimination in favor of certain classes in order to correct the supposed historical abuses of others. Instead, for the first time since the revolution, there is serious discussion of "social symmetry" as the equitable and consensual distribution of hardship.

What does the Mubarak regime have to offer Egypt's most influential groups in return for their cooperation in weathering unavoidable hard times and averting a possible revolution? When Sadat's assassination brought Mubarak to power, he pledged that he would redeem all three of his predecessor's historic promises to the Egyptian people, the promises of comprehensive peace, economic development, and democracy. Now it is clear that no Egyptian government will be able to attain the goals of peace and prosperity in the foreseeable future. Both of these objectives are intimately tied to Egypt's relations with the United States and Israel. With the steady deterioration of those relations, two of the unkept promises of the Sadat era are at the mercy of foreigners over whom Egypt's leaders have little control.

The only promise that remains is the one that depends solely on Egyptian initiative, the promise of democracy. Probably the only way that Mubarak can expect to elicit consent and support for painful and unpopular economic policies is to devolve greater responsibility for making and implementing those policies to the organized interests that have the most at stake. Naturally, Mubarak and his military-technocratic advisers do not relish the prospect of sharing power, but this could be the only card they have left to play. The diversity of political organization and the volatility of public opinion in Egypt today make repression far more costly and risky than expanding the modest experiments with "corporatist democracy" that were initiated and then abandoned by Sadat.

The following chapters will trace the evolution of associational life in twentieth century Egypt, arguing that corporatism has served to advance dependent development and authoritarianism in some ways while also helping to limit and transform them in other ways. Whereas theorists of the "semiperipheral syndrome" portray corporatism as a device for building narrow, transnational coalitions that promote inequality, despotism, and cultural homogenization, this study seeks to demonstrate that it can also give rise to broad, nationalist countercoalitions demanding greater social justice, democracy, and cultural integrity.

Chapter 2 discusses the socioeconomic context of contemporary group conflict, focusing on the fitful and discontinuous nature of Egyptian industrialization since World War I. A noncumulative process of economic change marked by frequent policy reversals has produced only a modest level of industrialization, but it has promoted a high degree of conflict between social and economic groups that are intensely jealous of one another's privileges. Organized interests have become adept in enlisting state support to expand their spheres of influence, helping to create a mixed economy that has become partitioned into a number of self-contained compartments.

Chapter 3 traces the increasingly interventionist role of the state in molding and manipulating associational life as it has expanded and diversified during the last century. Modern public policy toward interest groups has preserved and consolidated an assortment of corporatist techniques inherited from Ottoman rule, the British occupation, the constitutional monarchy, and the Wafd. World War II and the Free Officers' Revolution greatly accelerated the process so that by the early 1960s corporatism had replaced pluralism as the dominant mode of representation. Nevertheless, there have been important differences in the timing and degree of corporatization in each sector that account for enduring variations in the autonomy and influence of contemporary groups. Three distinct patterns of associational evolution have produced what can be termed ''corporatist sectors,'' ''corporatized sectors,'' and ''hybrid sectors.''

The major associations that typify these three developmental patterns are compared in chapters 4, 5, and 6. Each category of groups provides a different type of arena for competition and bargaining between supporters and critics of the authoritarian elite. Groups in every arena have been penetrated and mobilized not only by the regime's allies but by its opponents as well. Enduring legal and structural disparities between groups in different arenas frustrate the coalition-building strategies of opposition leaders. At the same time, growing partisan and ideological divisions within each arena make it impossible for the authoritarian state to fashion any of them into a preserve of its supporters.

Chapter 4 examines the middle-class professional syndicates that have been organized along corporatist lines since their inception in prerevolutionary Egypt. Particular attention is given to the syndicates of lawyers, journalists, engineers, and commercial employees because they exemplify the wide range of political action and independence that has been tolerated by the state despite the similarity of corporatist structures and controls.

Chapter 5 compares labor unions and agricultural cooperatives as leading examples of spontaneous social movements that were gradually refashioned into nationwide corporatist hierarchies during the Nasser era. Although both of these sectors experienced a common transformation from pluralism to corporatism, the socialist revolution endowed them with very different political and economic resources. Consequently, under post-Nasserist governments union leaders have been fairly successful in preserving and in some cases expanding their revolutionary gains, whereas the cooperative movement has been emasculated and unable to prevent the return to openly inegalitarian, capitalist policies in the countryside.

Chapter 6 examines businessmen's associations and religious groups, sectors in which the persistence and revival of pluralism have promoted intense rivalries between autonomous groups created from below and semiofficial organizations controlled from above. In both cases the recent proliferation of groups has been a result of widespread dissatisfaction with the contrived nature of corporatist representation and its inability to reflect a growing diversity of interests and opinions. Yet the resurgence of pluralism has had very different consequences in each sector. Among organized Muslims it poses a defiant challenge for the regime to live up to its own democratic and religious rhetoric. Among organized capitalists it presents the ruling elite with a more confident coalition partner whose support is particularly welcome as the populist and socialist slogans of the revolution lose what little remains of their credibility.

Finally, chapter 7 discusses Egypt's diverse and "unruly" brand of corporatism in comparative perspective. The unsuccessful corporatist policies of Anwar Sadat are compared with similar examples of unstable and self-defeating corporatist experiments in three other authoritarian regimes in the Middle East and Asia—the experiments of Muhammad Riza Shah Pahlevi in Iran, Park Chung Hee in South Korea, and Indira Gandhi in India. Some common themes are identified concerning the most likely motivations and consequences of these ill-fated associational policies, concluding with speculation about what to expect after an unruly corporatist regime has been deeply shaken or overthrown.

2

Interrupted Industrialization and Economic Compartmentalization

Few non-Western countries have had a longer and more difficult experience with industrialization than Egypt. From Muhammad ʿAli to Ismaʿil Sidqi and Talʿat Harb, from Misr al-Fatat to Jamal ʿAbd al-Nasser and Husni Mubarak, Egyptian elites have identified the creation of modern industry not only as a hallmark of national power but as a matter of survival in the face of mounting pressures from overpopulation and diminishing returns in agriculture. Yet all of Egypt's recurrent projects of industrialization have generated severe political conflicts both with foreign governments, who have feared shifts in the regional balance of power, and with domestic constituencies, who have perceived themselves as the prospective beneficiaries or victims of fundamental economic change.

Since World War I the Egyptian impulse toward industrialization has been renewed periodically, each time with greater urgency and ambition. But each time this impulse eventually has become stalled or dissipated by some combination of foreign opposition and local upheaval. The result has been a long series of aborted and disconnected projects: the Commission on Commerce and Industry, Bank Misr, the Federation of Egyptian Industries, Ahmad Husayn's ''Piaster Project'' *(Mashruʿ al-Qirsh),* the Five Year Plans, and the open door policy. These initiatives have pro-

35

moted very different mixtures of public, private, and foreign ownership, and also have pursued incompatible strategies for redistributing wealth and power among different social classes.[1]

Sporadic growth coupled with frequent reversals in social and economic policy has produced a dangerous combination in Egypt. The country still has achieved only a modest level of industrialization, but it has accumulated an assortment of well-entrenched groups who have managed to retain a large portion of the wealth and privileges they acquired in the past and who are determined that future economic advances will not be made at their expense. Given the historical precariousness of wealth and power in Egyptian society, these groups are intensely jealous of one another's privileges and deeply suspicious of one another's intentions. Many of them have been able to protect (though not necessarily consolidate) their gains by embedding themselves in the state bureaucracy and the ruling party.

This is not to say that Egypt is dominated by what Mancur Olson has called "distributive coalitions"—powerful special interest groups that arose during an earlier period of prosperity only to foreclose future possibilities for innovation and competition.[2] In fact, Egypt has had more than its share of the wars and depressions, the revolutions and counterrevolutions that Olson views as indispensable to breaking down uncompromising defenders of the status quo and paving the way for creative responses to national crisis. Indeed, it is precisely the common memory of such upheavals that has created a pervasive sense of vulnerability among organized groups, making them mistrustful of each other and sensitive to the slightest changes in their relative positions.

The influence of organized interests in Egypt is manifested not in overt political hegemony but in a more subtle kind of economic partition—not in the ability of a particular coalition to impose its will on others but in the tacit agreement of diverse groups to parcel out authority and resources so that each can hope to construct a secure niche for itself. Noncumulative spurts of industrialization and inconsistent policies of social restratification have caused dramatic reversals of fortune for virtually all segments of Egyptian society. After long years of what was often portrayed as a life and death struggle between incompatible ideological and social forces, both the ruling elite and most organized interests now seem reconciled to the coexistence of a corrupt capitalism and a wasteful socialism that will inspire no developmental breakthroughs but that might at least allow diverse enterprises to make their own way without the constant fear that one sector will swallow the others.

During the past two decades a series of governments have sought to moderate political and class conflicts by encouraging a proliferation of economic sectors operating under different legal formulas and serving different constituencies. This has involved the careful preservation of basic distinctions between public and private enterprise as well as between national and foreign capital despite certain relaxations of the traditional barriers separating them. Moreover, the state has tolerated (and, in many cases, directly promoted) a more active entrepreneurial role for a variety of special groups, such as labor unions, professional syndicates, cooperatives, religious associations, the military, and the black market.

The authoritarian regime has consistently refused to permit interest groups to acquire an independent footing in the political system either by establishing separate political parties or by selecting occupational contingents to elected assemblies. But the regime has been quite willing to allow the same groups to establish important economic enclaves even when this requires turning a blind eye to the predictable spread of duplication, inefficiency, and corruption. Explicit, political corporatism has been rejected in favor of a more imperceptible and informal type of economic corporatism. Eager to prevent or at least deflect class confrontation in the political arena, Egypt's rulers have been more than willing to bear the costs of a gradual compartmentalization of the economy.

Such a strategy might provide the leaders of the most resourceful and influential groups with a greater stake in the system and, for a time, it may even create an illusion of multiple opportunities in what continues to be an economy of scarcity. However, a patchwork of uncoordinated economic sectors is neither a substitute for a ''new social contract'' nor an adequate response to demands for a more inclusive system of representation. Economic partition cannot generate enough wealth or devolve enough power to persuade Egyptians that their rulers have devised an ingenious variety of social democracy uniquely suited to their customs and temperaments. On the contrary, it is more likely to diminish the prospects for class collaboration and political consensus by reinforcing the already deep popular cynicism about the regime's capacity to resume industrialization and about the sincerity of its pledges to reestablish democracy.[3]

Long-Term Trends in Industrialization

The growth of modern industry in Egypt is a record of ups and downs, of brief surges punctuated by abrupt halts, of important advances followed by long periods of running in place. Import substitution in various

TABLE 2-1.   The Economically Active Population by Occupational Groups,
1907–1982 (Percentages)

	1907	1917	1927	1937	1947	1960	1966	1971	1976	1982
Agriculture	68.3	68.0	67.5	69.5	61.7	57.0	53.2	53.2	45.8	36.8
Manufacturing	8.3	8.5	8.3	6.2	8.6	9.5	13.1	12.4	14.1	14.7
Utilities	—	.1	.4	.4	.3	.5	.6	.3	.6	.7
Construction	2.1	1.4	1.6	2.0	1.7	2.1	2.5	2.3	4.3	5.3
Trans. and commun.	2.9	3.5	3.7	2.4	3.0	3.3	4.1	3.9	4.9	5.3
Trade and finance	4.7	7.5	8.7	7.5	8.9	8.3	7.2	9.6	8.6	10.0
Services	13.0	11.0	9.8	12.0	15.8	19.2	19.2	18.3	21.5	27.2
E.A.P. as percentage of total population	30.4	33.8	36.9	36.3	34.8	29.6	32.3	—	29.3	26.6

Sources: Samir Radwan, *Capital Formation in Egyptian Industry and Agriculture: 1882–1967* (London: Ithaca Press, 1974), p. 283; *Population Census of Egypt,* 1960, 1966, 1976; Khalid Ikram, *Egypt: Economic Management in a Period of Transition* (Baltimore: Johns Hopkins University Press, 1980), pp. 134–35; International Labor Organization, *Yearbook of Labor Statistics, 1985* (Geneva: I.L.O., 1985), p. 172.

guises has spanned three-quarters of a century. Current efforts to fashion a more sophisticated manufacturing base have built upon earlier achievements of the Nasser regime before the Six Day War, which, in turn, continued a series of more tentative advances spurred by World War I, the Great Depression, and World War II. Despite this long history, however, industrialization has never acquired a sustained momentum and its contributions to economic diversification have been modest and painfully slow.

The erratic nature of structural change is evident from recurrent fluctuations in the distribution of the work force across economic sectors (Table 2-1). Since the beginning of the century agriculture's share of total employment has declined steadily from about two-thirds to about one-third, with two important periods of retrenchment occurring during the depression and between the wars of 1967 and 1973. But the lion's share of the nonagricultural labor force has moved into various service occupations, not into manufacturing. Industrial employment has followed a wavelike pattern of growth: rising mildly during the two world wars, surging with the socialist experiments of the early 1960s, and barely holding its own afterward. During the *infitah* period manufacturing's share of employment has leveled off while the services have swollen to encompass nearly one-half of all workers.

Furthermore, manufacturing's contribution to total production is no greater than its share of total employment (Table 2-2). Official reports often cite industry as accounting for about 30 percent of the gross domestic product, but most of this is attributable to recent earnings from the petroleum sector. In fact, manufacturing's current share of production is only 13 percent, precisely what it was in the mid-1950s. As the relative importance of agriculture has declined, it has been overtaken by the service sectors, especially trade and finance, which have been the fastest growing areas of the economy since 1973.

Over the past three decades the structure of production has, indeed, diversified, but it has also become more fragmented. Services now contribute over 50 percent (including both public and private sectors), industry accounts for less than 30 percent (almost equally divided between petroleum and manufacturing), and agriculture has fallen to 20 percent. While Egypt's economy can no longer be described as resting on an agricultural center of gravity, it is more difficult than ever to argue that its driving force lies in the emergence of modern industry.

Within the manufacturing sector itself there is some evidence of long-term structural change, indicating the gradual development of a more complex division of labor. Before the 1952 revolution there were a number of often volatile shifts in the distribution of workers across the various branches of industry (Table 2-3). Since the revolution there has been a more decisive movement of workers from consumer industries to intermediate and investment industries, but that movement was almost entirely compressed within the first half of the 1960s (Table 2-4).[4]

In each era international and political factors have been decisive in

TABLE 2-2.   Distribution of Gross Domestic Product by Economic Sector, 1955–1982 (Percentages)

	1955	1960	1967	1973	1977	1982
Agriculture	34.4	31.5	29.0	26.0	24.5	19.8
Manufacturing	13.4	20.1	20.3	18.4	17.2	13.6
Petroleum	4.6			2.9	5.9	15.0
Utilities	.4	1.3	2.2	2.4	1.8	.6
Construction	9.6	9.2	9.3	8.8	8.4	6.6
Trans. and commun.	6.0	7.3	5.5	5.7	7.8	7.9
Trade and finance	11.0	10.4	9.3	9.2	15.6	18.3
Services	21.1	19.9	24.2	26.2	18.7	18.3

Sources: Robert Mabro and Samir Radwan, *The Industrialization of Egypt, 1939–1973* (London: Oxford University Press, 1976), p. 47; Arab Republic of Egypt, *Economic Report of the Ministry of Finance* (Cairo, 1983).

TABLE 2-3.   Diversification of Manufacturing, 1907–1952
(Employment by Sector—Percentages)

	1907	1917	1927	1937	1947	1952
Food			15.1	20.9	21.5	18.7
Beverages	17.0	17.2	9.6	.8	1.7	2.1
Tobacco				5.9	3.5	4.0
Textiles	34.0	20.3	22.4	26.1	48.3	43.8
Clothing	19.0	25.1	4.9	6.2	1.2	2.2
Wood	5.0	15.6	9.7	2.7	1.3	.4
Furniture						2.2
Paper	4.0	3.3	.6	1.6	1.6	2.0
Printing			5.6	4.4	1.9	2.8
Leather	.5	.7	1.6	.9	.7	.8
Rubber					.3	.3
Chemicals	.3	.6	3.0	4.1	5.7	4.2
Petrochemicals				.1	1.3	1.7
Nonmet. minerals	4.2	2.8	4.7	4.9	4.7	5.4
Basic metals				5.7	.4	1.4
Metal products	12.0	7.9	11.0		4.5	2.8
Nonelec. machinery						.2
Elec. machinery				1.6	.1	.4
Trans. equipment	2.0	1.2	11.2	10.0	.8	3.3
Miscellaneous	2.0	5.3	.4	3.8	.4	1.0
Consumer goods	70.0	62.6	52.0	59.9	76.2	70.8
Intermediate goods	14.0	23.0	25.2	24.4	17.9	21.2
Investment goods	12.0	9.1	22.2	11.6	5.4	6.7

Sources: Samir Radwan, *Capital Formation in Egyptian Industry and Agriculture: 1882–1967* (London: Ithaca Press, 1974), pp. 173, 179, 215; United Nations Department of Economic and Social Affairs, *The Development of the Manufacturing Industry in Egypt, Israel and Turkey* (New York, 1958), p. 104.

both stimulating and limiting industrial diversification. Throughout the first half of the century frequent disruptions in international trade created brief opportunities for import substitution, but semicolonial status accentuated and prolonged the vulnerability of infant industry. Since 1952 industrial development has closely paralleled the rapid burst and extended exhaustion of revolutionary energy, with the 1967 war standing as a clear point of demarcation.

During the first four decades of import substitution, when colonial Egypt was just beginning to reclaim control over its trade and fiscal polices, the shape of the industrial work force was periodically revised in response to fluctuations in the international environment. World War I encouraged a shift of workers from basic industries to woodworking, metallurgy, and transportation equipment. On the eve of the depression food processing, textiles, and clothing accounted for only about one-half of all manufacturing workers, as opposed to 70 percent before the war. This reflected a short-lived revival of several crafts and small workshops, as well as the rapid growth of vehicular repair, which at this stage included primarily maintenance workers instead of production workers.

During the depression and World War II this trend was sharply reversed as manufacturing became more and more centralized in larger textile plants. Advances among tailors, carpenters, smiths, and repairmen during the first war were erased even before the second began. By the

TABLE 2-4.   Diversification of Manufacturing, 1954–1980
(Employment by Sector—Percentages)

	1954	*1960*	*1966*	*1971*	*1977*	*1980*
Food	19.0	15.1	13.3	17.6	16.5	14.8
Beverages	1.5	1.2	1.0			1.7
Tobacco	3.4	2.8	2.0			2.0
Textiles	42.9	50.7	42.0	41.6	40.5	37.0
Clothing	2.3	1.3	1.7			1.9
Wood	.5	.4	1.4	1.5	1.4	.9
Furniture	2.1	2.2	1.5			.5
Paper	1.7	2.1	2.3	4.1	3.7	1.8
Printing	2.9	2.7	2.3			2.0
Leather	1.0	.6	.5			.5
Rubber	.3	.6	.7			.6
Chemicals	3.2	5.2	7.8	11.3	12.1	7.6
Petrochemicals	1.1	1.1	1.7			3.1
Nonmet. minerals	6.4	3.9	5.5	5.4	5.0	5.2
Basic metals	1.0	2.9	3.9	5.4	7.9	7.7
Metal products	4.3	2.4	4.3	12.5	12.7	3.6
Nonelec. machinery	.3	.8	1.5			2.4
Elec. machinery	.7	.6	1.9			2.2
Trans. equipment	4.3	2.0	3.2			3.9
Miscellaneous	.7	1.0	1.1	.3	.2	.1
Consumer goods	69.1	71.1	60.0	59.2	57.0	57.4
Intermediate goods	20.2	21.7	27.6	27.7	30.1	29.9
Investment goods	9.6	5.8	10.9	12.5	12.7	12.1

Sources: United Nations Department of Economic and Social Affairs, *The Development of the Manufacturing Industry in Egypt, Israel and Turkey* (New York, 1958), p. 104; Samir Radwan, *Capital Formation in Egyptian Industry and Agriculture: 1882–1967* (London: Ithaca Press, 1974), p. 215; Leroy P. Jones, "Improving the Operational Efficiency of Public Industrial Enterprise in Egypt" (Cairo: U.S. A.I.D., 1981), pp. A-32, A-34; Central Agency for Public Mobilization and Statistics, *Egypt: Statistical Indicators, 1980* (Cairo, 1980), p. 129.

end of World War II basic industries had reabsorbed an even larger portion of the work force than at the beginning of the century, with textiles alone claiming nearly one-half of the country's industrial workers. The transition from small-scale manufacturing to assembly line production involved an important restructuring of Egyptian industry, but it would be more accurate to describe this process as concentration rather than diversification.

After the Free Officers' Revolution there were renewed signs of industrial deepening until 1966, followed by a virtual freezing of the employment structure thereafter. The greatest movement was the relative decline of food processing in favor of chemicals, basic metals, and machinery. By the mid-1960s intermediate and investment industries included about 40 percent of all manufacturing workers, a distribution very similar to that on the eve of World War II. From 1966 through 1980, however, there was remarkably little change in the relative importance of the various branches of industry. Aside from a slight shift toward basic metals and petrochemicals, the picture is one of nearly complete stagnation throughout the *infitah* period.

To find more convincing evidence of industrial diversification, one must look at the pattern of investment instead of employment (Table 2-5).[5] Between 1952 and 1980 the distribution of value added shifted steadily from basic industries to intermediate and investment goods. The sole exception occurred between the 1967 and 1973 wars when change was confined to a brief reordering of investment within consumer goods industries, reemphasizing food and clothing over textiles. After 1973 the flow of capital to heavier industries resumed, particularly toward petrochemicals, machinery, and transportation equipment.

Beginning in the 1950s clear divergences appear between the distribution of employment and the distribution of investment, indicating a tendency toward greater capital intensiveness in the more complex branches of industry. Among the intermediate industries the shares of value added consistently exceeded the shares of employment, with the largest disparities appearing around 1960. In contrast, consumer industries consistently absorbed labor faster than they absorbed capital. By 1980 the divergence between more capital-intensive and more labor-intensive branches was advanced and unmistakable. For the first time, investment industries joined intermediate industries in claiming a larger share of value added than employment. Consumer industries, on the other hand, retained the bulk of workers even though their portion of total value added fell below 50 percent.[6]

Hence, the signs of industrial deepening during the *infitah* are far more

TABLE 2-5. Distribution of Industrial Investment, 1952–1980
(Value Added by Sector—Percentages)

	1952	1960	1966	1973	1980
Food	18.2	16.4	10.7	19.2	12.5
Beverages	4.2	2.3	1.2	1.1	1.9
Tobacco	7.4	5.9	4.4	3.2	1.8
Textiles	33.2	33.3	38.1	20.8	30.3
Clothing	1.9	1.0	1.2	7.0	1.5
Wood	.2	.1	.4	2.7	.4
Furniture	1.4	1.2	.8		.6
Paper	1.3	1.7	2.8	2.1	2.7
Printing	2.8	2.2	2.0	2.6	2.7
Leather	.6	.4	.4	1.3	.2
Rubber	.4	1.7	.9	.9	1.5
Chemicals	7.5	11.3	12.7	9.1	9.1
Petrochemicals	8.5	7.0	5.2	3.7	7.0
Nonmet. minerals	4.3	5.3	4.2	4.4	5.4
Basic metals	1.6	4.9	3.9	5.4	4.9
Metal products	1.7	1.3	3.3	3.0	3.2
Nonelec. machinery	.2	.4	1.1	1.2	4.6
Elec. machinery	.4	1.0	3.2	3.0	4.4
Trans. equipment	3.1	1.7	2.1	3.6	5.3
Miscellaneous	1.2	.9	1.1	5.8	.3
Consumer goods	64.9	59.9	55.6	51.3	48.0
Intermediate goods	28.6	35.8	33.3	32.2	34.3
Investment goods	5.4	4.4	9.7	10.8	17.5

Sources: Samir Radwan, *Capital Formation in Egyptian Industry and Agriculture: 1882–1967* (London: Ithaca Press, 1974), p. 211; Central Agency for Public Mobilization and Statistics, *Egypt: Statistical Indicators, 1980* (Cairo, 1980), p. 127; Khalid Ikram, *Egypt: Economic Management in a Period of Transition* (Baltimore: Johns Hopkins University Press, 1980), p. 242.

tentative and ambiguous than they were in the 1960s. The earlier period combined diversification of both employment and investment with rapid growth in industry's share of total economic production. Since 1973, however, diversification has occurred only in investment. The structure of the industrial work force and its share of total employment have not advanced beyond what they were on the eve of the Six Day War. Furthermore, when petroleum output is treated as a separate entry in the accounting, manufacturing's share of domestic production dropped by 1982 to its lowest point since the 1952 revolution.

The *infitah* is trying to pave the way for a more capital-intensive type of industrial development in which imported technology will play a larger

TABLE 2-6.   Foreign Exchange, Trade, and Debt, 1975–1984
(Millions of Dollars)

	1975	1978	1981	1984
Services and Remittances				
Suez Canal	85	514	664	1,050
Tourism	332	702	773	725
Workers' remittances	366	1,761	2,700	3,500
Exports				
Petroleum	710	1,080	3,150	2,300
All others	860	860	850	920
Foreign Trade				
Imports	3,940	4,740	7,920	7,540
Exports	1,570	1,940	4,000	3,320
Trade deficit	2,370	2,800	3,920	4,220
Foreign Debt				
External Debt	4,850	10,834	17,298	20,037
Debt service as percentage of commodity exports	38.5	113.9	104.7	180.6
Debt service as percentage of all exports	—	—	18.9	30.0

Sources: Friedemann Büttner, "A Country Scenario Analysis of Egypt," *Vierteljahresberichte* 96 (June 1984): 163–79; Chase Econometrics, *Economic Forecasts for Africa and the Middle East,* 1985 (Philadelphia, 1985); Karen Pfeifer, "Debt and Development in the Middle East," *MERIP Reports* (September 1983), p. 10; Khalid Ikram, *Egypt: Economic Management in a Period of Transition* (Baltimore: Johns Hopkins University Press, 1980), p. 349.

role. In time this new strategy might yield some important gains in productivity, but there is no reason to believe that it will generate anything approaching the volume of employment opportunities that are needed to match Egypt's high birth rate. On the contrary, the evidence thus far shows that the recent pattern of investment already has made Egyptian industry even less capable of absorbing the waves of new job seekers who are scraping out a living in marginal services or swelling the pool of migrant labor.[7]

The high cost of the snail's pace of industrialization is underscored by the dramatic rise in trade deficits and foreign indebtedness throughout the *infitah* period (Table 2-6). Between 1975 and 1984 Egypt's import bill doubled while the total value of manufacturing and agricultural exports remained nearly static. This explosion of domestic consumption has made Egypt more dependent than ever on new sources of foreign exchange. Rising revenues from the Suez Canal and tourism have helped, but by far the most critical earnings have come from petroleum exports and from remittances of the estimated 4 million Egyptians who have found employment out of the country.[8]

Although this combination of new revenues helped to carry Egypt through the 1970s, none of them can be considered a reliable source in the future. Indeed, by the early 1980s there were already signs that their earnings had peaked. Tourism dropped after the political crisis of 1981, aggravating the problem of excess capacity in a sector that had been expanded prematurely. Workers' remittances were cut in half during 1982 and resumed growth only after the government agreed to a drastic devaluation that allowed repatriation at the black market exchange rate. The most serious loss has been the decline in oil exports due to the rapid growth of domestic energy consumption, which now diverts almost one-half of Egypt's petroleum output.[9]

The Mubarak government has tried to compensate for the erratic performance of these foreign exchange earners by imposing new limitations on imports. But the government's room for maneuver in foreign trade has narrowed considerably because of Egypt's growing reliance on foreign sources of basic foodstuffs. Whereas Egypt was nearly self-sufficient for most food products during the early 1970s, food accounted for one-third of all imports in 1980 and one-half by 1984.[10] Thus, even with a new importing regime that severely penalizes luxury goods and gives preference to industrial inputs, Egypt's foreign debt doubled between 1978 and 1984. When Mubarak took office the ratio of debt service to commodity exports already exceeded 100 percent; by 1984 it was approaching 200 percent despite his promulgation of a "corrective" *infitah*.

Social Restratification and Economic Partition

During the periodic expansions and contractions of the economy the benefits and burdens of change have been unequally apportioned among social groups, economic sectors, and geographic regions. However, the degree and direction of inequality have fluctuated substantially as successive governments switched their strategies of development, their international alliances, and their bases of social support. Many constituencies have experienced enormous fluctuations in their relative fortunes, gaining advantages during one period only to see them lost or cut back as the uncertain political ground shifted under their feet.

This has resulted in an unstable and highly antagonistic class structure in which each regime has been perceived as promoting excessive and offensive privileges for favored groups at the expense of others. The monarchy supported a coalition of aristocrats, minority capitalists, and resident foreigners against the burgeoning nationalism of the native middle class and the labor movement. The revolutionary and socialist regimes lavished rewards on army officers, managers and engineers, and public sector workers while decimating big landlords and businessmen. The neocapitalist revival of the *infitah* has turned the tables once again by enriching an assortment of builders and bankers, butchers and plumbers to the detriment of the vast majority who cannot keep up with the spiraling cost of living.[11]

The regressive impact of the *infitah* policies on income distribution has been well documented by a number of economic and sociological studies. Geographically, the redirection of resources has benefited the towns (particularly the capital city) over the countryside, the Delta over Upper Egypt, the Canal Zone and frontier provinces over the Nile Valley.[12] In sectoral terms, agriculture and manufacturing have been neglected in favor of trade, finance, and construction while private enterprises have been given priority over public ones.[13] Sociologically, upper classes who retained wealth from the monarchy as well as those who acquired it after the revolution have prospered from the reintroduction of market forces in contrast to most urban wage earners who remain on fixed incomes. In the countryside the position of landowners has been strengthened against tenant farmers, and the gap has widened between larger operators with capital to invest in profitable livestock, citrus, and vegetables, and smaller farmers whose cultivation is limited to price controlled crops.[14]

The *infitah* has not entirely abandoned the Nasserist commitment to social equity, but it has clearly sought to subordinate equity to growth while reducing the mechanisms of state intervention that were designed to encourage social mobility. Instead of Nasser's ambitious programs of land reform, guaranteed employment, and universal education, his successors have been content to define social opportunity in terms of food subsidies for the poor, migration for the skilled, and second-class jobs in foreign firms for those with special language abilities. The heads of urban middle-class and working-class households that benefited most from the reforms of the 1950s and 1960s have not witnessed similar mobility among their children. "Feudalist" families, thought to have been destroyed by the revolution, have bounced back, displaying an aristocratic passion for free-for-all capitalism that more than equals that of the *nouveaux riches*.[15]

This recurrent inversion of social and economic opportunities has produced a society in which examples of status incongruity abound. Family income and consumption correlate less with occupational prestige or level of education than with the ability to survive and exploit the vicissitudes of the marketplace. Construction workers may earn more than experienced engineers. Bilingual secretaries and bank clerks may be paid double the salaries of their university professors, who must moonlight at other schools and give private courses to make ends meet. The children of butchers and electricians drive their Mercedeses to the universities, social clubs, and hotel discotheques where they mingle with disdainful descendants of the *bashawaat*. Teachers, managers, and technicians leave their families for lower-level jobs in the Gulf countries, where they can build a nest egg while their skills deteriorate.[16]

As the growing inequities of the *infitah* aggravated class antagonisms, Sadat and his critics advanced contradictory explanations for the increasing incidence of violent social protest. The president dismissed the 1977 riots as an "uprising of thieves"—a criminal outburst of riffraff and malcontents whose rejection of natural hierarchy inevitably drove them to insolence and anarchy. During the next four years his marathon television addresses regularly included stern lectures to the Egyptian people, scolding them for harboring feelings of spite and resentment *(hiqd)* against the more successful and enterprising elements that had been unleashed by his bold economic reforms.[17]

Time and again Sadat reminded his audiences of his historic role in breaking the back of the monarchy, the aristocracy, and the foreign capitalists. Having given Egypt its independence and its social revolution, he would not tolerate allegations that he was selling the country to foreigners and restoring their agents to power. Egyptians, he insisted, had to overcome their "psychological complexes" against the accumulation of wealth so that hard work could receive its just rewards.

Sadat's critics, on the other hand, accused him of creating a system of "economic apartheid" in which the majority of Egyptians were becoming second-class citizens in their own country. In their view, "economic liberalization" had become a euphemism for deliberate social discrimination. The *infitah*, they asserted, was steepening the class pyramid through a number of blatant devices that were bound to be particularly offensive in an intensely nationalistic and status-conscious society: reestablishing special privileges for foreigners; nurturing the most greedy and unscrupulous segments of the business world; slashing the purchasing power of the salaried middle class precisely when the country was being flooded with luxury imports; and undercutting the already desperate position of the working poor.[18]

Sadat's condemnation of social jealousies and psychological complexes as well as his critics' allusions to economic apartheid both portrayed the *infitah* as accomplishing a fundamental transformation in Egypt's economy from socialism to capitalism. However much they disagreed about the merits and costs of such a development, each side spoke as though it were witnessing a painful but decisive shift in the balance of power between two mutually incompatible systems for organizing the economy as a whole. Indeed, this common perception of the regime and its leading opponents was largely responsible for Sadat's growing conviction that social peace could be preserved only with an arsenal of new laws limiting the freedom of association, freezing the formation of political parties, and tightening government control of the press.[19]

In retrospect it appears that both sides attributed far more credit (or blame) to the *infitah* than it deserved. Throughout Sadat's reign, and particularly under his successor, Egypt's economy became more "mixed" than ever before. While Egyptian governments were reassuring international creditors and private sector allies of their commitment to free market capitalism, they quietly promoted several different types of enterprises, hoping to mollify, if not to reconcile, the demands of diverse constituencies for a more active role in the emerging economic order. While the critics of the *infitah* were highlighting its aggravation of older horizontal and class cleavages, they generally overlooked its simultaneous encouragement of vertical and sectoral partition.

One reason that the regime's tolerance of centrifugal tendencies in the economy has been underestimated is that it contrasts so sharply with the extreme caution of the ruling elite in pursuing political liberalization. Most observers of Egypt's political economy have focused their attention on the supposed eclipse of the old socialism by the new capitalism and on its likely implications for the struggle between authoritarianism and democracy. Both in Egypt and abroad debate has revolved around the question of whether capitalist development would be compatible with further democratization (an eventual bourgeois revolution) or whether it would require an extended interlude of even greater political repression (an Egyptian version of bureaucratic authoritarianism).[20]

Although this stark framing of alternatives seemed justified in light of the political crisis that culminated in Sadat's assassination, economic changes before and after those events indicate that for some time the regime has been groping for a way to avoid both of these choices by allowing the economy to fragment into separate spheres of influence. Economic partition has been encouraged by two interrelated tendencies. First, there has been a notable scaling down of expectations about the possibilities for direct collaboration between the three largest and most powerful types of enterprises—the public, private, and foreign sectors.

Second, there has been a steady growth of entrepreneurial activity among a variety of smaller sectors geared to particular social groups and seeking to rectify or exploit the perceived deficiencies of the more dominant sectors.

Early expectations that the *infitah* would promote an easy intermingling of public, private, and foreign firms gradually gave way to a more sober recognition of their distinctive identities. Debate about the possible divestiture of state enterprises produced a backlash among labor leaders that eventually limited even more modest projects to sell a portion of their stock in open capital markets and to establish joint ventures with private and foreign investors. Efforts to reorganize public enterprises advanced only when the government assured the union hierarchy that divestiture was a dead issue and that the state would retain a controlling interest in any ventures involving existing public industries. Mubarak has increased state industry's share of planned investment and has tried to quiet labor leaders' lingering suspicions about the *infitah* by echoing their slogans that public enterprises constitute "the essential focus of national industry" and "the historic core of Egyptian socialism." [21]

Union leaders in the public sector have been willing to accept a number of unpopular reforms for the sake of greater productivity, including concessions on employment and wage levels as well as retraining programs to relocate redundant workers. In return, however, they have pressed hard for broader forms of codetermination that would grant the unions a measure of control over the selection of worker representatives. To moderate union demands for a greater voice in public sector management the government has encouraged the leaders of the labor movement to go into business for themselves. Since 1976 the labor confederation has been granted a variety of new powers, allowing it to expand the existing system of cooperatives and to use a combination of public funds and compulsory worker contributions in establishing its own economic enterprises. [22]

The private sector has been even more assertive in protecting its turf against the foreign investors who were thought to be its natural allies. Most of the capital attracted to joint venture firms has come from local rather than foreign investors; many of the enterprises are wholly owned by Egyptians seeking the exemptions and incentives accorded by special legal status without the interference of multinational partners. In several cases the original foreign exchange requirements for these enterprises have been relaxed, allowing local businessmen to set up their own "joint ventures" with soft currency. [23]

The importance of the joint venture formula in helping to consolidate

UNRULY CORPORATISM

TABLE 2-7.   Shares of State, Private, and Foreign Capital
in Joint Venture Projects
(Percentages by Sector through December 31, 1983)

	State	Private	Foreign	Arab	E.E.C.	U.S.	Other
Finance and Services							
Investment	18	23	59	55	1	0	3
Banking	40	39	21	7	5	3	6
Tourism	8	55	37	13	4	1	19
Transport	6	52	42	15	9	0	18
Health	21	53	26	8	4	3	11
Services	6	27	67	1	3	60	3
Subtotal	19	35	46	31	3	5	7
Agriculture and Construction							
Agriculture	40	40	20	8	4	4	4
Housing	11	64	25	21	2	0	2
Contracting	7	68	25	7	11	2	5
Consulting	21	42	37	2	10	9	16
Subtotal	21	56	23	13	5	2	3
Industry							
Textiles	31	34	35	11	1	8	15
Food	15	64	21	8	5	1	7
Chemicals	47	21	32	6	18	2	6
Wood	12	64	24	16	7	2	1
Engineering	20	42	38	8	19	7	4
Building materials	38	44	18	7	5	3	2
Metallurgy	46	26	28	16	4	1	7
Pharmaceuticals	22	54	24	1	7	9	7
Mining	91	7	2	1	0	0	1
Petroleum	12	3	85	0	85	0	0
Subtotal	35	37	28	8	11	3	6
Grand total	24	38	38	22	5	4	7

Source: Omar Saad el-Din, "The Role of State, Private, and Foreign Capital in Law 43 of 1974 Projects" (Master's thesis, Department of Economics and Political Science, American University in Cairo, 1984), pp. 28, 44.

the position of the native business community is evident from the relative weight of state, private, and foreign capital in new firms established with the permission of the Egyptian Investment Authority (Table 2-7). Total investment in all joint ventures is evenly divided between private and foreign capital, with the state acting as a junior partner. Within specific categories, however, the pattern of investment is clearly skewed toward the Egyptian private sector. The textile industry is the sole area in which all three sectors account for nearly equal shares of investment. In eight out of twenty categories Egyptian private investors account for a solid majority of capital and in three others they have contributed the predominant share. Moreover, the areas in which local capital prevails are quite evenly distributed among the services, construction, and various branches of manufacturing.

In contrast, the pattern of foreign and state investment is far more selective and specialized. Foreign investors dominate in only three categories, reflecting strong concentrations of European capital in petroleum, of American capital in government consulting, and of Arab capital in investment firms feeding housing and tourism. State investment is more oriented toward industry, where it dominates mining and, to a lesser extent, chemicals and metallurgy. In general, the participation of state capital seems geared not to establish public control but to supplement local private investment and to insure that control of nearly all categories remains in Egyptian hands.[24]

The Mubarak government has tried to strengthen the Egyptian element in the private sector equation even more by redefining the major role of foreign participation as the contribution of advanced technology instead of the mere provision of capital. By carving out a protected market for domestic producers in light industry, the architects of the ''productive *infitah*'' are hoping to direct toward manufacturing some of the local profits acquired during the earlier period of liberal importing. This amounts to a new division of labor in which foreign capital is being assigned the task of long-term industrial deepening while native capital is invited to turn toward lucrative import substitution. The result has been a clear ''re-Egyptianization'' of many consumer goods as foreign firms shift to the greater use of local inputs and as native manufacturers scramble for licenses and raw materials to produce more of what was formerly imported.

The renewed divergence of public, private, and foreign enterprises is symptomatic of a more general trend toward sectoral fragmentation that is evident in many other areas of the economy as well. The improved organization of big business has been accompanied by an expansion of the already vast and amorphous ''informal'' sector and by the emergence of a more complex and powerful black market.[25] Within the public sector the military has initiated several new projects to diversify the defense industry and to achieve self-sufficiency in many consumer goods. Perhaps the most striking innovation has been the rapid growth of a new type of associational capitalism exemplified in the wide assortment of enterprises that have been established by the syndical, cooperative, and Islamic movements.

This multiplication of actors and organized interests has presented the Mubarak government with a serious dilemma. Just when it is attempting to redress widespread grievances over the "economic anarchy" of the *infitah,* it confronts an array of compartmentalized sectors that are less amenable than ever to the reassertion of central planning and government regulation. Just as the state is preparing to reassert its role in overall economic coordination, its own agencies are becoming more susceptible to penetration by conflicting interests that seek to undermine official policy or to pull it in opposing directions.

Thus far, the state's relations with the more specialized economic sectors have varied widely from confrontation to direct subsidization to cautious watchfulness. The most striking example of confrontation concerns the extensive black market that has flourished on the illegal exchange of foreign currency. Egypt's economy has long supported a number of separate black markets trafficking in a broad range of goods, such as smuggled appliances and clothing, spare parts, public sector inputs and building materials, subsidized foodstuffs, cigarettes, and narcotics. During the *infitah,* however, illegal commerce has concentrated in well-organized currency smuggling operations funneling foreign exchange from migrant workers and foreign residents to importers in both public and private sectors.

When proregulation members of the Mubarak cabinet tried to strengthen the power of the Central Bank, they quickly discovered that the government could not even estimate, let alone control, the nation's money supply. After nearly three years of trying to smash the illegal subeconomy with police measures, they realized that its size and resilience could be countered only if the government enacted a series of devaluations that would make the official banking system competitive with its underground rivals. In the end it was the black market, not the state, that set the official rate of exchange. Private and foreign banks, which were originally to be subjected to tougher government controls, emerged with most of their privileges intact and welcomed a new set of ministers who viewed bankers not as adversaries and profiteers but as the most reliable agents for implementing financial policy.[26]

The leading cases in which the state has actively subsidized new entrepreneurial activities concern the military and the syndical movement. The Ministry of Defense and War Production operates a number of independent manufacturing establishments whose traditional output has been uniforms and munitions. Under the Mubarak government military commanders have been granted a larger share of public investment to develop a national arms industry, including ambitious plans to manufacture fighter planes in cooperation with France and Brazil. Military production has been diversifying considerably throughout the 1980s, moving into the provision of food and household appliances for the civilian market. Military managers characterize these newer activities as removing a burden from the private sector and as compensating temporarily for some of its specific weaknesses. Nevertheless, when the expanded industrial capacity of the armed forces is added to its far-reaching operations in public construction, utilities, and transportation, the military can be considered one of Egypt's fastest growing subeconomies.[27]

One of the most intriguing innovations of the post-Nasserist state is the creation of a broad network of business enterprises throughout the syndical movement. A new economic sector—an Egyptian variety of syndical capitalism—is emerging under the leadership of the labor unions and professional associations. The chief prototypes of associational entrepreneurship thus far are the Confederation of Labor and the Engineers' Syndicate. These organizations have received charters for special banks to finance their own trading companies, factories, construction firms, real estate corporations, hospitals and clinics, consumer and housing cooperatives, sporting and vacation facilities, and educational institutions. Capital subscriptions for these enterprises are derived from several sources: state banks, pension funds, compulsory levies on members, public stock offerings, and partnerships with private and foreign businessmen.[28]

Virtually all of the other professional associations have followed suit on a more modest level with projects offering a similar combination of special services and profit-making opportunities. Syndical capitalism has quietly superseded the old cooperative system that was launched with great expectations during the socialist era only to become a stepchild of the *infitah*. The Sadat and Mubarak regimes continued to pay lip service to the cooperatives as making up the third major sector of the Egyptian economy (after the public and private sectors) even as that role was being shifted to foreign capital. With the rise of the syndical sector, the cooperative movement was demoted once again. Deprived of substantial public resources, most cooperatives have been reduced to a vestige of socialism whose legal privileges and symbolic status are either exploited by private entrepreneurs or appropriated by the more powerful occupational associations.[29]

There is an additional type of investment activity that has developed with conspicuous independence of state support—what can be described as an emerging Islamic sector of the economy. From the inception of the *infitah* the marriage of religion and capitalism has been most visible in the growth of Islamic banking and in the prosperity of many businessmen in the Muslim Brotherhood. Both of these elements have strong connections to the economies of the Gulf states either through direct capitalization or because of longstanding commercial dealings. Islamic banks have already grown to account for 15 to 20 percent of all bank deposits. Sensing yet another threat to its control over the money supply, the government has halted the formation of new Islamic banks while directing some state banks to cut into their market by offering similar services.[30]

The success of Muslim businesses has encouraged many private religious groups to establish their own Islamic enterprises in direct competition with both the public and private sectors. The Islamic movement has opened several retail shops and small factories soliciting the patronage of pious sympathizers. A large portion of its investments also has gone into new clinics that generally are affiliated with private mosques in the big cities. Managed by the Islamic associations and financed with private charitable contributions, these clinics have attracted many patients from the provinces as well as the urban quarters who regard them as superior alternatives to the poor care of overcrowded state hospitals and the high costs of private physicians.[31]

The leaders of the Islamic associations note with some pride that they are improving medical care for the masses at no expense to the public treasury whereas nearly all other organized interests are queuing up with selfish demands for some form of state assistance. The government, of course, realizes that these expanding economic and philanthropic activities are providing religious groups with a popular following that extends far beyond their core members. It is precisely the success and independence of these groups that concerns the regime, creating predictable fears that the state will try to regulate, subsidize, and ultimately absorb their facilities.

The most controversial members of the Islamic sector are the "Islamic investment corporations" *(sharikaat tawzif al-amwal)*. These are generally family-run companies that imitate the interest-free principles of the traditional Islamic banks but that pay much larger dividends because of their high-risk involvement in gold speculation and foreign currency trade. Since the early 1980s about fifteen of these companies have attracted well over a million investors, raising estimates of their total assets to $15 billion or more. The combined appeal of religious imagery and high profits proved so popular among small investors and overseas workers that both nationalized and foreign banks began to pressure the Mubarak government to step in and restrain their Islamic competitors.[32]

In 1986 the governor of the Central Bank launched a campaign to crush the Islamic investment companies, but he was ousted from office after a counterattack from their defenders in the cabinet and the press who described them as the most important spontaneous development in the private sector since the emergence of Bank Misr. The following year the largest investment companies managed to break a wave of panic withdrawals by paying out an average of $11 million a day for nearly two weeks. When a new law finally was adopted in the summer of 1988 to regulate the investment corporations, its intent was not to eliminate them but to protect their investors and stabilize their operations by changing them into something approximating joint stock companies. The government insisted that this legislation was the product of bargaining and mutual agreement between the ruling party and the investment companies. This negotiation was described as a key to the maturation of the Islamic sector from an informal and extralegal "parallel economy" into a full-blown partner of state and foreign capital in joint ventures that would rechannel small savings to local industry.[33] When the largest of the Islamic investment companies collapsed at the end of 1988, the government took direct control of its assets and enterprises, indicating that other members of the Islamic sector might have to accept greater state regulation if they wished to avoid a similar fate.

The proliferation of so many different kinds of enterprises in Egypt's mixed economy can be interpreted as a sign of new vitality in several areas of civil society. The persistence of strong cleavages in class, ideology, and culture have in no way dampened economic innovation; indeed, they may have encouraged it in some surprising ways. The inherent tensions between socialist and capitalist principles have been skirted and finessed with a remarkable combination of practicality and hypocrisy, ingenuity and indifference. Instead of a society paralyzed by dissent and indecision, there is ample evidence of organizational sophistication among a number of groups that are moving ahead under their own steam and in their own directions.

Yet this optimistic assessment must be tempered by the recognition that economic partition also reflects enduring weaknesses in the political system. The multiplication of disjointed economic sectors has been a direct consequence of policy adopted by a stumbling authoritarian regime. This may be justly criticized as a tacit and timid policy, but it is a policy nonetheless. Divided over development strategy, fearful of recurrent social explosions, and unwilling either to dismantle or to galvanize an ineffective system of corporatist controls, Egypt's leaders have let initiative slip more and more into the hands of special interests. The procrastination and drift of the state contrast more glaringly than ever with the energy and impatience of organized society.

3

The State and the Organization of Interests

The development of associational life in Egypt has reflected an ongoing tension between the regeneration of the authoritarian state and the increasing organization of civil society. For at least a century there has been a continuous interplay between emerging groups and movements seeking to fashion representative institutions from below and ruling elites trying to mold and manipulate representation from above. Egyptian interest groups have evolved as a combined product of spontaneity and contrivance. Many organizations that originated as voluntary groups or popular movements have been reshaped into semiofficial appendages of the bureaucracy. Many others were conceived by the state as instruments of economic regulation and social control but then gradually took on a life of their own to become virtual veto groups in key areas of policymaking.

The autonomy of associations—as well as the autonomy of the state that has chartered and regulated them—has fluctuated periodically, often producing consequences that have been unintended and undesired by government and group leaders alike. When associations have flaunted their capacity for independent action or political opposition, they have provoked repression and extensive state interference in their internal affairs. Similarly, when ruling elites have devolved authority and resources in order to co-opt favored groups, they have created new centers of power that have bolstered authoritarian regimes in the short run while limiting their long-term maneuverability and adaptiveness.

Association leaders commonly are torn by incompatible demands to defend the interests of their constituents while simultaneously serving as agents of the government. Even leaders who are appointed by the state or slated by the ruling party frequently become forceful advocates for the very groups they are expected to regulate. Alternatively, leaders who are elected with clear popular support are regularly drafted into the cabinet, the government party, and the parliament, where they find it much more difficult to separate themselves from official policy and nearly impossible to identify with the political opposition. Incorporating members of the associational elite into the decision-making process has created a semblance of consultation with diverse interests, but saddling them with dual allegiances has alienated them from their constituencies and undermined their credibility as spokesmen for the groups they purport to represent.

The constant tug-of-war between the government's supporters and opponents for control of associations has shortened the careers of many leaders who sided too openly with rank-and-file revolts or who sold out their members for personal advancement. On the other hand, many group leaders have been able to exploit the inherent ambiguity of their roles by persuading disgruntled constituents that they need an influential voice at court and by warning the government that it must enhance the authority and privileges of the associations to prevent them from falling into the hands of troublemakers. Interest group leaders who have demonstrated an ability to feed off the mutual suspicions of their members and the ruling elites have managed to carve out a position of independence from both.

Throughout the twentieth century the counterpoint of state sponsorship and independent initiative has provided Egypt's associational life with a marked and persistent structural heterogeneity. From the British colonial administrations to the current Mubarak government, successive regimes have shifted back and forth between pluralism and corporatism as the preferred technique for organizing or disorganizing group activity, depending on their changing strategies of political domination and economic development. Consequently, a wide variety of pluralist, corporatist, and hybrid organizations have emerged as alternative channels of representation for different social and economic interests.

It is possible to identify particular historical periods and social sectors in which either pluralism or corporatism has been the predominant mode of representation. However, no regime has been able to mold the expanding associational universe into anything that approaches a coherent pluralist or corporatist design. Each government has tolerated organizational

vestiges inherited from earlier periods and each government has deliberately fostered glaring inconsistencies in the structure and influence of
groups representing different constituencies. Regardless of the overall thrust
of associational policy at any given time, many groups have retained an
idiosyncratic combination of privileges and constraints that are periodically renegotiated with the political authorities.

The Evolution of Public Policy toward Associations

Three types of sources are particularly useful in reconstructing the historical record of state intervention in promoting and restructuring associational life. Historians, social scientists, and association leaders have produced several valuable case studies covering group activity in individual
social sectors and specific historical periods. In addition, the state itself
has promulgated an enormous body of detailed legislation establishing
and reorganizing associations in all fields and closely regulating virtually
every aspect of their operations. Finally, many government agencies and
group headquarters have collected statistical information, including some
data acquired over the course of several decades, on the number of various associations, the growth of their memberships, and their changing
geographic distributions.

Piecing together these parts of the puzzle makes it possible to organize
a historical overview of public policy toward associations since the late
nineteenth century. A summary of the landmark statutes regulating interest group activity demonstrates the eclectic and shifting nature of state
intervention (Figure 3-1).[1] Over time Egypt's rulers have promoted very
different blends of pluralist and corporatist structures in particular interest
sectors and in the political system as a whole. In general, there have been
four fairly distinct periods during which important changes have occurred
in the relative preponderance of pluralist versus corporatist policies.

From the beginning of the British occupation until the establishment of
the constitutional monarchy associational life became increasingly heterogeneous as corporatist remnants of the traditional guild system survived
alongside new voluntary groups in labor, agriculture, and commerce. An
important stimulus for group formation came from Egypt's earliest political parties as they sought to mobilize working-class and middle-class
supporters both in the cities and in the countryside. At the same time the
government chartered the first modern corporatist association, the lawyers' syndicate, in order to regulate the new legal profession and to co-
opt the principal source of leadership for the burgeoning movement on
behalf of national independence.

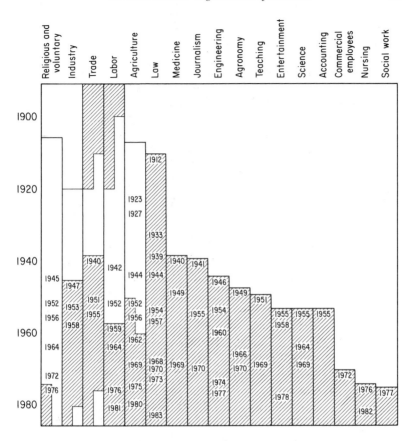

Figure 3.1 Evolution of Associational Legislation by Sector (corporatist sectors, shaded;, pluralist sectors, unshaded)

During the 1920s and 1930s, when popularly elected Wafdist parliaments were dissolved by a series of aristocratic dictatorships, pluralist policies clearly predominated. Both the Wafd and its enemies encouraged a feeble and fragmented collection of private, voluntary groups that were highly susceptible to repression by the state and to manipulation by party patrons. The major beneficiaries of this debilitating pluralism were urban protest movements such as Misr al-Fatat and the Muslim Brotherhood, which were able to organize on the fringes of the law, as well as the entrepreneurs of the Federation of Egyptian Industries, who developed close connections with the palace and its aristocratic allies.

With the onset of World War II the state began a gradual but decisive shift toward a more interventionist associational policy. In one sector after another new corporatist groups were established and existing voluntary associations were reorganized into semiofficial bodies. The recasting of associational life occurred in three successive waves of corporatization coinciding with World War II, the Free Officers' Revolution, and the socialist transformation of the 1960s. Many corporatist initiatives began as piecemeal and improvised responses to wartime emergencies and revolutionary crises. However, by the final years of the Nasserist era corporatism was portrayed as an essential aspect of Egyptian political culture, supporting a supposedly unique experiment in Arab socialism and providing the blueprint for a quasi-syndicalist republic.

In response to the recurrent political unrest that has jolted the authoritarian regime since the Six Day War, Egypt's rulers have advanced and buried a number of pseudoreforms involving various mixtures of both pluralism and corporatism. The edifice of corporatist associations has been retained and expanded to cover additional sectors, but it has become an increasingly inadequate device for insulating the ruling elite from the demands of special interests and political opponents. Several groups have been able to use the privileges of corporatism to extract greater resources from the state and to forge informal alliances with the opposition parties. Many businessmen and religious activists have broken out of the corporatist network altogether, establishing independent voluntary associations that openly compete with older, state-sponsored groups.

As post-Nasserist governments have oscillated between loosening and retightening restrictions on the freedom of association, the historic heterogeneity of group life has resurfaced. Now, more than at any time since the Free Officers' Revolution, civil society is organized around a mélange of corporatist, pluralist, and hybrid groups pressing similar kinds of demands despite enduring differences in their legal status and formal structures. While the authoritarian regime temporizes over the pace and direction of political reform, it is being forced more and more to balance and bargain with diverse interests instead of trying to repress them.

The Persistence of Traditional Corporatism and the Genesis of Modern Pluralism, 1882–1922

Although the modern occupational associations of the early twentieth century did not evolve from Egypt's traditional guild system, there were clear connections and similarities between them. Although it is often assumed that the guilds were destroyed by Muhammad 'Ali's experiments with modern industry, their decline was in fact a subtle and protracted process that continued well beyond the British occupation until the end of World War I. Despite the relatively early weakening of artisan organizations in the first half of the nineteenth century, many commercial, construction, transportation, and service guilds survived and continued to perform important public functions. As late as the 1880s Cairo and several other towns still possessed diversified guild networks encompassing the vast majority of the working population.[2]

Only in the last quarter of the nineteenth century did Egyptian governments begin to supplant the guilds' traditional role as administrative links and regulatory bodies with their own bureaucratic apparatus. Even as the guilds began to disappear, the state continued to rely on their assistance in providing labor and services, in fixing wages and prices, in implementing government directives, and in disciplining their members. The enduring utility of the guilds to the colonial administration helps to explain why they were never abolished by law, as in the other Ottoman provinces. Instead, they were allowed to linger and fade imperceptibly with the influx of European goods and settlers, the growth of a new urban work force fed by rural migration, and the appearance of modern labor and commercial associations.[3]

The malleability of the guilds and their ambivalent relations with the state distinguished traditional corporatism in Egypt from similar institutions elsewhere in the Ottoman Empire. Compared to the tightly controlled guilds of Istanbul and the autonomous guilds of Damascus, Egyptian guilds occupied an intermediate and uncertain status. The more centralized administration of the Ottoman capital permitted the state to devolve greater powers to the Turkish guilds during their heyday and to wipe them out more swiftly when they were deemed unnecessary. Alternatively, in Syria, where government was more decentralized than in Egypt, the guilds were less entwined with the state and more strongly supported by the local population. Thus, the Damascene guilds survived much longer than their Egyptian counterparts, continuing nearly two decades after they had been formally abolished.[4]

As World War I approached Egypt's withering guild system left two important legacies that helped to shape the rise of the earliest modern occupational associations, both pluralist and corporatist. To the nascent labor movement the guilds bequeathed a fragmented collection of artisans, journeymen, and shopkeepers from diverse religions and nationalities. Their vulnerability in the face of European trade created ample reason for social protest, but they were far less prone to collective action than the smaller groups of industrial workers who were often led by radical immigrants from Greece and Italy. The gap between the "guild mentality'' of the tradesmen and the ''imported anarchism'' of the factory workers split the union movement from the beginning. Even when native Egyptians came to constitute the bulk of the membership in subsequent years, the persistence of divergent union subcultures frustrated many efforts to establish nationwide federations.[5]

To the rising middle class of native professionals the guild system left a more subtle yet more enduring legacy—a prototype for the modern corporatist syndicates that authoritarian governments would use time and again to contain middle-class political ambitions while giving in to narrow demands for occupational recognition. When the lawyers' syndicate was chartered in 1912 as the first exclusively Egyptian corporatist association, its leaders protested that the government was trying to transplant the archaic and restrictive guild system to the liberal professions. Sa'd Zaghlul, who was minister of justice at the time, specifically objected to the charter's demeaning language, which dubbed the syndicate a *niqaba* and its president a *naqib*—terms that symbolically linked the new association with the subservient guilds and with the working class.[6]

Zaghlul understood that the special treatment accorded the lawyers was a mixed blessing, that the government was responding less to their elevated social status than to their political troublesomeness. A semiofficial syndicate allowed native professionals a measure of self-government, but it also gave the state broad regulatory powers over the segment of the middle class that was least dependent on government employment and most qualified to lead the nation's new political parties. Egyptian lawyers thought they were fighting for an occupational syndicate that would be modeled after the European-dominated Mixed Bar Association; instead, they had to settle for a neo-Ottoman formula that was carefully designed to increase state control over the livlihood of politically assertive nationalists.

Government fears about the interconnection between occupational organization and political mobilization were well founded. Even sporadic tolerance of press and associational freedoms was enough to stimulate a nascent pluralism in which short-lived political parties sought alliances with new voluntary associations. Indeed, the state's efforts to preserve and refurbish corporatism can be seen as a defense mechanism against the early success of the nationalist parties in promoting and infiltrating several kinds of occupational groups.

Before World War I the Nationalist Party (Hizb al-Watani) played an important role in organizing some of the first labor unions and agricultural cooperatives. Especially when leadership passed to Muhammad Farid, the party attempted to move beyond its urban middle-class base and to build mass support for the nationalist movement. The Nationalist Party was particularly successful in penetrating the early craft unions. It helped to establish the first union federation, the Manual Workers' Union, which remained the leading labor organization until the war. Party activists ran a network of People's Night Schools, with branches in the provinces, that offered a combination of vocational, legal, and religious training. During the first two decades of the labor movement these schools served as the major bridge between the party-sponsored craft federation and the independent transport and railway unions.[7]

While the Nationalist Party was attempting to reach out to the lower classes, the National Party (Hizb al-Umma) was expanding its domination of provincial politics and of the Legislative Assembly by forging links with new associations of professionals, landowners, and merchants. Umma Party leaders were prominent among the founding members of the press union, the lawyers' syndicate, the cotton growers' society, and the Egyptian chambers of commerce that sprang up in many of the provincial capitals. Although the Umma Party represented the large landholding families who were the principal beneficiaries of British rule, they relied upon the new economic associations to extract greater concessions from the colonial administration, especially as the war approached. In exchange for their endorsement of a formal protectorate in 1914, for example, the British agreed to a generous package of tax and debt deferrals, long-term loans, and guaranteed crop purchases.[8]

The most powerful convergence of associational and political activity occurred during the Nationalist Revolution of 1919. This time, however, the emergence of a new party was more the product than the cause of widespread group agitation. Except for the planned demonstrations of lawyers and students who had been close allies of the Hizb al-Watani, the early uprisings of the revolution were not controlled by the Wafd leadership. Indeed, it was the unanticipated spontaneity and diversity of mass protest that spurred the Wafd to develop quickly a complex infrastructure that could sustain and direct the nationalist movement and gradually shape it into a popular base for Egypt's first nationwide party organization. Throughout its rapid transformation from a peaceful petition campaign to a revolutionary steering committee and then to a powerful electoral machine, the Wafd was constantly trying to catch up with the very social forces it sought to represent.

The domestic organization of the Wafd was led by a central committee and a secret apparatus, both of which relied heavily on existing associations to coordinate support for Zaghlul and his colleagues while they were in exile or in Europe. The central committee had a predominantly rural composition, in contrast to the more urban and professional orientation of the top leadership abroad. It was particularly effective in mobilizing financial support from the countryside by enlisting the aid of the village headmen (*'umdas*) who controlled the provincial administrations. In the cities, however, the central committee operated more as a liaison than as a directorate. Its major activity was orchestrating strikes and boycotts that were carried out by a host of sympathetic but independent groups, including civil servants, professionals, Azharis, the Coptic churches, students, unions, merchants, and women.[9]

The Wafd's tenuous control over the diverse associational life of the cities was underlined by its frequent resort to intimidation and terror via a special underground organization. The most spectacular operations of the secret apparatus were a series of assassination plots against politicians who were willing to enter interim governments and bargain with the British behind Zaghlul's back. Ironically, the secret organization did not succeed in killing a single minister, but it was quite effective in forcing merchants to close down their shops and in drawing workers into party-sponsored labor unions. The secret organization provided the Wafd with its first foothold in the union movement, initiating a tutelary and paternalistic relationship with organized labor that party leaders would expand considerably over the next two decades.[10]

Palace Pluralism, 1923–1939

The period during which associational policy was most reliant on pluralism was also the period in which the constitutional monarchy most frequently lapsed into aristocratic dictatorship. During the 1920s and 1930s the state chartered no new corporatist organizations and provided no legal guarantees for the freedom of association. Each government tolerated a shifting assortment of private, voluntary groups that could be manipulated in an arbitrary and discriminatory manner. Hampered by primitive organization and a precarious legal status, most groups remained vulnerable to repression, police infiltration, and suspensions of public subsidies. Groups that sought to overcome these inherent weaknesses by forming alliances with political parties often became even more crippled and divided as they were drawn into the partisan squabbles of their overbearing patrons.

The debilitating nature of Egyptian pluralism contributed to royal absolutism and dependent capitalist development in several ways. First, it prevented the Wafd from developing a reliable network of associational support either in its constant battles with the king and the British or in its mounting street skirmishes with more radical segments of the nationalist movement. Unable to translate its clear electoral majorities into an organized social coalition, the Wafd became alienated from more and more of its urban supporters and was forced to collaborate with the semicolonial regime it had vowed to destroy.

Second, palace pluralism fostered a pronounced class bias in the art of association. Although the state quietly encouraged the development of a centralized set of businessmen's associations, it forcefully intervened to frustrate the consolidation of the labor movement. In exchange for their support of dictatorship, native industrialists won approval of their demands for protectionism and import substitution while repeatedly vetoing initiatives favoring union recognition and social welfare.

Third, a fragmented and lopsided pluralism disorganized society to the point that authoritarian governments felt no compelling need to construct a more elaborate system of corporatist controls. Instead of chartering new associations that would require the explicit recognition of group privileges, the king and his allies tolerated divided unions and militant social movements that were able to launch sporadic campaigns of nationalist, religious, and economic protest. Only in the late 1930s, when mass movements reached new levels of organized violence, did the aristocratic dictatorships begin to advance corporatist strategies for restructuring associational life. As powerful clandestine organizations superseded the discredited party system, pluralism developed revolutionary potentials that demanded innovative countermeasures. Gradually, the regime began to abandon palace pluralism in favor of new state-sponsored groups that were intended to serve as supporting elements of a more popular authoritarian order.

Throughout the interwar period the Wafd's key associational alliances remained limited to three extremely vulnerable groups: the lawyers' syndicate, a series of short-lived union federations that were largely the creation of the party itself, and an agricultural cooperative movement that was dependent on irregular flows of credit from the state. By far the most dependable of these groups was the lawyers' syndicate, which quickly became a cocoon sheltering Wafdist leaders whenever they were driven from the government. Within the bar council the Wafd's deposed ministers regularly regrouped as a shadow cabinet, launched attacks on their enemies, and planned a return to power after new elections. Yet, no matter how useful the syndicate was to the Wafd, it never became a safe haven. By waging political warfare from within a corporatist enclave, the

Wafdists selected a battlefield where the state also enjoyed guaranteed access and where it could constantly revise the rules of combat to suit its own purposes.[11]

Liberal historians have highlighted the syndicate's role in rallying opposition that cut short at least two authoritarian governments and helped to restore the constitution. In the long-term, however, the syndicate paid a high price for these political victories. Each time the Wafd's enemies returned to power they resumed their attacks on the syndicate with greater vigor, interfering in syndical elections, packing its membership with government supporters, and trimming its statutory powers. By the end of the 1930s the Wafd had lost control of its only associational stronghold. The bar council came to represent a coalition of partisan tendencies, including new factions within the Wafd itself. Faced with a divided council, the government was able to enact a new syndical law limiting the syndicate president to two terms and establishing a mixed system of elected and appointed leadership.[12]

By turning the corporatist privileges of the lawyers' syndicate against the state, the Wafd virtually insured that no other professional group would be accorded a similar status for many years. Although the Wafd enjoyed strong support among the liberal professions, its fusion of syndical and party politics hampered the many private professional societies that were seeking official recognition and support in the interwar period. After 1940, when Egypt's rulers revived their interest in corporatism, the taming of the bar association provided a chastening reminder of what other professions could expect if they tried to follow the lawyers' example.

In the labor movement the Wafd occupied a far more precarious position that was under constant assault. One of the earliest decisions of the Zaghlul government in 1924 was to dispatch the police against factory occupations led by his rivals in the socialist unions. Thereafter the Wafd set up new labor federations whenever it came to power, but they quickly weakened as soon as it was forced back into opposition. For struggling labor leaders seeking a reliable source of patronage, the Wafd offered the worst of both worlds. Its labor advisers insisted on party supervision of strike activity and union finances, but they never controlled the state long enough to redeem even modest pledges of social reform. Affiliation with the Wafd merely increased labor's vulnerability to government repression. When the depression hit, the union movement was virtually defenseless against the combined attack of the Sidqi government and the Federation of Egyptian Industries.[13]

During the 1930s much of the decimated labor movement began to regroup around the patronage of 'Abbas Halim, the flamboyant outcast of the royal family who openly challenged Wafdist hegemony over the unions. Halim is often portrayed as a spoiler who divided the labor movement in order to advance his own claims to the throne. Yet his federation provided an attractive alternative for many unionists whether they sought a more effective link to the palace or a more tolerant protector who would foster an independent union leadership drawn from the workers themselves.

Despite his princely origins and monarchist pretensions, Halim became a powerful symbol of working-class autonomy. He was often accused of being a stalking-horse for the palace, but his earliest success in a union election represented a clear worker repudiation of a candidate who had been handpicked by King Fu'ad. Halim did conclude an understanding with Ahmad Husayn that his legal advisers would be chosen from the members of Misr al-Fatat, but this appeared to be nothing more than a tactical alliance permitting him greater independence from the Wafd. Unlike the other patrons of the labor movement, he recruited his assistants largely from workers rather than party lawyers.[14]

Halim's federation was a crucial training ground for a whole generation of labor leaders who felt stifled by the Wafd's persistent tutelage and betrayed by its increasing social conservatism. It was Halim's comrades, not the Wafdists, who led the famous hunger strikes of 1939 that finally achieved Egypt's first prounion legislation. Halim retained a following in the labor movement during World War II despite his imprisonment at the hands of the Wafdist government that had been installed by the British. Many of his associates emerged from the war to head powerful union factions of their own. These included both radicals who reestablished socialist unionism in the private textile plants as well as opportunists who fashioned the public transport unions into a key political force that could be wielded by or against the government of the day.[15]

Perhaps the bitterest disappointment for the Wafd was its inability to sustain a foothold in the agricultural cooperatives—the very groups that could have solidified its support among its natural constituency in the countryside. Here, more than in any other sector, the Wafd's failure to control the public purse was decisive. The meager flow of state credits to the cooperatives tended to rise precisely when the Wafdists were ousted from power. Muhammad Mahmud was eager to persuade rural voters that the suspension of the constitution would bring new prosperity to the villages. He sponsored a number of public works programs and irrigation projects, following them up with campaign forays into some of the Wafd's strongest provincial bases. Even the Wafdist project to establish an agricultural bank was ultimately stolen by its enemies. In 1931 the Sidqi government turned over controlling interest in the new Bank of Agricultural Credit to foreign bankers and private investors and then posed as the farmers' savior during the darkest days of the depression.[16]

While aristocratic governments increased the cooperatives' credits, they also raised the minimum holdings that were required for eligible borrowers. What had always been intended as a safety net for small cultivators who could not qualify for loans from foreign banks gradually became a source of cheap credit for the grandees who were buying up the most productive land. As the state delivered the cooperatives into the hands of the rural notables, it hastened the growth of large estates and the fragmentation of small holdings. In time the corruption of the cooperatives also helped to shift the balance of power within the Wafd itself. By strengthening the hand of the party's conservative agrarian wing, the dictatorships of the 1920s and 1930s all but insured that the postwar Wafd would eventually try to kill its own proposals for land reform.[17]

The social biases of palace pluralism are most obvious when the ups and downs of professional, worker, and farmer groups are contrasted with the impressive progress of native businessmen's associations. Even before World War I private Egyptian business groups began to proliferate alongside the several European chambers of commerce that had operated since the late nineteenth century. Soon after the war Bank Misr tried to accelerate and diversify the organization of local capitalists by sponsoring new chambers of commerce and agricultural cooperatives in the provinces. Tal'at Harb and the Misr group managed to build substantial support for their nationalist campaign on behalf of a purely Egyptian industrial policy. However, by far the most successful associational venture came not from the handful of new Muslim entrepreneurs who wished to break European economic hegemony but from the more cosmopolitan group of "Egyptianized" foreigners (al-mutamassiryun) who were content to renegotiate the terms of that hegemony in light of the postwar changes in Egypt's semicolonial status.[18]

The principal agency for organizing these cosmopolitan interests into the dominant faction of Egyptian capitalism was the Federation of Egyptian Industries. Established in 1922, the federation developed a highly centralized structure grouping industrialists in over twenty specialized branches. During the interwar years, it was indisputably the most influential and effective occupational group in the nation. The federation led the fight to abolish customs duties on local manufactures and to replace them with protective tariffs. It repeatedly nullified union and welfare legislation that would have reduced the competitive advantages of Egypt's cheap and docile labor force. It carefully straddled the battles between the Misr group and the group's foreign competitors until it was able to depose Tal'at Harb and replace him with its own board of directors. Finally, it deflected efforts to broaden the state's direct participation in industrialization until World War II, when it had consolidated its position as the leading spokesman for private enterprise.[19]

The ongoing symbiosis of European, minority, and state interests was vividly personified in the three figures who guided the association's development for nearly thirty years: Henri Naus, Isaac Levy, and Isma'il Sidqi. Naus, the president of the federation, was a Belgian industrialist who operated a lucrative sugar monopoly. He had come to Egypt at the turn of the century after working as an engineer for a Belgian sugar company in Indonesia. Of the many foreign communities in Egypt at the time, the Belgians were one of the smallest and least assimilated, retaining particularly strong ties with European finance. Although Naus was one of the first Belgians to establish firm roots in Egypt, he nevertheless remained a vigilant defender of Europe's local agents.[20] Although a state concessionaire himself and the manager of many government subsidies to the federation, Naus vigorously protested public assistance to the Misr enterprises, especially when they began to take over foreign firms that had been weakened by the depression.[21]

Levy, the general secretary, was the federation's chief economic adviser, organizational strategist, and propagandist. A Jew born in Istanbul and trained in Italy in political economy and oriental languages, he served in the Egyptian bureaucracy for more than a decade before helping to found the federation. Levy was an energetic essayist who expressed his views on all aspects of social and industrial policy as editor of the association's journal and through a number of independent economic reviews. He is recognized as the principal architect and negotiator of the German-style compacts in which federation members agreed to discourage competition in favor of market sharing, price fixing, and cartelization.[22]

The federation's key link to native capitalists and to the state was Isma'il Sidqi, by all accounts a consummate bureaucrat, a financial virtuoso, and an inveterate reactionary. Along with Tal'at Harb, Sidqi was probably the most important driving force behind Egyptian industrialization before the Free Officers' Revolution. Unlike the Misr group, however, Sidqi favored a gradualist policy of industrialization that would not threaten European investment but merely attempt to decentralize it and subject it to government regulation.[23] He aimed to crush what remained of the nationalist movement so that the state and the aristocracy could reap what he regarded as the major fruit of its limited victory—a compromised yet profitable autonomy that allowed local control over trade and fiscal policy.

Sidqi's strategy of industrialization was as much political as economic in inspiration. A master manipulator of men and money, he combined his government and association posts to smooth over constant conflicts of interest between the often reluctant members of Egypt's industrial coalition. By identifying himself as the tireless enforcer of a precarious social peace, he was able to persuade foreign investors that they must accede to moderate nationalist demands for taxation of their profits and for greater collaboration with local partners. By carving out sinecures for landlords and palace favorites in corporate management, he lined the pockets of the aristocrats who had the most to fear from the growth of modern industry. And by steadily strengthening the presence of native Egyptians in the federation leadership, he paved his own path to the presidency of the association after Naus's death in 1938.

Even as the federation prospered in a pluralist climate that disorganized its adversaries, its leaders began to propose a more comprehensive and cohesive framework of associations that would have amounted to a corporatist state. The earliest description of this project was advanced in 1935 by Isaac Levy, the Neapolitan-trained organizer and publicist, who undoubtedly expected it to find favor in a palace that was increasingly infatuated with Italian ideas and manners. Convinced that even the most discriminatory forms of pluralism could not deflect social unrest indefinitely, Levy called for a network of professional, labor, and employers' associations that would be bound in "mutualism and collaboration under the state." Concerning industrial relations, he specifically suggested that managers and workers be organized in mixed corporations over which the state would preside as "moderator, animator, and supreme arbiter."[24]

Levy's call for a self-conscious strategy of social engineering represented an open admission that by the 1930s the fragmenting impact of palace pluralism had reached its limits and was beginning to produce dangerous side effects. Although restrictions on the freedom of association hamstrung the Wafd and its would-be allies, they were also encouraging the rise of radical social movements and secret societies bent on completing the unfinished business of the nationalist revolution. The most popular mass movements, Misr al-Fatat and the Muslim Brotherhood, alternatively competed and cooperated in mobilizing an entire generation of young Egyptians who had no stake in the phony democracy of the parties or the pseudoindependence of their constitution.

Both groups were fed by the steady politicization of secondary school and university graduates who could not find employment during the depression. Both were led by young professionals and teachers who combined religious and anti-imperialist protest with the organization of independent economic enterprises and social welfare agencies. In 1935 and 1936 they helped to lead violent demonstrations of students and workers that forced the established parties into a brief national front to negotiate a new Anglo-Egyptian treaty. Enraged with the concessions made to the British, the new movements became even more militant, forming paramilitary groups that openly battled the Wafd and the palace for control of the streets.[25]

The rise of mass movements in the major cities led Egypt's rulers to reevaluate their traditional hostility to civil society. Confronted with more dangerous forms of opposition capable of sustaining elaborate underground organizations, the regime slowly realized that legal associations might become more effective means of social control if they were carefully regulated and co-opted instead of being continually denied and repressed. Before the late 1930s the legitimation of associational life was not seriously contemplated; all governments provided ad hoc benefits in exchange for the support of specific groups, but none was willing to grant anything approaching official recognition or institutionalized privilege.

Each of the palace coups that suspended the constitution in 1925, 1928, and 1931 was accompanied by a more restrictive law of associations. The Ziwar government (1924–1926) cultivated an anti-Wafdist coalition among Azharis, royalist army officers, and a number of state-funded professional and cultural societies. But it virtually abolished the freedom of assembly with a new statue (contemptuously known as the ''Ziwar law'') that remained in force through the rest of the 1920s. Wafdist efforts to liberalize the law were resisted by the British, who asserted that the proposed changes would pose new threats to foreign lives and interests. The issue helped to precipitate the coup of Muhammad Mahmud (1928–1929), who tried to balance the renewed repression of urban groups with increased public spending in the countryside.[26]

The most thorough purge of associational life was conducted by the government of Isma'il Sidqi (1930–1933). Sidqi's assault on his opponents was equally relentless in the cities and in the provinces, challenging every organized group except the business community. He combined mass arrests of union leaders with a new electoral law that disenfranchised over 80 percent of the population. Whereas Muhammad Mahmud had used state largess to pry a rural constituency away from the Wafd, Sidqi used agricultural credit to ensnare farmers into greater debts that could be recalled or extended according to the farmers' political leanings. In response to the growing radicalism of young educated Egyptians, he specifically excluded from parliament all members of the liberal professions who lived outside Cairo. Foreign residents could note without exaggeration that "Egypt was living under a businessmen's government."[27]

Sidqi's counterrevolution left a legacy of social protest so powerful that his successors no longer dared rely solely on the strength of the state to dominate society by disorganizing it. The "reform" governments of ʿAli Mahir (1936 and 1939–1940) signaled the first attempt to bolster authoritarianism by sponsoring a legitimist set of interest groups and creating the illusion of a modern welfare state. As early as 1935 the British knew that ʿAli Mahir was contemplating the formation of a "corporative parliament" in which government-approved deputies would be chosen from various occupational groups instead of from geographic districts. ʿAli Mahir was never able to implement this sort of overt political corporatism, but before the British deposed him for his secret diplomacy with Mussolini, he managed to set in place the building blocks of what would eventually become an elaborate system of state-sponsored associations.[28]

ʿAli Mahir established the Ministry of Social Affairs to control private voluntary groups, including labor unions, which were on the verge of receiving official recognition. He encouraged the formation of the first new corporatist syndicates for professionals since the creation of the bar association in 1912. By the time he was driven from office, legislation already had been drafted for separate syndicates of journalists, doctors, dentists, pharmacists, and veterinarians. Planning for increased government regulation of a wartime economy, his administration prepared the statute that converted the Egyptian chambers of commerce into corporatist groups that were even more centralized than the guilds of the nineteenth century.[29]

The Rise of Modern Corporatism, 1940–1967

The transformation of associational life from pluralist to corporatist lines was a slow and steady process that unfolded over a quarter of a century. From the beginning of World War II until the mid-1960s group activity was gradually restructured in one sector after another, producing a nearly universal system of functional representation under state control. In each occupational category succeeding governments tried to limit representation to a single association that went through a series of legislated reorganizations until it conformed to a fairly uniform model of corporatism. Although corporatism spread across sectors at different rates and to different degrees, there was a clear convergence of previously diverse and fragmented groups around a remarkably homogenous set of structures.

The typical corporatist association in Egypt is created by statute and endowed with a formal monopoly of representation for all who work in its field of jurisdiction. Membership is generally compulsory, in fact if not in law, providing the group with a guaranteed income that is supplemented by government subsidies. Organizational structure is almost always hierarchical or, as the trade unions statute puts it, "pyramid shaped." Local units are tied to functional and regional branches, which are centralized under a national confederation with headquarters in the capital city. The confederation, in turn, is linked with a parent ministry that supervises its finances and activities, consults with its leaders on public policy, and delegates quasi-governmental powers of economic regulation and professional discipline.

Association leaders are generally selected through a shifting combination of appointment and election. Often the law stipulates a complex system of proportional representation, distributing posts among occupational categories, regions, and age groups. Many confederation councils also have special seats reserved for ministry appointees, making them more like "mixed commissions" than elected boards of directors. Even where the leadership is formally chosen by the rank and file, it is common practice for candidates to be nominated by the government party or to be screened by the police. The arbitrary nature of these formulas for leadership selection insures that each association will retain a distinctive political life beneath the outward uniformity of legal codes and organization charts. The ceaseless juggling and reshuffling of group representation reflects a constant tension between partisan factions, each of which is attempting to stack the deck in its own favor.

Although the advance of corporatism thoroughly reshaped the representation of interests, it hardly signified the unfolding of a preconceived plan. The early projects of Isaac Levy and 'Ali Mahir gradually gave way to a number of competing notions that had no clear connection to either Italian or neo-Ottoman models. Some association leaders had aspirations of reorganizing their particular sectors, but not society as a whole. Egyptian industrialists had long admired the centralization of German employers' associations. Before the revolution many union leaders hoped to build partisan alliances similar to those of the British and Continental labor movements. Later, during the nationalization of industry, they were eager to replicate the managerial role of Yugoslavia's workers' councils.[30]

Ruling elites often debated more comprehensive designs of group representation, but these varied widely even within the same government. The Wafd emerged from its experience in wartime regulation with rudimentary plans for tripartite control of industrial relations. These were quickly frustrated, however, by the postwar radicalization of the unions and by its own weakness in the face of deepening class conflict. The Nasserists considered several foreign models for tying corporatist associations to a single party apparatus, yet they never agreed to import any ready-made authoritarian or socialist blueprint. Their enthusiasm constantly wavered between a Peronist populism and a Portuguese police state, between an Eastern European tolerance of semiautonomous power centers and a Soviet-style insistence on transmission belts and a command economy.[31]

Modern corporatism in Egypt arose as the cumulative product of a number of discrete and largely improvised responses to the challenges of wartime emergency, revolutionary consolidation, and socialist planning. Its common legal and administrative forms were inherited from colonial and Ottoman times. Its specific economic and political relationships have been fashioned and revised by constant collusion, bargaining, and struggle between modern governments and association leaders in each sector. Its theoretical and ideological justifications are recent accretions, added after the fact to legitimize pragmatic arrangements in terms of the public interest and social justice, historical necessity and cultural authenticity.

The expansion of corporatism across social and economic sectors occurred in three successive phases, corresponding roughly with the final decade of the monarchy, the early reforms of the 1952 revolution, and the socialist experiments of the 1960s. Modern corporatism originated during World War II on the familiar turf of government regulation of business, journalism, and public health. As soon as the war broke out, the chambers of commerce were reorganized and enlisted to implement supposedly temporary measures such as price controls, import licensing, and rationing in connection with the Middle East Supply Center. All of these policies survived the wartime administration to become routine responsibilities of corporatist businessmen's associations. The Middle East Supply Center never accomplished the transition from improvised regulation on a country-by-country basis to its ambitious goal of regional economic integration, but it did provide new models for coordination and planning between local governments and private business groups that were expanded after the war. This was particularly true in Egypt, where the Supply Center's headquarters were located and where the native chambers of commerce were entrusted with a key role in managing the wartime economy.[32]

The war also encouraged new experiments in the political control of the press. A new journalists' syndicate was delegated broad powers to set professional ethics and working conditions. The syndicate's leaders were expected to assume greater responsibility for self-censorship in exchange for an assortment of special privileges ranging from cut-rate phone service and train fares to journalism prizes and government-supported advertisements. The founders of the journalists' syndicate were newspaper owners and editors rather than reporters; some of them were from Levantine families that had adopted Egyptian citizenship. All of the twelve original members of the syndical council were chosen by the king rather than by the journalists. The first president, Edgar Jallad, was the same man the palace had tried to install earlier as head of the union confederation that was taken over by ʿAbbas Halim.

From the beginning the syndicate's leaders had to maneuver carefully between trying to limit censorship and sharing in its enforcement. Although the syndicate defended journalists when they had scrapes with the law, the early domination of newspaper managers made it more an employers' association than a reporters' guild. As its presidency passed from palace appointees to pro-Wafdist editors, the syndicate became a less reliable instrument of self-discipline. But the syndicate's board of directors continued to be dominated by enemies of the Wafd who had no intention of jeopardizing their government connections by joining in battles to revise the press law.[33]

As soon as the war ended, the Federation of Egyptian Industries reorganized itself into a semipublic body, hoping to attract new investment subsidies and greater state support for its campaign to further Egyptianize corporate management. In this instance, the initiative for corporatist reorganization came more from the industrialists themselves than from the government. The terms of the federation's charter were negotiated precisely when Ismaʿil Sidqi moved from the presidency of the F.E.I. to the prime ministership. Although Sidqi's hold on power was brief, he had a decisive impact on postwar industrial relations. He gave big business new means to press its arguments for the primacy of industrialization at the same time that he was arresting union leaders for trying to establish a national labor confederation.[34]

The growing self-confidence of native industry was reflected in the federation's espousal of a new technocratic ethos, emphasizing collaboration between business and the state as the critical factor in launching an Egyptian renaissance. This was particularly evident in the writings of Subhi Wahida, the man who succeeded Isaac Levy as the federation's general secretary. Like Levy, Wahida was also an Italian trained economist who believed that economic development could be achieved only if the state intervened to overcome the pervasive disorganization of Egyptian society. However, Wahida portrayed his project not as an imitation of a European model of corporatism but as a return to an ancient tradition of Egyptian statecraft that had been disrupted by centuries of misrule at the hands of foreigners. In his view, the reorganization of society had to begin at the top with a close alliance of business and political elites that would slowly be broadened to encompass other groups as well. Seeking the justification for this alliance in native culture and history, Wahida redefined the celebrated "Egyptian problem" of the postwar era as a matter of state-led industrialization and class collaboration instead of a struggle for complete national independence.[35]

Wahida's vision was not very different from the actual shape of associational policy during the final years of the monarchy. After the war corporatism moved beyond regulating businessmen and private practitioners to focus on organizing civil servants. In addition to the new syndicates of journalists and medical personnel, similar groups were established for engineers, agronomists, and teachers, most of whom were employed by the state. For the first time comprehensive regulations were issued for voluntary associations, labor unions, and agricultural cooperatives, but these private groups were not entitled to the same privileges that were being extended to businessmen, professionals, and civil servants. Hence, prerevolutionary corporatism was expanded in a highly selective manner, insuring that it would retain an unmistakably bourgeois flavor.

Pluralism survived and expanded, especially in the labor movement, but it appeared more and more to be the vestigial preserve of a disorganized underclass that was forced to rely on its own meager resources. As the newly corporatized associations of the upper and middle classes became increasingly enmeshed with the state bureaucracy, the weaker voluntary groups of the lower classes were being torn apart by open warfare between the police and revolutionary socialist and religious movements. Before World War II class biases had been informally promoted by clear inequalities in the art of association. After the war, however, these biases became more openly institutionalized in the growing dualism between a corporatist arena that was favored by the state and a pluralist arena that was a breeding ground for radical political opposition.

As the revolutionary regime of the Free Officers consolidated power, it gradually eliminated this associational dualism and moved toward a more comprehensive corporatist policy. The Free Officers eliminated the pluralist arena by abolishing political parties, suppressing the Muslim

Brotherhood, and purging the left wing of the labor movement. At the same time, they sponsored new corporatist initiatives to build supporting constituencies among workers and peasants, to throttle the professional middle class, and to strengthen government controls over private business. Nasser did not create modern Egyptian corporatism. Rather, he inherited an expanding corporatist infrastructure that he strengthened and extended into new social sectors until, by the end of the 1950s, corporatism clearly had replaced pluralism as the predominant mode of interest representation.

The revolution was far more swift and deliberate in extinguishing older pluralist groups than in replacing them with strong corporatist organizations. Throughout his first decade in power Nasser was reluctant to construct any powerful and centralized interest group until he was confident that it would not be infiltrated by his enemies or manipulated by his colleagues. Although several ambitious corporatist projects were initiated during the 1950s, they all remained partial and tentative. In many cases the implementation of corporatist legislation was delayed for several years while the regime made and broke promises to its associational allies and competing government agencies squabbled for control of potential clienteles.

Nasser's early enthusiasm to build corporatist structures was weakest regarding the social groups that had the most to gain from the revolution and strongest regarding the groups who had the most to lose. The most decisive measures were directed at the chambers of commerce and the Federation of Egyptian Industries, which had already become semipublic entities before the revolution. New legislation was adopted for both businessmen's groups, stipulating compulsory membership and increasing ministerial representation in their directorships. Professional groups were subjected to fewer and generally less intrusive laws. The lawyers', journalists', and engineers' syndicates were modified to increase the representation of civil servants. But new professional organizations were limited to a handful of small syndicates for entertainers, scientists, and accountants.

The most hesitant and ambivalent corporatist projects were undertaken for peasants and workers—the very groups the revolution claimed as its natural constituency. In the agricultural sector the regime created a new dualism between land reform cooperatives and credit cooperatives. The former were compulsory groups for peasants who received expropriated lands that they cultivated under state supervision. The latter were a continuation of the older, voluntary cooperatives that were modified to require the delivery of cash crops at controlled prices in exchange for government-supplied inputs. Both systems extended state control over the surplus and methods of Egyptian farmers, but they also insured that the cooperative movement would remain divided and decentralized, split by bureaucratic infighting at the top and by the power struggles of influential families in the villages.[36]

Nasser was particularly cautious in his efforts to rebuild the Egyptian labor movement. In the earliest days of the revolution the Free Officers demonstrated their determination to crush union radicalism by executing leftists implicated in the riots at Kafr al-Dawwar. During the decisive "March crisis" of 1954 the anticommunist leaders of the powerful transport workers' union mobilized timely support for Nasser against rival commanders who favored an early return to parliamentary democracy. Muhammad Najib and Khalid Muhi al-Din led a broad coalition of the old parties, the Muslim Brotherhood, and the professional syndicates that was on the verge of deposing Nasser until his union allies struck in defense of the revolution. Thus, next to the army itself, Nasser had good reason to regard the labor movement as a key factor in either consolidating power or losing it altogether.[37]

Nasser's sensitivity to the potential power of the workers helps to explain his desire to reorganize the unions into a reliable base of support as well as his even greater fear that these groups might ultimately be turned against him. Consequently, Nasser put off the creation of a national labor confederation until 1957, even though this had been one of the regime's first pledges to unionists in 1952. Instead, he encouraged his labor allies to establish an international Confederation of Arab Unions in order to advance Egypt's pan-Arab policies among foreign petroleum workers. Meanwhile, Nasser sponsored the formation of many small unions at home, but he did not authorize large, nationwide industrial federations until a comprehensive labor code was adopted in 1959.

Egypt's new labor law was a landmark piece of corporatist legislation that was strikingly similar to the labor code of the Brazilian Estado Novo. Although the government quickly implemented its broad reforms of social welfare and working conditions, the provisions for union reorganization were shelved for several years while the Ministries of Interior and Labor debated the political implications of strengthening the union movement. Nasser finally agreed to proceed with the plan only when Syrian police officials assured him that new corporatist unions had greatly simplified the task of political surveillance in their region of the United Arab Republic. By consolidating union activity in a handful of big federations, the Syrians explained, the new labor law had eliminated many of the local nesting areas that served as the traditional refuges of Ba'thist and communist troublemakers.[38]

Encouraged by these favorable reports from Damascus, Nasser instructed his own police and union allies to carry through with the corporatist reforms in Egypt as well. In 1962 the Egyptian Confederation of Labor was reorganized around only fifty-nine industrial affiliates; by 1964 their number had been reduced again to a mere twenty-seven. At the same time Nasser extended his campaign of economic nationalization from foreign to Egyptian enterprises and initiated a program of worker participation in the management of state-owned industries. Unions were not authorized to select the worker representatives for these management councils, but the simultaneous creation of a corporatist labor movement and a large public sector inevitably bred expectations that some form of industrial codetermination would be put on the bargaining table.

The corporatization of the unions signified the consummation of an important ''gentlemen's agreement'' between Nasser and noncommunist labor leaders after a full decade of mutual suspicion and frustrating bargaining. On one hand, the regime had eliminated the most radical and independent elements from the upper reaches of the union hierarchy. On the other hand, loyalist labor leaders had at last secured through state sponsorship the authority and resources they knew they could never achieve unilaterally. Of course, the state continued to withhold the right to strike or to engage in true collective bargaining. Nevertheless, at the time many unionists felt they had won at least a partial victory and, in view of the revolution's rapid drift toward socialism, they had reason to believe that additional gains would soon be within their grasp.

Egyptian corporatism reached its apogee during the socialist transformation of the 1960s. The principal additions to corporatism during this period were ideological and symbolic rather than organizational. By the beginning of the decade the associational building blocks of corporatism were already established in all of the key economic sectors. Remaining gaps in the system were lessened somewhat by adopting compulsory membership for agricultural cooperatives, by reorganizing al-Azhar into a semiofficial religious establishment, and by amalgamating voluntary associations in regional federations sponsored by the Ministry of Social Affairs.

The key innovation of the 1960s, however, was the elaboration of an organic vision of society and an explicitly syndicalist path of political development. Throughout the decade Nasserism became increasingly identified with a comprehensive system of functional representation that

was portrayed as the key instrument for "melting" traditional class antagonisms into a new era of class collaboration. Moreover, many Nasserists insisted that Egyptian corporatism was an inherently democratic force—
by promoting social justice and harmony, it would also be paving the
way for a gradual devolution of power from the "transitional" authoritarian state to a self-governing alliance of "popular working forces."[39]

The task of endowing a preexisting and largely improvised edifice of
corporatist associations with an ideological justification and a historical
purpose was taken up by the National Congress of Popular Forces, the
Charter of National Action, and the Arab Socialist Union. Each, in turn,
struggled to devise a formula of proportional representation that could be
defended as a weighted balancing of "natural" social elements with one
another and with the state. Each relied upon an arbitrary mixture of criteria for identifying constituencies and ranking their order of importance.
These criteria included demographic size, the extent of current enrollment
in corporatist associations, and relative contribution to the national income—the sum of which was then subject to "political correction" according to each group's supposed commitment to the goals of the revolution.[40]

As the Arab Socialist Union extended its supervision of syndical activity, political correction lapsed more and more into party control. The
pretense of corporatist partnership and social balance was brushed aside
in favor of greater state intrusion in syndical affairs. Proportional representation became a device for uprooting independent leaders and install-
ing party-slated rivals. Professional groups were purged of "feudalist"
and "bourgeois" elements and packed with new members from the civil
service and the working class. Businessmen's associations were handed
over to technocrats and managers of state enterprises. Training programs
for the leaders of agricultural cooperatives and youth organizations were
turned into schools for revolutionaries. Union leaders also were threatened with an attempted party takeover of their elections and educational
programs, but they were able to appeal to powerful military allies such
as Kamal Rif'at, the minister of labor and ideological chief of the A.S.U.,
who urged Nasser to restrain the growing power of the 'Ali Sabri faction.[41]

The heavy-handed implementation of Nasser's corporatism left association leaders with no illusions that a syndicalist republic was at hand.
Nevertheless, many of them continued to adhere to the associational principles of the Charter of National Action, believing that the leaders of the
A.S.U. had subverted Nasser's vision instead of executing it. Consequently, Nasserism's combination of syndicalist rhetoric and organization

building left an enduring legacy that has influenced (and often plagued) relations between governments and organized interests ever since. This legacy is not a built-in demand for "permanent revolution" or a road map toward a uniquely Egyptian brand of "social democracy" but a heightened set of expectations about the representative role of organized groups that are largely the creation of the state itself.

The significance of Nasser's corporatist experiments can be seen in a number of mutually reinforcing perceptions that have become increasingly widespread among association leaders during the past two decades. Even group leaders who remain unsympathetic to Nasser often interpret his associational policies as an open admission of the need to search for some type of "social contract" between the authoritarian state and civil society. From this perspective, the Nasserist emphasis on syndical organization is viewed as a tacit acknowledgment of the legitimacy and utility of functional representation in a political system where parties and parliaments traditionally have been suspended or corrupted. The very creation of new representative institutions is construed as a "promissory note" that might be redeemed in the future to permit greater consultation and cooperation with corporatist groups in shaping policies that directly affect their interests.[42]

Alternatively, even group leaders who look back upon the 1960s with rose-colored glasses generally admit that the Nasserists erred by not allowing the representatives of each sector to be chosen freely by their own members. Many syndical leaders who rose to head the organizations inherited from the Nasser era express regret or resentment over what they regard as the unkept promise of the revolution: it would and should lead to a gradual sharing of power between the state and organized groups that demonstrate a clear regard for the public interest.[43]

The Protracted Crisis and Pseudoreform of Populist Authoritarianism (1968–the present)

The crushing defeat of the 1967 War was a turning point in the authoritarian state's relations with civil society. It was a blow from which Egypt's rulers have never fully recovered—a severe setback that forced them to come to terms with their own populist pretensions and to admit, at last, the need for fundamental political reform. Nasser, Sadat, and Mubarak stumbled from one crisis to another over the past two decades, groping for a system of representation that could absorb or deflect the ceaseless rise of social protest and political opposition. Yet no such system has been devised despite the regime's repeated assurances of its commitment to democratization. The very sense of weakness and insecurity that has compelled the authoritarian elite to reach out for greater popular support has also caused it to sabotage its own modest plans for sharing power with newly organized groups and interests.

While promising a steady movement toward political liberalization, the regime has zigzagged between loosening and restricting freedom of association with a chain of disconnected and mutually incompatible projects that have combined both pluralist and corporatist techniques. In Nasser's Declaration of March 30, 1968, in Sadat's "Corrective Revolution," and then in Mubarak's "Era of Good Feeling," each gesture of reform and consensus building has been countered by an attempt to patch up the battered structures of authoritarianism. A competitive multiparty system has grown up alongside a co-optive corporatist parliament; invitations to engage in dialogue and debate have been coupled with increasing resort to tyranny by plebiscite; strengthening the rule of law has gone hand in hand with new justifications for special tribunals and a constant state of emergency.

During his final three years in power, Nasser held up a remote vision of pluralist democracy while making belated and tentative efforts to breathe new life into the overly centralized system of corporatist representation. However, his attention focused on reforming the A.S.U., not the syndicates. By allowing freer elections that increased worker and peasant leadership throughout the A.S.U. hierarchy, he tried to revive the image of a mass based party against the prevailing line that favored a vanguard organization controlled by well-indoctrinated cadres and secret members. Although he wished to encourage factional rivalry within the ruling party, Nasser was far more cautious toward demands for greater group autonomy.[44]

Immediately after the war elections for most syndicates were postponed indefinitely and the terms of their sitting leaders were extended by decree. New elections were not permitted until 1971, when Sadat sought syndical support during the power struggle that accompanied his succession. Although Nasser encouraged labor leaders to play a greater role in party affairs, he explicitly rejected their pleas for increased responsibility in the management of state enterprises. Instead, he promoted a confusing system of overlapping jurisdictions that divided authority in the workplace between unions, managers, elected worker representatives, and party-led production committees.[45]

Even as he began to adopt the vocabulary of pluralism in his public discussions of party reform, Nasser made two final attempts to consolidate the existing corporatist design of group representation. Hoping to contain and perhaps exploit the powerful upsurge of religious sentiment that followed Egypt's military defeat, Nasser initiated a project to reorganize the popular mystical fraternities into a state-chartered federation of Sufi orders. Less than two years after launching his second wave of arrests and executions against the Muslim Brotherhood, Nasser decided to subsidize the mystics' festivals and parades on a grand scale, allowing greater mass religious demonstrations but channeling them in a direction that would be far less threatening to the regime.

The combination of financial support and official licensing quickly induced the fragmented Sufi leaders to accept a new corporatist framework that would effectively annex them into the state-sponsored religious establishment. However, the most powerful member of that establishment, the *'ulama'* of al-Azhar, insisted that their authority not be undercut by the regime's eagerness to conclude an alliance with heterodox religious groups that might encourage popular superstition. The Azharis managed to delay the reorganization of the Sufi orders until several years after Nasser's death. Because of their objections, Nasser's original proposal was rewritten to insure that the governing board of the new Sufi federation would include several *ex officio* representatives of al-Azhar who would closely supervise the orders' activities and publications.[46]

Nasser's final attempt at associational reform came in the very last week of his life. In September 1970 he authorized the establishment of the Confederation of Agricultural Cooperatives, hoping to provide the disorganized cooperative movement with the kind of nationwide structure and political influence that the labor unions had possessed for more than a decade. Among Nasser's many corporatist initiatives this was by far the least successful, and it was the only one that failed to survive him. As Sadat prepared for the parliamentary elections of 1976, he became convinced that a strong cooperative movement would help to mobilize local support for his rivals, particularly for the early reemergence of the Wafd. In the midst of the electoral campaign Sadat abolished the cooperative confederation and brought its leaders to trial under charges of corruption.

Sadat did not allow establishment of another confederation of cooperatives until 1980. By that time, however, most of the funds and buildings of the local cooperatives had been turned over to a new set of "village banks" that operated not as government credit agencies but as local investment banks promoting the business ventures of Sadat's supporters among the rural middle class. The Nasserists quickly responded by forming an independent farmers' federation that claimed to be the true inheritor of the cooperative movement despite its purely private status. Realizing that they had been shut out of the very corporatist groups they had helped to create, the Nasserists were forced to build an alternative network of voluntary organizations alongside the state-sponsored cooperatives. Thus, in the agricultural sector, Nasserism became increasingly identified with pluralism as Sadat crippled and then appropriated the Nasserists' original corporatist projects.[47]

Throughout the 1970s Sadat steadily reoriented his strategy of political reform from pluralist to corporatist programs. From 1970 until 1976 he perceived most corporatist associations as potentially menacing "centers of power" that could be used to mobilize support for his opponents on both the left and the right. Sadat was not eager to endorse any pluralist reform of the party and electoral systems until he was confident that these groups would not fall into the hands of the Nasserists, communists, and Wafdists. Accordingly, he moved swiftly to purge and thoroughly restructure the union and cooperative movements while allowing one committee after another to debate countless proposals for the transition from single-party dictatorship to multiparty democracy.

As soon as the 1976 elections were over, Sadat began a clear retreat from encouraging the emergence of a pluralist process that was certain to be exploited and perhaps controlled by his opponents. During 1977 a combination of new threats convinced him that a genuine pluralist democracy would quickly slip from his control: the riots touched off in several cities by attempts to reduce food subsidies; the powerful display of popular support for the New Wafd Party; and the murder of a former minister of *Awqaf* by an underground religious society. Throughout his remaining years in power Sadat gradually abandoned his efforts to launch a new system of competitive parties and turned instead toward reshaping the existing set of corporatist associations into more reliable instruments of control and co-optation. By the time of his death, Egyptian corporatism had taken on a distinctive Sadatist coloring that had little connection to the socialist and syndicalist slogans of the Nasser era.

First, the presidential personality was increasingly endowed with neotraditionalist attributes of religiosity and paternalism. The president was now known as "the believing president" *(al-ra'is al-mu'min), Muhammad* Anwar Sadat. He referred to himself as "the elder of the Egyptian family" *(kabir al-'a'ila al-misriya)* and the guardian of authentic national morals, which supposedly were best exemplified in the unspoiled fabric of village society. Weekend newscasts invariably were dominated by films of the president performing the Friday noon prayer in his family's village of Mit Abu al-Kum and then appearing, clad in his *gallabiya* and holding his walking staff, to "consult" with members of the village council.

Second, the electoral and judicial processes were distorted to reflect these presidentially personified values and to enforce the tyranny of the provincial majority. A long list of plebiscites produced predictable but incredible majorities ratifying constitutional amendments that included restrictions on political party formation, abridgements of the freedom of association, and new means of press censorship. The new Law for the Preservation of Values (dubbed the "Law of Shame" by its opponents) established a special court to deal with dissenters who "defamed" the nation, especially those who criticized Sadat's "normalization" of relations with Israel.

Third, Sadat sponsored another corporatist reorganization of the union movement, greatly enhancing the powers and privileges of the Confederation of Labor while cutting it off from its own constituency. The creation of attractive sinecures for a self-recruited union elite was intended to compensate for the abolition of the A.S.U. and the adoption of capitalist economic policies. Insulating the union hierarchy from rank-and-file pressures did not prevent wildcat strikes and worker support for opposition parties. Nevertheless, Sadat's ability to isolate working-class discontent was strengthened by his encapsulation and neutralization of the top union leaders who, in turn, played upon the government's insecurities to extract still more concessions and resources for their organizations.

Fourth, Sadat made an energetic effort to form alliances with several corporatist associations in the business community and among middle-class professionals. The chambers of commerce were put in charge of "National Development Banks" that funneled cheap credit to provincial businessmen who led the local organizations of the ruling party. New interchamber federations were formed among related syndicates in the health and technical professions. These, in turn, were encouraged to collaborate with the private sector in establishing their own profit-making enterprises. Sadat also organized a powerful new constituency for the *infitah* by creating a huge syndicate for commercial employees, most of whom were connected with private banks and joint venture firms. By the early 1980s its membership exceeded 160,000, making it the second largest professional syndicate in the nation.

On the other hand, many of Sadat's dealings with professional groups were so high-handed that they bred more scandal and resentment than support. Association leaders had long been accustomed to the government's mobilization of civil servants during syndical elections, but they were flabbergasted by the busloads of army engineers who were sent to vote for Sadat's handpicked candidates. Sadat also revived Isma'il Sidqi's tactic of playing on regional rivalries between Cairo and the provinces. However, whereas Sidqi disenfranchised the Wafd's supporters in the countryside, Sadat regularly relied on the votes of new syndical members in the provincial capitals to cancel out his opponents' superiority in Cairo.

Fifth, Sadat made a grand though halfhearted display of his willingness to share power with the leaders of occupational associations in a kind of "corporatist democracy." During the holy month of Ramadan in 1979 he met each evening after the *iftar* (fast-breaking) meal with a different assemblage of interest group leaders to discuss creating an "upper" chamber of the legislature whose members would be drawn primarily from the corporatist associations. Business representatives were particularly candid and straightforward in outlining their view of the president's alternatives for structuring the new Majlis al-Shura (consultative assembly). If the chamber was to be a true syndical parliament with legislative powers, they said, then its members should be elected from the various functional groups composing the "Egyptian family." However, if the chamber was to be a ceremonial body, then the president should appoint its members and leave the syndicates out of the matter altogether.[48]

Typically, Sadat chose neither of these clear alternatives; instead, he announced a hybrid formula that eventually alienated most of the groups it was designed to co-opt. The Majlis al-Shura was created in 1980 as a consultative chamber with very limited policy-making powers that amounted to supervising a cumbersome new system of press censorship. Half of its members were elected not from corporatist syndicates but from party lists in geographic districts, as in the People's Assembly. The other half of its members were appointed by the president as representatives of key occupational groups and national institutions. The syndical leaders had no role in the selection of deputies, and there was no effort to revive any of the quota systems or schemes of functional representation that Nasser had devised in the 1960s. All of the opposition parties boycotted the elections to the Majlis al-Shura and several prominent presidential appointees declined their seats. Hence, the net product of Sadat's experiment in corporatist democracy was a collection of local party functionaries and aged luminaries who represented no one and who had virtually nothing to do.

Disappointed with these meager results, Sadat launched a frontal assault on all associations that had provided an outlet for any type of political dissent. From the founding of the Majlis al-Shura in November 1980 until his assassination in October 1981, he attacked one group after another: the journalists' and lawyers' syndicates, the party press and uni-

versities, and religious associations of both Copts and Muslims. The cul-
mination of the yearlong political crisis came just one month before his
murder. In a furious television address he announced the imprisonment
of more than 1,500 people whose views spanned the entire spectrum of
Egyptian public opinion. At the same time he revealed a particularly audacious plan to nationalize every mosque in the country, including thousands of private mosques, which by that time represented Egypt's last
islands of associational freedom.[49]

When Mubarak assumed power, his campaign of national reconciliation quickly turned toward the creation of an extraparliamentary forum
for consulting the opposition parties and the major interest groups. Early
in 1982 he convened an economic summit conference to air longstanding
criticisms of the *infitah* and to lay down guidelines for a new type of
"guided capitalism." Although a handful of association leaders were invited, the summit was dominated by about two hundred professional
economists who carefully expressed their political differences with the
government in muted technocratic language. Conferees from varied ideological and academic backgrounds attacked Sadat's "anarchic" *infitah*
and generally agreed that it had to be corrected by a return to some form
of central and comprehensive planning.

Many of the conferees also argued that renewed state intervention in
the economy could succeed only if it was accompanied by greater collaboration between the government and informed public opinion, including
organized interests as well as trained experts. Several Western European
examples of economic planning were mentioned as possible alternatives
to Egypt's unhappy experiences with stifling socialism and unbridled capitalism. Many speakers noted that Egypt's troubled and mixed economy
could no longer tolerate the mismanagement of authoritarian rulers who
rejected sound counsel when it did not serve their political ambitions.
The summit concluded with a remarkably candid admission of its own
inadequacy to provide the sort of guidance and advice that it regarded as
indispensable. It recommended that additional conferences be scheduled
to include a major role for the leaders of the political parties and occupational associations.[50]

At first Mubarak endorsed this proposal with great enthusiasm, assuming that it would allow him to preside over a well-orchestrated critique of
his unpopular predecessor while shaping a national consensus for economic reform. The government announced that it would convene a whole
series of expanded summit meetings to discuss "The Egypt of Tomorrow."
The first of these was to be organized around special policy committees,
each of which would be chaired by the leader of a different political party

and composed of representatives from corporatist chambers and syndicates.[51]

All of these highly publicized plans for economic summitry and pact-making evaporated the moment Mubarak acceded to the Sadatists' pleas that he take up the leadership of the National Democratic Party. Sadat's followers conceded the need for changes in economic policy, but they insisted that the president could find all the advice and diversity of opinion he needed in the special committees of the ruling party and in both houses of parliament. Once he abandoned his formal stance of nonpartisanship, Mubarak saw no advantage in creating new opportunities for his competitors to discuss the nation's future with cabinet officers and interest group leaders.

Thenceforth, organized interests would be invited to participate in policymaking either by their approaching government agencies directly or through the good offices of the ruling party. Any group wishing to strengthen its voice with the support of a rival party could take its chances in the competitive atmosphere of the electoral arena, but not under the cover of state-sponsored commissions. "The Egypt of Tomorrow" conferences were quietly shelved and never again mentioned by the government. During the next several years, however, the opposition parties often referred to them as a worthy experiment that had been sabotaged because Mubarak was forced to sell out to the Sadatists. Many opposition leaders assured the president that they were willing to revive the project whenever he wished, especially if he gained greater independence from his adopted party or if he felt that summits could be helpful in times of national crisis.

Mubarak has never openly accepted such invitations, but he has prudently left the door ajar. Throughout his first term in office he preferred to deal with interest groups in a series of isolated encounters, trying to assure them that their competing demands could be reconciled by direct bargaining with the state rather than by confrontation with one another. In fact, this strategy has tended to intensify group competition, not to moderate it. The result has been a number of embarrassing reversals in economic policy as well as deepening divisions within the government itself as more and more ministries seek to veto initiatives that threaten the entrenched interests of their bureaus and clienteles.

In preparing for election to a second term, however, Mubarak revived the themes of social partnership and economic cooperation that marked the earliest months of his presidency. Instead of denouncing the opposition parties for endangering his plans for democracy with "irresponsible" behavior, he allowed them to increase their representation in parliament in the April 1987 elections and then invited them to a more open debate of economic reform. Instead of admonishing special interests for their selfish demands and lack of public spirit, he acknowledged that Egypt was a "pluralist" and "civil" society composed of many organized groups with legitimate rights that must be respected by the state.[52]

Mubarak continues to define Egypt's crisis in economic rather than political terms and he insists that further democratization must be preceded by the implementation of unpopular austerity measures. Yet he also realizes that austerity must be negotiated because the authoritarian state is no longer powerful enough to impose it unilaterally. If austerity is to have any chance of success, it must have a credible appearance of equity and consensus that can be provided only by multilateral bargaining between the government and an assortment of well-organized interests. Nasserists once were fond of the grim slogan "Justice is equality in the face of dictatorship"; it seems that Mubarak and his advisers are trying to move the country toward a more "liberal" reformulation: "Democracy is participation in the negotiation of austerity."

4

Corporatist Sectors: Professional Syndicates

The associations of the professional middle class are the groups that have conformed most clearly and consistently to corporatist principles of organization. Whereas associational development in most other sectors has combined changing mixtures of pluralism and corporatism, the professional syndicates have evolved as a distinct corporatist subsystem that has been molded and steadily expanded by colonial, monarchist, and revolutionary regimes. Unlike labor unions and agricultural cooperatives, which originated as voluntary social movements, all of the professional syndicates have been corporatist groups from their inception. In contrast to the historical heterogeneity of the business and religious sectors, where the recent proliferation of new groups has generated intense competition and conflict, the middle-class syndicates have retained their monopolistic status. Even when the struggle for power between rival syndical factions has approached open warfare, it has remained within the traditional corporatist framework instead of spawning defections and splinter groups.

The striking durability of corporatism among the professions is a consequence of authoritarian rulers' persistent fears about the political ambitions of the native middle class combined with the continuing dependence of these groups on the privileges and powers that can be afforded only by state-sponsored associations. Egypt's rulers have harbored an enduring suspicion of organized professionals. Succeeding regimes have viewed them as the vanguard of the nationalist movement, as a key component of the Wafdist coalition, as a breeding ground for bourgeois counter-revolution, and most menacingly, as an alternative elite likely to control any genuine multiparty system. On several occasions even the limited independence of professional syndicates has been perceived as an intolerable threat. The monarchy froze their development for nearly three decades. Nasser contemplated abolishing them altogether or absorbing them into the labor movement. Sadat warned that parliament could strip them of their privileges and reduce them to private clubs. At no time, however, has any regime seriously considered replacing the syndicates with the kind of multiple and competing associations that have been permitted in many other sectors.

Alternatively, Egyptian professionals have never been willing or able to forgo the benefits of corporatism in favor of private and autonomous collective action. No matter how constraining its tethers, they have found the syndical system to be indispensable in accomplishing several important objectives: in overcoming their traditional inferiority vis-à-vis resident foreigners, in acquiring a measure of occupational self-regulation, in building patronage networks inside the ruling circle and the state bureaucracy, and in preserving thinly disguised enclaves of partisan loyalty that have managed to survive even the most tumultuous purges and transformations of the political system. Hence, both the state and the professions have developed a strong interest in preserving the syndicates. The mutual suspicions of ruling and associational elites have been channeled into constant battles for position and frequent renegotiations of syndical operations but not, as in other sectors, into fundamental attacks on corporatist representation. However much they may disagree about the relative merits of pluralism versus corporatism in the political system as a whole, neither side has displayed much appetite for dismantling Egypt's modern counterpart of the guild system.

Although the lawyers' syndicate was an important political arena throughout the constitutional monarchy, the widespread politicization of professional syndicates was a belated consequence of the 1952 revolution. This was by no means the intent of the Free Officers' regime during its first decade in power. Indeed, Nasser particularly distrusted the professional associations because of their close connections with the old parties and aristocracy and because the lawyers', teachers', and journalists' syndicates openly collaborated with the pro-Najib coalition during the leadership struggle of 1954. Thereafter, Nasser adopted a defensive strategy toward the syndicates, aimed at demobilizing or ''containing'' them instead of attempting to enlist them as active allies of the revolution. Particular groups were managed in very different manners, depending on the perceived likelihood that they would promote further opposition. The most extensive purges and controls were directed at lawyers and journalists. Less threatening groups, such as the syndicates of teachers, doctors, and agronomists, were taken under the protection of high-ranking military officers who cultivated them as patronage networks and secondary power bases.[1]

When Nasser began to think seriously about a comprehensive plan of corporatism in the early 1960s, his first inclination was to exclude the professional syndicates from the new arrangements. Many syndical leaders connected with the prerevolutionary parties had worked their way into the National Union, the loosely structured official party that monopolized political activity in the 1950s. During the deliberations of the National Congress of Popular Forces they embarrassed the regime by demanding greater freedom of association and by openly calling for a return to parliamentary democracy. Nasser responded by attacking the syndicates as vestiges of "professional feudalism" and "reactionary capitalism." Their survival, he insisted, would merely preserve opportunities for class exploitation and introduce a dangerous "dualism" into the institutions of a socialist society. The melting of social conflicts, he suggested, required new, multiclass syndicates organized according to the principle of "the democratic unity of labor" and gathering in a single functional group all "workers" from holders of advanced degrees all the way down to janitors.[2]

Ultimately, the professional syndicates were saved, but this was not due to the intervention of their military patrons nor because the regime feared alienating the skilled personnel it required for economic development. What rescued the professional associations was the rise of leftist leadership in the new Arab Socialist Union that believed that the syndicates could be refashioned into useful channels of controlled political participation. Just as Syrian police officials earlier persuaded Nasser that corporatism would improve the political surveillance of the labor movement, the left wing of the A.S.U., which included a number of former communists, convinced him that an ideologically inspired party vanguard could penetrate the professional syndicates and mobilize them in the struggle for socialism.[3]

The A.S.U.'s campaign to reform professional groups was actually quite short-lived, lasting only from about 1964 until shortly after the June war. Nevertheless, it was a powerful assault that jolted and antagonized many groups, setting off a chain reaction of political struggles that spilled over to the regimes of Nasser's successors. Even before the June war, there were signs that the A.S.U.'s initiatives were meeting particularly strong resistance in the lawyers' and journalists' syndicates. On several occasions the government nullified or rigged elections only to see its own candidates emerge as new critics echoing many of the same complaints that had been voiced by the A.S.U.'s opponents. Syndicate presidents such as ʿAbd al-ʿAziz Shurbaji and Ahmad Baha' al-Din were clearly A.S.U. choices, but they quickly developed reputations as independent Nasserists who could operate as group spokesmen rather than government plants. While Baha' al-Din led the journalists' syndicate, for example, it publicly endorsed the student demonstrations of 1968 and claimed part of the credit for the March 30 Declaration's promises to move toward greater syndical democracy. These setbacks forced the A.S.U. to impose younger and more pliable party representatives, such as Ahmad al-Khawaja in the lawyers' syndicate and Kamal Zuhairi in the journalists' syndicate. Like their predecessors, however, both of these men gradually built alliances with internal syndicate factions and developed into two of the strongest critics of the Sadat regime in the late 1970s.[4]

Sadat supported a mild reassertion of syndical autonomy when he first came to power, but tried to restrain and then crush it during most of his presidency. As soon as Sadat arrested the heads of the A.S.U. in 1971, he encouraged the syndicates to conduct a "purge from below" by allowing new elections that replaced many of the party-imposed slates with coalition councils representing several contending factions. While Sadat strengthened his grip on power after the 1973 war, he skillfully directed the resentment of the "liberated" syndicates in weakening and gradually abolishing the A.S.U.[5] As they began to take his proposals for a multiparty system more seriously than he wished, he combined political pressures and economic incentives to reward the more loyal syndicates and to divide the more unruly ones. When strong pockets of syndical opposition developed against his economic policies, his separate peace with Israel, and his turn toward autocracy, he steamrollered the most outspoken groups with a decisiveness that went far beyond the earlier forays of the A.S.U. "vanguardists."

Mubarak has generally sought to avoid such head-on confrontations with professional groups. Instead of trying to silence criticism with punitive legislation and appointed leaderships, he has relied on the ruling party organization to outmaneuver a variety of opposition factions in syndical elections. In many cases the Mubarak government has settled for partial victories, hoping that freer competition between partisan rivals would dilute their criticisms of particular policies and prevent the emergence of opposition fronts. Consequently, debates in syndical elections and councils are often more animated than those in the party system and parliament where the government has insisted on retaining a much firmer grip on power.

In contrast to Sadat, Mubarak has not perceived occasional reversals and embarrassments in the sideshows of syndical politics as jeopardizing his control over the political system as a whole. Indeed, by giving his critics greater leeway in syndical affairs, he has tried to offer partial compensation for the continued artificiality and rigidity of the party and electoral processes. Partisan movements such as the Nasserists and the Muslim Brotherhood, which are still prohibited from operating as independent parties, have been granted considerable freedom to test their strength in the quasi-pluralist atmosphere of professional politics.

The Growth and Politicization of Professional Syndicates

The cumulative impact of these shifting policies has been to endow the corporatist associations of the middle class with a political importance that they did not possess before the 1952 revolution. "Containment," "mobilization," "liberation," and "selective confrontation" have produced a diverse and highly politicized set of professional groups whose significance far surpasses that of the celebrated alliance between the Wafd and the bar association under the monarchy. Especially since the 1960s increased state intervention in syndical affairs has promoted a number of mutually reinforcing processes that have strengthened professional organizations and enhanced their political influence. These processes are the rapid expansion of syndical membership, the more balanced representation of occupational subgroups and regional branches, the emergence of a more stable factionalism in syndical councils, and the gradual commercialization of professional associations in conjunction with the growing private sector.

Total syndical membership nearly quadrupled between 1963 and 1978; by the end of Sadat's reign, over 700,000 professionals had been enrolled in eighteen separate organizations (Table 4-1).[6] The rapid growth of overall membership during the Nasser era was quickened by Sadat, demonstrating that corporatism had lost none of its appeal with the shift from socialism to capitalism and from a single-party to a multiparty system. Furthermore, in both periods, all of the syndicates connected with the mass media (journalism, acting, cinema, and music) retained small and unusually stable memberships. Although other features of the syndical structure were modified to suit changing political and economic objec-

TABLE 4-1. Membership in Professional Syndicates, 1963–1978
(Members and Percentage of Total)

	1963		1971		1978	
Medicine	11,538	6.4	11,848	3.8	34,170	5.0
Dentistry	1,013	.6	4,728	1.5	4,595	.7
Pharmacy	3,191	1.8	5,520	1.8	13,150	1.9
Veterinary	1,055	.6	2,369	.8	6,251	.9
Nursing	—	—	—	—	4,120	.6
Law	6,872	3.8	9,816	3.2	13,283	1.9
Journalism	1,166	.6	1,503	.5	1,999	.3
Acting	940	.5	890	.3	1,182	.2
Cinema	472	.3	612	.2	701	.1
Music	935	.5	904	.3	945	.1
Engineering	18,387	10.2	36,774	12.0	95,039	13.8
Applied arts	—	—	—	—	17,911	2.6
Agronomy	11,277	6.3	36,370	11.8	94,262	13.7
Science	1,121	.6	4,108	1.3	1,466	.2
Education	120,477	67.0	190,740	62.0	290,450	42.2
Accounting and commerce	1,424	.8	1,635	.5	108,831	15.8
Total	179,838	100.0	307,817	100.0	688,355	100.0

Sources: United Arab Republic, General Agency of Statistics, *Statistical Annual, 1966* (Cairo, 1966), pp. 356–57; and Central Agency for Public Mobilization and Statistics, *Egypt: Statistical Indicators,* 1973, p. 189; and 1980 (Cairo, 1973, 1980), p. 189.

tives, in these fields corporatism continued to operate as part of a larger system of propaganda and censorship.

Despite this evidence of continuity, however, important differences in the development of specific syndicates reflected divergent strategies of coalition building under the two regimes. During the 1960s the greatest increases in membership were among technicians and civil servants, especially engineers, agronomists, scientists, and teachers. The prestigious medical and legal groups grew at far more modest rates, with the doctors' syndicate remaining virtually stagnant as it battled to resist socialized medicine. During the 1970s the medical professions gained new strength from the construction of private hospitals and clinics. Doctors and pharmacists quickly joined the technicians as the fastest-growing groups. New syndicates were established for related paraprofessionals such as nurses and draftsmen, while greater freedom of migration seriously depleted the dental and scientific associations.

The most striking change during the 1970s was the rise of a large new syndicate of commercial employees, representing a younger generation of university graduates who worked primarily in private and foreign establishments. Throughout the decade the Nasserist favoritism of civil servants over private practitioners was greatly reduced and a sizeable constituency was fashioned from the children of the *infitah*. Threats to swamp the "elitist" professions with clerical and working-class majorities were abandoned and five new associations were created to absorb graduates of the special academies and technical institutes. By the time Mubarak assumed power, the syndical movement had been expanded to represent a broad mixture of public and private employees, small businessmen and technical assistants, holders of advanced degrees and secondary school graduates.

Syndical growth has been accompanied by a number of legislated reorganizations that have encouraged greater continuity of leadership while providing various forms of proportional representation for occupational categories, age groups, and geographic regions. The terms of elected presidents and councils have been gradually lengthened from one or two years to three or four years. In some groups presidencies have been limited to two terms, yet the net result is still greater stability than the earlier practice of annual or semiannual elections that were commonly postponed and nullified.

The impact of proportional representation has been much more problematic. Improvements in the diversification of leadership have often been outweighed by bitter infighting between older and newer members. Both Nasser and Sadat tried to pack or fragment many syndicates by increasing enrollments of public employees and residents of the provincial capitals. Established syndicate leaders initiated several lawsuits to exclude many of these members or to deny them full voting rights. Some organizations, such as the bar association, continue to produce multiple membership rosters, all of which vary substantially from the government's enumerations. As a result, syndical elections are commonly challenged in court as defeated candidates claim fraud and each category of members demands a reallocation of scheduled posts.

While many syndicates have struggled to integrate the influx of new members, the reemergence of partisan competition since the 1970s has not disrupted their activities as much as the government desired. In many associations power is shared by the ruling party and an assortment of opposition factions, including groups that can be traced back to the prerevolutionary parties, as well as newer groups that are products of the Nasser and Sadat eras. Even where the National Democratic Party has been victorious, it faces regular challenges from followers of the New Wafd, the Socialist Action Party (which is a direct descendent of Misr al-Fatat), the Muslim Brotherhood, various types of Nasserists, former communists, and a new generation of independent Islamic groups.

The ruling party clearly expected these factions to devour one another, thereby allowing the government to divide the syndicates it could not directly control. However, to its surprise and frequent dismay, this has generally not occurred. Instead of reviving bitter memories of their pre-revolutionary battles and dwelling on their ideological differences, opposition groups have striven to accommodate one another's aspirations for a greater voice in syndical affairs. In many syndicates the coexistence of opposition factions has bred a remarkable degree of tolerance and an exchange of views on several issues where they disagree with the government more than one another. It has become commonplace for rival groups to rotate the use of syndical headquarters for their public seminars, to share podiums and assembly halls in joint conferences, to invite outside speakers affiliated with different political parties, and to publish in one another's journals and newspapers.

At times these factions have moved beyond coexistence and tolerance to cooperate in coordinating oppositional activity not only within particular syndicates but among the party leaderships as well. Particularly during the political crisis that preceded Sadat's death, many syndicates became rallying points for opposition groups that had been presumed to be irreconcilable enemies. As that crisis unfolded, the Socialist Action Party came to play a central role in encouraging a common front against Sadat's attacks on civil liberties and associational freedom. Ever since then the Socialist Action Party has led all other opposition parties in cultivating ties with a wide range of interest groups, including professional syndicates, labor unions, and religious associations.[7]

The strength and diversity of these associational ties has made the Socialist Action Party a major player in the post-Sadat party system. All of Egypt's political parties contain formal elements of corporatist organization for members of different functional groups. However, except for the government party, which enjoys privileged access to all corporatist structures, no opposition group has worked more seriously and effectively than the Socialist Party to breathe life into its specialized branches and committees. These efforts helped the Socialist Party to overcome its original image as Sadat's "domesticated opposition" and to make it a valuable coalition partner for any group that could identify with its blend of socialist and Islamic principles. Thus, the party's leaders were both early proponents and major beneficiaries of the factional collaboration that developed within the syndical movement. This success was instrumental in paving the way for the party's coalition with the Muslim Brotherhood in the new "Islamic Alliance," which displaced the New Wafd after the 1987 parliamentary elections as Egypt's leading opposition force.

Finally, the politicization of professional groups has also been stimulated by the growth of commercial activities and enterprises that the Sadat and Mubarak governments have promoted throughout the syndical movement. Virtually all of the professional syndicates have turned to investment and profit-making ventures during the *infitah*. The scope of their projects depends not only on the size of their pension funds and the extent of their landholdings but also on their ability to raise external capital through connections with the private sector and the government. Associational capitalism has enhanced the resources and prestige of many syndicates, but it has also provoked intense debate about how the investment funds are being managed. Syndical factions have become drawn into constant disagreements about whether profit making is appropriate, about the performance and utility of particular projects, and most of all, about conflicts of interest involving association leaders with overlapping positions in the business world and the ruling party.

When professional associations were weaker and poorer, the patronage of well-connected leaders was often viewed as a valuable asset to the group as a whole. However, as many syndicates have become indistinguishable from business enterprises, their would-be patrons have come under increasing scrutiny and suspicion. Leaders who might earlier have been viewed as offering benevolent protection are now seen as opportunists trying to enrich their cronies and advance their own political careers. Hence, commercialization has produced both new possibilities for scandal and new demands for accountable leadership. The crystallization of more stable factions has been accompanied by a dramatic increase in the stakes of their competition. Consequently, the political life of many syndicates has acquired a vigor that parallels and occasionally exceeds that of the party system itself.

The Sadat government had great difficulty in trying to manage professional associations during this period of growth and transformation, as has the Mubarak government. Over the past two decades most syndicates have experienced a notable increase in political activity by both opponents and supporters of the regime. This has led to wide variations in the balance of power between competing factions in several important professional groups. These heightened factional conflicts reflect ongoing struggles to expand or contain isolated beachheads of associational autonomy. In a larger sense, however, they also reflect attempts to fashion new types of corporatist arrangements that the regime and its rivals would like to hold up as alternative models for the future development of the syndical system as a whole.

Four professional associations have become particularly important battlegrounds: the syndicates of lawyers, journalists, engineers, and commercial employees. Opposition forces have made the greatest inroads in the lawyers' and journalists' syndicates, while the regime has managed to reshape the engineers' and commercial employees' syndicates into strongholds for some of its key allies in the private sector. Yet each group has developed a distinctive style of opposition or support. Together, their experiences illustrate the growing diversity of corporatist relationships as well as the likely consequences awaiting other syndicates that might wish to emulate them.

The lawyers' syndicate has developed into an unusual example of radical opposition, whereas the journalists' syndicate has become a house divided in which the government and its rivals oscillate between informal power-sharing arrangements and open warfare. For a time it appeared that the engineers' syndicate might become a showpiece of political loyalty and capitalist innovation, but instead it proved to be merely an embarrassing example of favoritism and intolerance. At first the commercial employees' syndicate seemed to be nothing more than an artificial creature of the state, designed to drum up white-collar support for the *infitah*. In time, however, the syndicate's leaders developed minds of their own and helped to prevent Mubarak from scrapping some of his predecessor's most controversial economic policies.

The Lawyers' Syndicate

Since the 1952 revolution the lawyers' syndicate has been involved in repeated and increasingly serious collisions with the regime. Over the past thirty years it has become by far the boldest and most persistent professional critic of government policies, demonstrating time and again that lawyers remain the weakest link in the extensive system of corporatist controls and that the preservation of that system has been possible only because of the state's willingness to employ rising levels of coercion. The experience of the bar association exemplifies the wide room for maneuver available to particularly tenacious opposition groups as well as the limits of the regime's tolerance of political threats that might quickly spill over to other syndicates and encourage their alliance with opposition parties.

The conflicts between the bar association and the government can be traced by comparing the colorful careers of Mustafa al-Baradi'i and Ahmad al-Khawaja—the two men who, with brief interruptions, dominated the syndicate presidency during the past three decades. Between 1958 and 1985 both men won election five times; both also managed to make impressive political comebacks after twice being ousted from office. Al-Baradi'i's terms covered 1958–1962, 1964–1966, and 1971 until his death in office in 1977. Al-Khawaja's presidencies have spanned 1966–1971, 1978–1981, and 1983 until the present.

Although both leaders experienced several ups and downs in their relations with the regime, they followed very different political paths. Al-Baradi'i was an early sympathizer of the Wafd and the Sa'dists who remained a consistent defender of judicial autonomy and parliamentary democracy as well as an implacable opponent of socialist threats to the quality of legal education and to the economic status of private practitioners. His changing political fortunes reflected not the adjustment of his independent opinions but the waverings and contradictions of successive governments that found it more or less useful to tolerate those views.

In 1962 al-Baradi'i clashed with Nasser when he was designated as the spokesman for several professional syndicates objecting to the requirement that workers and peasants make up 50 percent of all popularly elected bodies. This, coupled with his continued demands for a return to a multiparty system, led to his replacement by 'Abd al-'Aziz Shurbaji, a friend of Nasser's who had joined a "Free Lawyers" group in the early days of the revolution. When Shurbaji's quarrels with the government weakened his military support, al-Baradi'i quickly regained the presidency and mounted a blistering attack on several socialist policies until he was deposed by an A.S.U. counterassault in 1966.[8]

As soon as Sadat came to power, al-Baradi'i was rehabilitated and appointed to the committee for the reorganization of the A.S.U. Repeating his performance of a decade earlier during preparation of the Charter of National Action, he openly ridiculed all reforms that stopped short of multiparty competition. When it became clear that Sadat favored a halfway measure allowing state-sponsored "platforms" to emerge within the A.S.U., al-Baradi'i noted caustically that he did not understand what "platforms" were because democracy had no meaning without free political parties.[9]

Considering al-Baradi'i ungrateful for the renewed prosperity that private practitioners enjoyed with the return to capitalism, Sadat encouraged several rivals to challenge him in the 1975 syndical elections. Despite a closely contested race, al-Baradi'i won a second-round victory and became an even more outspoken critic of the man who had restored him to power. Just before his death in 1977 al-Baradiʿi led the bar association in rebuking the government's violation of civil liberties after the January riots and then gave Fu'ad Saraj al-Din a forum at the syndicate's headquarters for his provocative speech announcing the formation of the New Wafd Party.

Al-Khawaja, on the other hand, is a classic example of a political entrepreneur who has ridden several tigers without as yet being devoured by any of them. By disguising his partisan loyalties and altering his policy positions, al-Khawaja has been able to thrive on the rivalries and shifting alliances of the numerous factions that have arisen within the syndicate over the past two decades. In contrast to al-Baradiʿi, whose liberalism and independence were irrepressible, al-Khawaja has passed through several incarnations: as a stalking horse for the A.S.U., as a compromise candidate accepted though seldom trusted by the regime and its most ardent opponents, and in recent years, as a master of brinkmanship who has tested and helped to stretch the limits of permissable criticism.

Al-Khawaja began his syndical career as a creature of the A.S.U. who unseated al-Baradiʿi with powerful party backing. A member of the prerevolutionary Wafdist Vanguard, al-Khawaja fashioned a loose coalition of Wafdists, leftists, and young public sector lawyers who saw him as a useful alternative capable of softening the socialist assault on the syndicate and improving its strained relations with the government. During the final years of the Nasser regime, he effectively neutralized the bar association, preventing any resistance to the "massacre of the judges" of 1969 when the Ministry of Justice seized exclusive control over judicial appointments by summarily dismissing half of the Court of Cassation and the Judges Club.[10]

Al-Khawaja tried to remain neutral during the power struggle between Sadat and the ʿAli Sabri group, but he was purged anyway because of his close identification with the A.S.U. When Sadat became annoyed with al-Baradiʿi's demands for an immediate transition to democracy, al-Khawaja received tacit government support for his attempted comeback in the 1975 syndicate election.[11] Al-Khawaja became an even more appealing candidate to the government in 1978, after al-Baradiʿi died and a special election had to be arranged to choose his successor. Sadat was particularly concerned to prevent the victory of ʿAbd al-ʿAziz Shurbaji, who had developed a strong following among Nasserists and leftists because of his outspoken opposition to the Jerusalem trip and the Camp David talks. Al-Khawaja resisted overtures to run as a member of the ruling party, preferring instead to cast himself in the double role of "fusion candidate" and unofficial government representative.[12]

In 1979 al-Khawaja was reelected to a full term as syndicate president, but by this time the peace treaty with Israel had been finalized and he was finding it increasingly difficult to maintain his pose as the common spokesman of the Wafd, the Nasserists, and the National Democratic Party. After several efforts to dodge the issue during his campaign meetings, al-Khawaja finally admitted that Sadat had been "undemocratic" in concluding the treaty without consulting parliament, yet he scrupulously avoided criticizing the treaty itself. At this point the government was still more than willing to meet al-Khawaja halfway. Indeed, Sadat seemed to appreciate that his muted and technical criticisms of the treaty at the Federation of Arab Lawyers conference in Tunis ran against the more militant tide of opposition that was building within the Egyptian syndicate.[13]

During 1980, however, Sadat began to plan a showdown with the bar association that quickly pushed the reluctant al-Khawaja into alliance with, and then leadership of, the syndicate's most radical forces. At another meeting of Arab lawyers in Rabat, Egypt was represented by two delegations—one from the bar association and one sent by the government to counter criticisms of Sadat's separate peace. Even though al-Khawaja urged the conferees to stop short of direct censure of Egypt, as soon as they returned home he and several other syndicate leaders were denounced as traitors who should be tried for "defaming" the nation. Beginning in October 1980, al-Khawaja decided that the lawyers' best defense was to launch a vigorous counterattack against the government. He gave approval for regular biweekly seminars at the syndicate headquarters at which overflow crowds gathered to hear Sadat's foreign and domestic policies denounced by spokesmen of every opposition group in the country.[14]

Over the next six months the lawyers' seminars held center stage in educated Cairene society. Beginning as an underground debating club, they quickly snowballed into a combination of catharsis and guerilla theater, releasing a decade of pent-up resentment against the regime. Scheduled forums were commonly delayed two hours or more, giving various causes ample time to work the packed assembly hall with petitions and solicitations for funds. Speaking time and seating at the rostrum were carefully arranged to give an appearance of harmony among the syndicate's rival factions, though ex-communists were the most likely to be shortchanged when heated sessions ran well beyond midnight or when police presence was particularly conspicuous.

Week after week the Thursday night seminars dissected every aspect of the "Sadatist tyranny" with extraordinary skill and sarcasm—the "Law of Shame," the scandals of the *infitah,* the phoney party system, the plan to divert Nile waters to Israel, the persecutions of journalists, the exploitation of religious tensions, the growing indebtedness to foreigners, and the "Americanization" of economic and foreign policy. Whatever the scheduled topic, discussion always led back to the Camp David accords and the "normalization" of relations with Israel. In the early months of 1981, as the Israeli embassy opened in Cairo and another anniversary of the treaty approached, the syndicate focused more and more on the Begin government's settlement of the occupied territories and its incursions into south Lebanon. Just as Sadat had referred to the participants in the Rabat conference as traitors, now the lawyers began to return the insult, vowing that it was the "treasonous president" who would be brought to trial for welcoming the "enemy" in Egypt while Arab lands were being threatened with annexation.

Sadat soon decided to escalate the conflict by mobilizing his own contingents of lawyers and urging them to "cleanse" the syndicate. On the tenth anniversary of the "Corrective Revolution" Sadat delivered a long and menacing address to the Alexandria bar association that was televised throughout the country. Bedecked with the sash of a high-court judge and seated behind a valuable Qur'an presented to him by the syndicate president, Sadat recalled the many steps he had taken to make Egypt a "state of institutions" in which people no longer had to live in fear of "midnight visitors." He made a particular point of reminding his nationwide audience that he had closed the detention camps and helped to tear them down with his own hands.[15]

Yet the obvious strain and emotion in his voice during this portion of the speech inevitably raised a question that escaped no one even if they dared not ask it aloud: Did he not still have the power to change his mind and open the camps once again? The lawyers in the audience knew very well that the issue of the detention camps had already been raised by one of their own colleagues who had accused Sadat of preparing for a new wave of political arrests. Then, with the ease and self-confidence of a man who knew precisely what he had up his sleeve, Sadat noted that although the lawyers' syndicate in Cairo had fallen into the hands of a small group of troublemakers, they would soon learn the same lesson he had taught the insolent leaders of the engineers' and journalists' syndicates.

Sadat's performance before the Alexandria bar was part of a broad initiative to rally several special groups of lawyers against the syndicate leadership. He promised new graduates that the government would require all joint venture firms to hire Egyptian counsel. He told public sector lawyers that they would be granted full membership rights in the syndicate and that they would be allotted additional seats in the bar council. Most important, he pledged that parliament would rewrite the syndicate's statute to provide for equal representation of all provincial branches even though about 65 percent of the nation's lawyers were still registered in the Cairo bar.[16]

About one month after the Alexandria speech, the ruling party led members of all of these groups (as well as a number of secret police posing as lawyers) in a march on the syndicate headquarters. Forcing their way into the building, they held a rump meeting that declared a vote of no confidence in the elected syndicate board. Sadat promptly intervened, dissolving the bar council and appointing a provisional board headed by Jamal al-'Utayfi, a prominent *infitah* lawyer who had been Sadat's point man in drafting Egypt's new constitution with minimal input from the legal community. Sadat then announced the formation of a special parliamentary committee charged with investigating the "illegal political activities" of the bar and with preparing a new syndical law that would never again allow the association to be used as an "informal political party." When Sadat rounded up his political opponents in September 1981, five members of the elected bar council were imprisoned and the syndicate appeared to be locked into a prolonged period of government receivership intended to deter other professional groups that might wish to follow its example.[17]

During the first year and a half of Mubarak's reign the syndicate was torn by constant battles between its dual leadership—the appointed council and the government insisted that new elections be postponed until the new syndical law was adopted whereas the elected council pressed the courts for a speedy nullification of Sadat's intervention. By early 1983 members of al-Khawaja's group were confident that the courts would reinstate them, but they claimed that the ruling party was pressuring Mubarak to influence the outcome and to defy the judgment if it went against the government. The elected council began to organize its own invasions of the syndicate headquarters, reconvening its regular meetings and then marching to the courts in demonstrations for judicial independence. Al-Khawaja made a special effort to elicit statements of support from the provincial bar associations in order to convince the government that it could not isolate opposition in the capital.[18]

During the spring a compromise solution took shape. The elected council was restored for the full remainder of its term, but it was forced to accept a more restrictive syndicate law implementing most of the reforms demanded by Sadat, including explicit controls over the bar's affiliations with international organizations. In fact, by this time Egypt's relations with Israel and the United States had deteriorated to the point that Mubarak was extremely reluctant to enforce his broadened power over the syndicate. The very year the new law was adopted, al-Khawaja was elected president of the Arab Federation of Lawyers, whose meetings had prompted Sadat's confrontation with the Egyptian bar in the first place.[19]

Before long the lawyers' syndicate was denouncing the treaty and the normalization policy more openly and vigorously than ever. Indeed, it began boasting that Mubarak's "correction" of Egyptian foreign policy had vindicated the objections that lawyers had been stating for years. The syndicate announced that it would take disciplinary action against any members who accepted invitations to travel to Israel or even to participate in international conferences in Egypt where Israelis were in attendance. Annual celebrations in honor of Wafdist and Watani leaders now included public commemorations of Nasser's birthday as well.[20]

In October 1985 the syndicate held a special seminar to organize the legal defense of Sulayman Khatar, the policeman who had fired on Israeli tourists in Sinai after Israel's air raid on the P.L.O. headquarters in Tunis. The title of the seminar, which received wide press coverage throughout the Arab world, was an echo of the old Nasserist slogan from the days of the war of attrition, "No peace, no recognition, no negotiation." Leaders from every opposition party in the nation appeared, including a representative of the new Nasserist organization, which was still prohibited from operating as a formal party. After each party spokesman stated his well-known criticisms of Egyptian foreign policy, al-Khawaja seemed determined to outbid his guests in provocative oratory. First, he reminded them that the syndicate's headquarters was virtually the only building in the Arab world where the Egyptian and Palestinian flags flew side by side. Then, instead of repeating the long-standing demand for abrogation of the Camp David accords, he called for the nullification of article one of the 1974 disengagement agreement that had ended the state of war between Egypt and Israel. Finally, al-Khawaja asked why Arab governments were purchasing millions of dollars' worth of arms and using them against their own people instead of against the U.S. and Israeli "enemies." Every Arab citizen, he said, must ask his government one question: "Where are the arms to fight Israel?"[21]

Al-Khawaja's demonstration of contempt for the relative caution of the opposition parties paid off handsomely in the upcoming syndicate elections. Shortly after his fiery performance at the October seminar, al-

Khawaja was elected to his fifth term as president, receiving over 75 percent of the vote. He proclaimed that his landslide victory and international notoriety were testimony to the growing "political and national *(qawmi)* role of the bar association."[22] Sadat's punitive syndical legislation not only proved to be a dead letter but also helped to turn a longtime opportunist and former regime pawn into a darling of the opposition whose activities are followed closely in the Arab press. Al-Khawaja's appetite for brinkmanship may again push him into waters that are over his head, but so far his criticisms have paralleled public opinion and tacit changes in government policy just enough to save him from renewed persecution.

The Journalists' Syndicate

The journalists' syndicate has been neither a reliable instrument of government control nor an effective means for redressing the many grievances of the press. Since its inception several governments have tried to involve the syndicate in various schemes of self-censorship and professional discipline, but these have never been more than a small part of Egypt's increasingly elaborate systems of media regulation. The focus of state control over the press has shifted periodically from the Ministry of Information to the Arab Socialist Union and, most recently, to the Majlis al-Shura and the managers of state-owned publishing houses. However, the syndicate has never played a serious role in shaping any of these systems, and it has been vested with no clear authority to assist in their enforcement. Viewing the syndicate as inherently untrustworthy, ruling elites have continued to depend on penal codes and censorship bureaus, dismissals and forced transfers, publishing bans and exile.

Journalists have developed an even more cynical view of the syndicate's usefulness in advancing their interests and defending their freedom. Many writers seek a degree of independence by aligning themselves with a particular faction of the ruling elite and expressing critical views they know are being voiced inside the government itself. Their ability to survive and prosper depends not only on their willingness to respect the tacit limits of tolerable debate but also on the accuracy of their "inside" information about the changing balance of power within the ruling circle. Weaker and less tractable writers are more likely to view the syndicate as a valuable forum for protesting government abuses, but when push comes to shove, journalists in trouble with the law generally look elsewhere for support and protection.

When these journalists appeal to syndicate leaders it is often with the intention of embarrassing them by exposing their impotence in defending the profession or their complicity in throttling it. By and large, journalists seek their main lines of defense not in the syndicate but in the courts, in sympathetic lawyers and opposition parties, and in alternative channels of publication and employment in the Arab and European press. When these lines of defense are available, journalists may choose to bypass the syndicate altogether. For example, when anti-Sadatist writers went to court to win the release of colleagues arrested during the crisis of September 1981, they explicitly rejected the syndicate's offer to cosponsor the suit, declaring that several syndicate leaders had helped to prepare the government's blacklist in the first place.

The degree to which independent journalists have become alienated from their own association was poignantly demonstrated by a series of acerbic exchanges between Sadat and Mustafa Amin concerning the most recent ''reform'' of the press in 1980 and 1981. When Sadat learned that the journalists' syndicate intended to resist his plans, he threatened to turn it into a private club. Amin suggested instead that it be turned into a casino. When Sadat claimed that the press was about to become the ''fourth power of the state,'' Amin said that his remarks would be misunderstood in unvoweled Arabic print because people would read the word ''power'' *(sulta)* as ''salad'' *(salata)*. When Sadat announced the formation of the largely government-appointed Higher Council for the Press, Amin observed that it should, indeed, be named the ''higher'' council because its meeting room would be on the eleventh floor.[23]

Despite the syndicate's obvious marginality as either a regulatory or a representative body, it has become one of the nation's most important political battlegrounds. Although the government and its opponents constantly complain about the syndicate's shortcomings, neither side is prepared to see it fall decisively into enemy hands. Hence, the syndicate has been the site for frequent skirmishes and tests of strength between progovernment and antigovernment factions in which temporary victories and truces have merely spurred new attempts to alter the balance of forces. Throughout most of its history, the syndicate leadership has represented an uneasy division of power between one faction in control of the presidency and a number of rival factions controlling the syndical council.

Before 1955 the presidency alternated between Mahmud Abu al-Fatah and his brother Husayn Abu al-Fatah of the Wafd and Fikri Abaza of the Hizb al-Watani. However, Wafdist influence was always checked by council majorities representing the weaker right-wing parties, which were more dependent on the goodwill of the government. Since 1955 the pattern has been reversed—the presidency has generally been controlled by progovernment candidates while the council has included representatives of several factions who have frequently equaled or outnumbered supporters of the regime.[24]

On two occasions this informal condominium arrangement broke down when opposition groups managed to elect the president as well as the majority of the council. From 1964 to 1966 the syndicate was headed by Hafiz Mahmud, a former member of the Liberal Constitutionalist Party and ally of Misr al-Fatat, who strongly criticized Nasser's management of the press and tried to establish an independent alliance of professional syndicates. Again, in 1980, opposition forces elected Kamal Zuhairi who, like Ahmad al-Khawaja, was originally a member of the A.S.U. Vanguard but then reemerged as a leading critic of Sadat's foreign policy and press reforms.

In both cases the threat of a consolidated opposition provoked a major assault from the regime that restored government control over the syndicate presidency. However, both assaults also spurred rival factions to redouble their efforts to secure representation on the syndical council. The result has been a steady increase of competitiveness and polarization, making the journalists' elections the closest and most bitterly fought contests in the entire syndical system.

Hafiz Mahmud was the only freely elected president of the syndicate during the 1960s. His term coincided with the important period of transition between the nationalization of the press in 1960 and the consolidation of A.S.U. control over the media toward the middle of the decade. Mahmud was the author of a short-lived attempt in 1964 to set up an interchamber federation of professional groups with himself as president and including Ibrahim Shukri of the agronomists' syndicate and Fu'ad Muhi al-Din of the doctors' syndicate. All three leaders had been connected with Misr al-Fatat before the revolution and were eager to develop an independent initiative toward syndical coordination before the rising group of leftists in the A.S.U. were able to launch their own program. Although this plan progressed further than al-Baradi'i's earlier effort to link professional associations, it too was killed soon after 'Ali Sabri learned of the "federation's" first meeting.

This skirmish was followed by a more serious confrontation in 1965 when the journalists' syndicate voted down the government's plans to place both ownership and supervision of the press in the hands of the A.S.U. Even though 'Ali Sabri managed to dismiss Mahmud and introduce many Marxists into the press corps, he was unable to prevent journalists from electing councils that reflected a variety of views, ranging from Wafdists and professional syndicalists to more conservative Nasserists who found support among Sabri's rivals in the army and the cabinet. Between 1965 and 1971 the A.S.U. tried to extend its control over the syndicate in a step-by-step manner. It dissolved elected syndical councils two years in a row before the June war and then allowed new elections in 1967, advancing Ahmad Baha' al-Din as a compromise candidate who was acceptable to both the A.S.U. Vanguard and the syndicate. When the syndicate endorsed the student demonstrations of 1968, the A.S.U. decided to impose its own list of candidates headed by Kamal Zuhairi.[25]

Zuhairi helped to author a new syndicate law designed to oust the older generation of A.S.U. opponents while formalizing the syndicate's role in representing journalists who were charged in criminal proceedings. Syndicate leaders were finally granted a bare majority of seats on the mixed committees that govern membership and disciplinary actions. Membership was henceforth restricted to university graduates and several seats on the syndical council were reserved for young journalists with less than fifteen years' experience. In a unique provision found in no other associational statute, the syndicate president was specifically required to be present during all interrogations of arrested journalists.

Although Zuhairi has always tried to characterize these changes as an important victory for the syndicate, they were in fact extremely modest improvements that implicated the syndicate president more directly than ever in party-ordered purges and prosecutions. Ironically, the "Zuhairi law" proved to be a weapon that was wielded primarily against its own authors. After Zuhairi himself was purged in the Corrective Revolution, the Nasserist and leftist elements that he headed continued to occupy about half of the seats on the syndicate council throughout the 1970s. But as they became more outspoken critics of the Sadat regime, they found the syndicate useless in defending them against retaliation.

When the syndicate again supported student demonstrations in 1972 and 1973, over a hundred journalists, including several council members, were fired and expelled from the A.S.U. Although they were given amnesty just before the October war, many left the country and were joined by yet another exodus after the Camp David accords. Leftists kept electing representatives to the syndicate's councils only to see its presidents stand by as the government drove them out of one publication after another—from *al-Katib* to *al-Tali'a*, from *al-Tali'a* to *Ruz al-Yusuf*, and, finally, from *Ruz al-Yusuf* to *al-Ahali*. After 1977 the ruling party began to recruit more and more of its syndical candidates from the very editors who had been most closely identified with these purges. Leading examples included Yusuf al-Saba'i, the former Minister of Culture and editor of *al-Ahram*, Muhammad 'Abd al-Jawad, the head of the state news agency, and Salah Jalal, the science writer who transformed *al-Tali'a* into a popular photo review.[26]

Sadat's desire to fill the syndicate leadership with more of his own men was part of a larger plan to reorganize the whole system of press regulation. The dissolution of the A.S.U.—the former owner of all Egyptian newspapers—together with the development of a new party press had created a number of legal and political problems that the government wanted to sort out once and for all. In an era when censorship supposedly had been abolished, Sadat was constantly being forced to take personal responsibility for newspaper seizures and questionable criminal actions against journalists who took his pronouncements about freedom of the press seriously. Every writer of prominence seemed to be held to a different and completely subjective standard. Muhammad Hasanayn Haykal could publish critical pieces abroad, but he was often told not to leave the country. Mustafa Amin continued to write in *al-Akhbar,* but he was privately scolded when he said the wrong things. Ahmad Baha' al-Din was thriving in Kuwait and saw no reason to lead other exiled journalists into a trap by accepting empty invitations to return to Egypt.

During 1979 and 1980 Sadat and his leading editors advanced a number of measures they claimed would clear the air. In fact, these were poorly disguised attempts to reintroduce censorship through the back door while spreading out responsibility for enforcement among a number of bewildering institutions with overlapping powers. Newspapers were to be licensed under three separate categories of ownership—state, party, and syndical—but privately owned newspapers were still prohibited. Formal ownership of the state newspapers inherited from the A.S.U. was vested in the new Majlis al-Shura, a consultative assembly in which half of the members were appointed by the president.[27]

All three types of newspapers were supervised by the Higher Council for the Press, an enormous mixed commission with about fifty members headed by the president of the Majlis al-Shura. One half of the Higher Council members were appointed by the Majlis al-Shura; the other half were *ex officio* members drawn mainly from editors and managers of state newspaper and broadcasting bureaus. In an earlier incarnation, one-third of the Higher Council for the Press had been leaders of the journalists' syndicate. In the expanded formula, the syndicate and the party newspapers were each allowed one seat. The Majlis al-Shura was also empowered to appoint most members of the state publishing houses' management councils and to supervise elections of the remaining members by the employees.[28]

These arrangements placed control of the press more firmly than ever in the hands of nonjournalists and diminished the syndicate's already marginal authority to the vanishing point. Journalists were thoroughly at the mercy of their editors and appointed management boards that included many members from outside the profession. They could moonlight for the party newspapers and write what they wished, but they might still be charged with "defamation" under the new "Law of Shame." Furthermore, the new system required prior approval from the Higher Council for anyone who wanted to publish abroad—a muzzle that Haykal boasted had been tailor-made for him alone.

Journalists' resentment over these measures were an important factor in Kamal Zuhairi's comeback victory in the syndical election of 1980. The government was caught off guard after the tragic death of Yusuf al-Saba'i, Sadat's handpicked syndicate president who was killed in Cyprus when Egyptian commandos stormed an airliner that had been hijacked by Palestinian guerrillas. Zuhairi was joined on the new syndical council by a large group of opposition journalists, including Amina Shafiq and Husayn 'Abd al-Raziq of the left-wing Tajammu' Party.

Zuhairi soon became a regular participant in the bar association's evening seminars, where he denounced the new press laws and discussed his book attacking the planned diversion of Nile waters to Israel. He also pushed through the syndical council a resolution threatening disciplinary action against journalists who cooperated in the normalization of relations with Israel. By the beginning of 1981, when the government was preparing to enforce the new press system, the journalists' and lawyers' syndicates had formed an open alliance to resist it in the courts. Moreover, they had clear backing from at least two of the opposition parties that were printing lengthy exposés of the conflict in their weekly newspapers.[29]

Sadat had little difficulty in organizing his own supporters to vote Zuhairi out of office in the spring of 1981. "Nationalist" journalists were mobilized by the ruling party and the heads of the state publishing houses, led by Makram Muhammad Ahmad, the manager of *Dar al-Hilal* and editor of *al-Musawwar*. In an election that saw the highest turnout in the syndicate's history, the government candidate, Salah Jalal, won handily while opposition votes were split between Zuhairi and Jalal al-Hamamsi, a former Wafdist. Shortly after the election, Sadat demonstrated his gratitude by granting the syndicate ownership of the land on which its headquarters were located. A few weeks later, in a triumphant meeting to commemorate "national journalists' day," the president reminded Egyptian writers that the first guarantee of their liberties was "a responsible conscience and respect for morality."[30]

The relative ease with which Sadat regained control over the journalists' syndicate strengthened his determination to take on the more defiant
lawyers and emboldened him to use increasingly heavy-handed tactics
against all of his other critics. After the assassination, however, government control over the syndicate began to deteriorate again as Mubarak
eased up on the party press and Sadatist editors pointed the finger at one
another for their alleged roles in persecuting opposition writers. In 1983
Salah Jalal and Kamal Zuhairi had a rematch in which Jalal won reelection by a mere three votes—476 to 473.[31]

During the campaign Jalal complained to Prime Minister Fu'ad Muhi
al-Din that the ruling party was dragging its feet because the government
editors were still nursing grudges from the crisis of September 1981. Jalal
had leaked a story to *al-Ahrar,* the Liberal Party paper, asserting that
Sadat had consulted with his press advisors before ordering the mass
arrests. According to Jalal, he and Makram Muhammad Ahmad had both
opposed the plan, but their objections had been overridden by Musa Sabri, the editor of *al-Akhbar,* who had insisted that the time had come to
put the president's critics behind bars.[32]

Musa Sabri was already locked in a vicious public feud with Haykal
who had made similar allegations in his book, *The Autumn of Fury.* Sabri
was also fighting court orders to pay huge damages to young journalists
who had accused him of mistreatment as an employer. In Sabri's view,
Jalal had fabricated the story and planted it in the opposition press in
order to squeak through a difficult election at his expense. Sabri claimed
that no one, Jalal included, had dared to express any objection to Sadat's
plan, knowing very well that the president had already made up his mind
and was merely testing the loyalty of his closest advisers.

Convinced that Musa Sabri was trying to sabotage his reelection, Jalal
appealed to Fu'ad Muhi al-Din to hold an emergency meeting with the
other government editors and to instruct them that he was the official
candidate of the ruling party. Turnout in the election was aided by the
intervention of Muhsin Muhammad and Ibrahim Nafi ', the editors of *al-
Jumhuriya* and *al-Ahram,* and by the last-minute announcement of increased government contributions to the syndicate's pension fund. Even
so, on election day the polling had to be postponed several hours because
of the absence of a legal quorum at the syndicate headquarters.[33]

Jalal's reelection victory was a narrow one and a hollow one as well.
He did his best to convince journalists that he could be a ''bridge'' between the syndicate and the government, pointing to the material benefits
that had flowed from his willingness to reach ''friendly solutions'' with
the Mubarak administration. Pensions were increased 50 percent. Mini-

mum wages and severance pay rose along with subsidies for housing, medical treatment, and travel. Government editors, he said, were at last being told that they could not treat their establishments and employees like personal possessions. Most important, the syndicate was beginning to attain financial independence. Mubarak had agreed to give the syndicate a share of advertising revenues from all state-owned publications. These funds would be used to finance a new seventeen-story office building that would bring in still more money from commercial tenants.[34]

Nevertheless, at least half of the syndical council once again was controlled by journalists representing various opposition parties. They described Jalal's "bridges" as costly invasion routes through which the ruling party was trying to occupy the syndicate and turn it into another business enterprise resembling the engineers' syndicate. They vowed to preserve their association as a "syndicate of opinion" *(niqaba al-ra'i)* in which political activities would always overshadow economic ventures.[35] The more Salah Jalal tried to reshape the journalists' syndicate into a replica of the engineers' society, the more his opponents struggled to prove that it was an inseparable sister of the bar association.

Jalal's opponents on the syndical council made a particular point of embarrassing him by reaffirming the syndicate's rejection of relations with Israel. Then, in early 1984, they claimed that he was cooperating with the U.S. embassy to promote normalization behind the council's back. The syndicate's cultural committee had agreed to sponsor a competition to select a delegation of young journalists for a goodwill visit to the United States. However, during the tour they discovered that their program included a meeting with an Israeli professor. When the delegation returned to Egypt, they complained to the cultural committee, which then demanded an apology from the embassy and an assurance that similar meetings would not be repeated on future trips. Instead, the cultural committee was informed that it would no longer be involved in the selection process because Salah Jalal had already agreed privately that, henceforth, visiting journalists should be chosen by the embassy itself.[36]

Since Sadat's assassination there has been a notable increase of cooperation among opposition journalists to insure representation of diverse views on the syndical council. Members of rival parties have clearly been supporting one another's candidates. In addition, more and more journalists have been splitting their votes, backing progovernment candidates in close presidential races while giving large majorities to outspoken opponents running for council seats. In the 1983 elections the leading vote-getter was Amina Shafiq, a veteran woman syndicalist and Tajammu' activist who cosponsored the lawsuit against Sadat's arrests and forced transfers of journalists. She has become a popular advocate of associational pluralism, writing widely about the need to strengthen all types of professional and voluntary groups alongside the political parties.[37]

In 1985 an even more lopsided majority elected a new face from the Islamic movement: Muhammad ʿAbd al-Qaddus, the son of Ihsan ʿAbd al-Qaddus and a young member of the Muslim Brotherhood. ʿAbd al-Qaddus received nearly eight hundred votes—about two-thirds of all votes cast and more than twice as many as the leading candidates of the ruling party. ʿAbd al-Qaddus has become a regular contributor to all of the opposition papers, where he has tried to demonstrate the Muslim Brotherhood's commitment to liberal democracy and its willingness to build alliances within the existing party system. He has been particularly active in trying to revive the syndicate's ties with university students, demanding the reinstatement of the elected student unions that were abolished by Sadat.[38]

The Engineers' Syndicate

One reason that lawyers and journalists have become more politically assertive is that they believe they have special rights and responsibilities to defend independent opinions. Equally important, however, is their determination to prevent the rest of the syndical movement from following the recent evolution of the engineers' syndicate, which the Sadat and Mubarak governments have touted as a model association that should be emulated by all other occupational groups. For those who believe that Egyptian corporatism, with its traditional diversity and flexibility, contains the seeds of pluralist democracy, the example of the engineers' syndicate is not merely an embarrassing contradiction but a serious threat as well.

Before 1979 the ups and downs of the engineers' syndicate were of little consequence to other associations or to the political system in general. From the beginning the syndicate was deeply divided by rivalries between branch organizations representing different specializations and grades. Even when industrialization and nationalization seemed to enhance the prestige of native engineers, most of them remained government employees with little influence over policy-making and no right to conclude collective agreements. During the Nasser era the syndicate presidency was passed back and forth between well-connected army engineers and ministers, cushioning it somewhat from the political miscues and assaults that upset other professional groups. Yet this was an unusually indifferent sort of patronage that provided few benefits besides free education while endorsing the virtual conscription of engineers by state agencies before the syndicate had time to certify them. Indeed, Nasser eventually diminished the syndicate's control over its own members to the point that many no longer bothered to enroll.[39]

The Corrective Revolution breathed momentary life into the syndicate when its president, 'Abd al-Khaliq al-Shinnawi, began to voice a number of demands and criticisms not directly against Sadat but against his prime minister, 'Aziz Sidqi. Al-Shinnawi demanded that the syndicate be empowered to regulate all native and foreign engineers, and that it also be allowed to review the government's development projects. He was particularly critical of programs involving Soviet technical assistance and of the plan to bypass the Suez Canal with an expensive oil pipeline to the Mediterranean Sea. Moreover, he had joined the leaders of the lawyers' and journalists' syndicates in endorsing the student demonstrators who attacked the government for delaying democratic reform and for prolonging the agony of "no war, no peace" before the October war.[40]

These problems did not grow into the sort of confrontations that Sadat had with other professional groups, but they did prompt a major reorganization of the engineers' syndicate under new leaders who were becoming key members of Sadat's inner circle. The reorganization was outlined in a new syndical law adopted in 1974 and implemented by a new syndicate president, Mustafa Khalil, who eventually became prime minister and a leading strategist of the National Democratic Party. Khalil's reforms helped to rescue the syndicate from its previous oblivion and put it on the way to becoming a showpiece of corporatist privilege for those who were ready to fall in step with the new policies of capitalist development.

The statute contains lengthy and detailed descriptions of the syndicate's powers, including an explicit prohibition against government employment of any engineer who is not a paid up and certified member of the association. All foreign engineers are also required to join the syndicate and to obtain temporary work permits that must be reviewed periodically. The term of elected presidents and councils was lengthened from two years to four and several new syndicate-wide committees were created, cutting across the old divisions between specialized branches. A separate syndicate was established for technical school graduates and draftsmen *(niqabat al-tatbiqiyin)*, who were allowed to become junior affiliates in a multichamber federation. Affiliations with other occupational associations outside the technical professions were specifically encouraged.[41]

Financial provisions constitute a large portion of the statute. The syndicate was provided a guaranteed income not only from dues and direct government subsidies but from numerous stamp taxes as well as special levies on all locally produced cement and steel. Government and employer contributions to the pension fund were raised substantially, and the syndicate council was granted broad authority to invest all revenues in profit-making enterprises, including those owned directly by the association. Authorized expenditures include (but are not limited to) housing cooperatives, clinics and hospitals, insurance, supermarkets, social clubs, sporting facilities, and vacation resorts.[42]

Although Mustafa Khalil laid the groundwork for an entrepreneurial syndicate, it was 'Uthman Ahmad 'Uthman who brought it to life and made it a center of controversy for the entire syndical movement. Shortly after 'Uthman's election as syndicate president in 1979, Sadat donated title to the land on which the association's headquarters are located. Within the next few years 'Uthman rapidly turned the engineers' syndicate into a financial conglomerate that paralleled and frequently overlapped his previous creation, the Arab Contractors' Group.

The keystone of the system is the Engineers' Bank, which is a principal shareholder in several other syndicate companies: insurance, housing, food production, macaroni and starches, bricks, information services, and a joint venture bottling company with Schweppes. These subsidiaries, in turn, have invested in other joint ventures with Pepsi-Cola and Mercedes-Benz and with the government in developing new cities such as "The Sixth of October City." They have also participated in "food security," tourism, and transportation projects in several provinces, including Isma'iliya, Suez, Port Sa'id, Beni Swayf, and Fayyum.

The syndicate has built one of Egypt's best equipped and most expensive private hospitals. It has purchased land from the state and the army at "symbolic prices" for new apartment complexes. It has made special arrangements with the Ministry of Industry for priority deliveries of locally produced automobiles. It has set up international telex and telephone services in the syndicate headquarters. It has opened a repair shop for household appliances. It operates a discount trade center and a full-service supermarket complete with door-to-door delivery. And it has been constructing vacation facilities on the Mediterranean and Red Sea.[43]

The scale and innovation of these enterprises won wide acclaim from syndicate members and the public alike, especially as Sadat made increasingly flattering references to the engineers during his attacks on more troublesome groups. But this acclaim went hand in hand with incessant accusations of favoritism and mismanagement. Revenues from the subsidiary companies flowed not only to the syndicate and its bank but also to the Arab Contractors' Group, which was a partner in several of the new firms. The control of funds was vested in the syndical council, which was filled with 'Uthman's relatives and business associates. Council members were paid special salaries and fees for running the syndicate's operations.[44]

Many engineers complained about the low profitability of the enterprises. Through 1983 profits were reported as ranging between 3 percent and 8 percent, while savings accounts were earning about 13 percent. At these rates, it was said, the syndicate was actually losing several hundred thousand pounds each year and jeopardizing its pension fund for the sake of short-term publicity. There was also a good deal of disappointment about the rising cost of services provided by the syndicate, especially when the price of apartments for young engineers doubled despite the acquisition of public lands at virtually no expense. Some engineers charged that the prices had been inflated because the syndicate awarded the building contract to a Saudi Arabian firm in which 'Uthman had an interest even though lower bids had been submitted. Worst of all, the syndicate's bank was making large, unsecured loans to private businessmen for projects that had nothing to do with its own enterprises. One of the biggest beneficiaries was Tawfiq 'Abd al-Hay, who used a \$2 million "food security" loan to import several tons of rancid poultry and then fled the country to avoid prosecution.[45]

Unfortunately for the syndicate, all of these problems coincided with a cascade of business scandals that Mubarak allowed to be publicized in order to distance himself from the more corrupt elements of the ruling party. The 'Abd al-Hay fiasco was quickly followed by the arrest of Rashad 'Uthman, a former dock worker in the port of Alexandria who became a multimillionaire by bribing customs officials on behalf of businessmen connected with the local branch of the National Democratic Party. Both of these affairs were then topped by government seizures of the estates of 'Ismat Sadat and his relatives, who had made even larger fortunes by trading on the name of the former president. In these circumstances it was inevitable that the syndicate's enterprises would come under still greater scrutiny, particularly since their creator was linked at every turn with the business committees of the ruling party, with the binational chambers of commerce, and with the Sadat family itself.

As 'Uthman's policies came under stronger attack in parliament and in the press, his followers moved to tighten their grip on the engineers' syndicate and to smother dissent before it could get out of hand. When the syndical council presented its reports to general assembly meetings, small groups of members demanded fuller financial disclosures only to be muscled out of the hall for creating a public disturbance. Eventually, general assembly meetings were limited to two hour readings of the council's reports, followed by a recess for the noontime prayer and then by a sudden cancellation of the afternoon sessions.[46]

When ʿUthman ran for reelection in 1983, Mubarak refused to endorse him as the official candidate of the government party. Dissident engineers invited several former ministers to challenge him (including ʿAziz Sidqi, ʿAbd al-Khaliq al-Shinnawi, and Sidqi Sulayman), but they all declined. Only about 10 percent of the 127,000 registered engineers participated in the polling, yet ʿUthman won over 85 percent of the vote. Some of ʿUthman's strongest support was attributed to a group of army engineers who were given a week's leave just before the election, supposedly so that they could repay his endorsement of their commanding officer as head of the syndicate's architectural branch.[47]

Looking ahead to the day when ʿUthman would be unable to run for a third consecutive term, his allies looked to parliament for an insurance policy that would preserve their control over the syndicate's council and, of course, over its economic interests. Parliament amended the syndicate statute, allowing sitting council members to succeed themselves in office several times. The same parliament had just prohibited multiple successions in the lawyers' and journalists' syndicates, hoping to disrupt opposition inroads into those councils.

The economic activities of the engineers' syndicate have inspired a proliferation of profit-making ventures by several other occupational groups. The chambers of commerce have joined the ruling party in promoting "Popular Development Banks" to capitalize small businessmen in the provinces.[48] The commercial employees' syndicate heads a new Trade and Development Bank that is also financed by contributions from seven other syndicates. This interchamber bank runs five major corporations: a trading company supplying household appliances to provincial branches of syndicate cooperatives, an import-export firm, an Islamic trading company, a livestock and poultry company, and a publication and computer center.[49] The largest and wealthiest professional association, the teachers' syndicate, has one of the most diversified portfolios, which is now managed according to a special "economic development plan." In addition to its hotel near the Gazira Club, the teachers' syndicate has sizeable holdings in the intersyndical bank, in the Halwan iron and steel complex, and in Bisku Misr, one of the country's biggest food producers.[50]

Smaller syndicates are discussing more modest projects, some of which are already on the drawing board. The draftsmen's syndicate is constructing a large office building in ʿAbbasiya. It has also started a joint venture with foreign investors to build a furniture factory that intends to open branches in several provincial capitals.[51] The doctors' syndicate wants to build a private hospital and may use the profits to buy into the pharmaceutical industry. The agronomists' syndicate has obtained land in Sinai for a desert reclamation program, intending to market its own produce under the "food security" program.[52] Even the tiny cinematographers' syndicate would like to go into business, but the government has already earmarked a special tax on movie tickets for the policemen's association.[53]

Although capitalism is flourishing in the syndical movement, it is also extracting a high price. In every one of these organizations the debate over profit-making ventures has become a potent campaign issue, polarizing the members and weakening many long-standing syndicate leaders. With each election there are more and more candidates who assert that the representative functions of their syndicates are being eclipsed by the scramble for land and capital, for licenses and subsidies, for partners and markets. The experience of the engineers' syndicate is frequently cited in these debates, but now even the defenders of associational capitalism are likely to point to it as a model they wish to avoid.

The Commercial Employees' Syndicate

The most important new professional syndicate created during the Sadat era was the association of commercial employees. A reformed version of the original accountants' syndicate, this group was designed to encompass employees of the Finance Ministry along with the new waves of university graduates who were being channeled into the private sector. Although the syndicate has succeeded in organizing a vast constituency on behalf of the *infitah,* its leadership has always been out of step with the government's economic policies.

Indeed, the syndicate presidency has consistently served as a platform for private sector spokesmen who were dismissed from the government after losing important policy debates. Two of the most notable casualties of the Sadat administration—ʿAbd al-ʿAziz Hijazi and ʿAbd al-Razaq ʿAbd al-Majid—have used the syndicate to make surprising political comebacks and to renew the battle over the role of the private sector. What might have been an even more reliable base of government support than the engineers' syndicate became instead a growing embarrassment to the regime and then a leading critic of its development strategy.

The father of the syndicate was ʿAbd al-ʿAziz Hijazi, a former dean of the faculties of commerce at Cairo and ʿAin Shams Universities who served as minister of finance from 1968 until 1973 and then as prime minister during the original formulation of the open door policy. Hijazi sponsored the syndicate's reorganization as minister of finance. When Sadat removed him from the prime ministership for not implementing economic reforms quickly enough, he began to expand his own business contacts with the Gulf countries and was elected to successive terms as head of the commercial syndicate until 1983.

As the membership and economic interests of the syndicate blossomed, Hijazi became a gadfly whose criticisms of the *infitah* resonated many themes of the Nasserist and leftist opposition. Although he always identified himself as an original proponent of the open door policy, his mounting complaints added up to a lengthy indictment of Sadat's management of the economy. The government, he said, was not really pursuing economic liberalization but tolerating the growth of monopoly and tax evasion in all sectors. He charged that the government was giving top jobs to foreign consultants while failing to update the educational system so that new graduates would have adequate language and management skills.[54]

Hijazi constantly attacked the inaccuracy of official statistics, the incomprehensible language of bureaucratic regulations, and the lack of concern for quality control. Pointing to his success with the intersyndical bank, he declared that Egypt had billions of dollars in idle capital that was being overlooked as her leaders piled up more and more foreign debts. These same leaders, he said, were obsessed with the issue of population control. In his opinion Egypt's large population should be considered "a national treasure," but policymakers were imprisoned by a mentality that viewed it only as a liability.[55]

Soon after the new Mubarak government consolidated power, it began looking for a more dependable successor to Hijazi, but he made it clear that he would not go without a fight. In 1982 the syndicate council revised its bylaws and Hijazi asserted that he would be eligible for yet another term as president. When he was overruled in court the ruling party began to promote the candidacy of Hassan Tawfiq, director of the Central Agency of Management. Tawfiq's candidacy was designed to tap the support of public sector employees in the syndicate and to shore up the Finance Ministry's sagging control over the organization. Hijazi responded by endorsing ʿAbd al-Razaq ʿAbd al-Majid, a former minister of planning and economic affairs, whose dismissal in the final days of the Sadat administration had been accompanied by far greater public humiliation than his own.

In many ways ʿAbd al-Majid appeared to be a most unlikely choice for

Hijazi. Hijazi was an advocate of enlightened regulation, while ʿAbd al-Majid was a free marketer par excellence. Hijazi's overseas contacts were strongest in the Gulf region, whereas ʿAbd al-Majid had long ties with the United Nations and the International Monetary Fund. Hijazi was a well-known critic of excessive foreign borrowing and government "disinformation" in economic reporting, yet ʿAbd al-Majid had gotten into trouble by telling parliament that Egypt's balance of payments was in the black without mentioning that his accounting included external loans. Stranger still, while Hijazi was vigorously demanding a crackdown on tax cheaters, ʿAbd al-Majid had been under indictment for allowing Rashad ʿUthman to import millions of dollars' worth of wood duty-free.

Aside from their common desire for personal vindication, what brought these two men together was their determination to keep the syndicate out of the government's hands while Mubarak and his advisors were trying to assert new controls over the banking and importing systems. Their alliance was cemented when ʿAbd al-Majid's successor as minister of economy, Mustafa Saʿid, began to assert that the commercial and banking sectors had made no real contributions to Egypt's development in the preceding decade. Saʿid's attacks, combined with what appeared to be a handpicked candidate of the Finance Ministry, helped to turn the 1983 syndicate election into a minireferendum on the integrity of the private sector.[56]

The ensuing contest was so corrupt and drawn out that both sides compromised the integrity of the syndicate, making it and themselves the object of constant ridicule for an entire year. ʿAbd al-Majid's opponents circulated rumors that a "well-known contractor and engineer" was financing his campaign, fearing that his defeat would seal the fate of the *infitah*. Hassan Tawfiq said that the syndicate's leaders had omitted many public sector employees from the membership roster, and that when he examined the voters' list he could not even find his own name. ʿAbd al-Majid charged that three thousand illegal votes had been sent in from Sharqiya, Tawfiq's home province. The syndicate threw out the Sharqiya votes and declared ʿAbd al-Majid the winner. Tawfiq got a restraining order and the minister of finance declared him the winner.[57]

The stalemate dragged on for several months as each faction appealed the latest court ruling and ministerial pronouncement. Another election was scheduled but never held. At one point Tawfiq stormed the syndicate headquarters with sixty supporters, breaking up a council meeting and cutting the telephone lines. Journalists began comparing the row in the syndicate to the family fights depicted in television soap operas.[58] Ahmad Baha' al-Din wrote a marvelous parody, describing the conflict as Egypt's counterpart to the battles of West Beirut and Suq al-Gharb. Why, he asked, was 'Abd al-Majid visiting the United States when Tawfiq's "militia" occupied the syndicate? Was it to seek Security Council mediation or to convince Ronald Reagan to bomb the enemy's positions? Were the Cairo police acting as an "emergency peacekeeping force" or as the government's militia? Were the causes of the "civil war" strictly internal or were the rival factions being supported by "great powers" behind the scenes?[59]

During all of this commotion over the presidency, most people had failed to notice that ten of the thirty-eight seats on the syndicate council had been won by members of the opposition parties. These included two professors from Cairo University who were among the most outspoken critics of the Sadat regime—Ibrahim Saqr of the law and political science faculties and Juda 'Abd al-Khaliq of the economics faculty. What were political science and economics graduates doing in the commercial employees' syndicate? Sadat himself had put them there because he did not want them to have their own syndicate and he assumed that they would be lost in the crowd among the "natural" supporters of his economic policies. Ironically, Ibrahim Saqr was one of the professors whom Sadat had tried to remove from the university during the September 1981 purges. Reinstated after the assassination, he and several other faculty members set out to turn one of the syndicate's orphan branches into a potent critic of the regime.[60]

In the end 'Abd al-Majid not only won the disputed presidency but also used it effectively in a campaign to depose the man who had taken his job as minister of economy. In the spring of 1984 'Abd al-Majid obtained a final judgment upholding his claim to head the syndicate. He then joined forces with the chambers of commerce, the chambers of industry, the foreign banks, and the Egyptian Businessmen's Association to attack Mustafa Sa'id, who was already locked in battle with the black market money changers. In early 1985, when Sa'id tried to implement his promised reforms of the banking and foreign trade systems, the Mubarak government reversed itself and abruptly repudiated the measures. Then, just a few weeks after his defeat, Sa'id was dismissed under charges that he and his wife had been involved in foreign currency smuggling.

In little more than a decade the commercial employees' syndicate had undergone several remarkable changes. It had grown rapidly into one of the country's largest professional associations, second only to the teachers' syndicate. Its entrepreneurial activities were not as grandiose as those of the engineers, but they were much more successful in eliciting intersyndical collaboration. It had survived a traumatic succession crisis that in many ways paralleled the difficult transfer of power in the regime itself.

The syndicate resisted Mubarak's halfhearted efforts to curb its budding autonomy and, by cooperating with the main line businessmen's groups, persuaded him to back away from a drastic revision of the *infitah*. Finally, in contrast to the hardening of the engineers' syndicate, it even made room in its council for a sizeable contingent that opposed many of the private sector interests it was supposed to represent. None of this indicated that the corporatist subsystem of professional syndicates was about to break down. But it did suggest that Mubarak was willing to tolerate a more flexible type of corporatism, closer to the visions of the lawyers and journalists than to those of Sadat and 'Uthman.

5

Corporatized Sectors: Labor Unions and Agricultural Cooperatives

The periodic tightening and loosening of corporatist controls over the professional syndicates have been quite modest compared to the sweeping transformations of the labor and cooperative movements. The introduction of corporatism into workers' and peasants' associations was a relatively recent and gradual process that unfolded slowly as the revolutionary regime tried to define and readjust its social bases and economic objectives. Efforts to reshape these groups from pluralist to corporatist lines were unquestionably the most ambitious associational projects of the Nasser era. Yet the two projects produced remarkably different results. The new labor confederation survived the Nasser regime and developed into the largest and most powerful corporatist group in the nation. The cooperative confederation, on the other hand, was one of the last associations created by Nasser and one of the first to be abolished by Sadat.

The reorganization of unions and cooperatives was a particularly delicate matter for the Free Officers. Both types of groups had a long history of struggle dating back to the earliest years of the twentieth century. They exemplified the inherent weakness and disorganization that plagued pluralist associations under the monarchy, yet they also had important moments of independent leadership that drew them into the country's tur-

124

bulent partisan and ideological conflicts. Furthermore, they represented incipient social movements of the very lower-class elements who were supposed to become the principal beneficiaries and mass constituencies of the revolution.

Hence, in labor and agriculture more than in any other sectors the new regime inevitably confronted the classic dilemmas of fashioning a populist authoritarian order.[1] Politically, the Free Officers sought to increase state controls over these groups while simultaneously turning them into reliable bases of support. Preexisting associations had to be strengthened and expanded, but not empowered to the point where their leaders could expect to be treated as veto groups or coalition partners. Moreover, these political and organizational problems had to be resolved in a manner that would be consistent with long-term aspirations for economic development. The regime had to use corporatist institutions to confer new material benefits that would be substantial enough to win genuine loyalty yet not so generous and irrevocable as to close off options for the future reform of economic policy. In short, the challenge that Egypt's authoritarian rulers created for themselves was to remold the country's oldest pluralist groups into a new variety of corporatism that would somehow help to consolidate and preserve the revolution without compromising the autonomy of the state.

The divergent fates of the union and cooperative movements have produced entirely contradictory criticisms of Nasser's corporatist legacy. Critics of the labor movement generally agree that corporatism went too far, but they fault it for very different reasons. Those who emphasize the growing independence of the prerevolutionary unions argue that Nasser corrupted and nearly destroyed the labor movement by strangling it in the state bureaucracy. They note that corporatist unions have not smothered class struggle but merely helped to deepen it and drive it underground by forcing workers to develop informal and illegal organizations of their own. However, those who emphasize the continuing failures of industrialization contend that Nasser gave the new unions too much. In their view the revolution prematurely devolved excessive power and privileges to organized labor, leaving a dead weight around the necks of post-Nasserist rulers that can be eliminated only at the cost of great social turmoil.[2]

On the other hand, most critics of the cooperative movement argue that corporatism did not go far enough. They portray the agrarian reforms as a fleeting interlude conferring so little new wealth and authority that their intended beneficiaries could never hope to defend even modest revolutionary gains. Many factors help to explain why the development of cooperatives persistently lagged behind the development of the unions.

The regime was more interested in controlling agricultural surplus than in redistributing it. Financing industry and feeding the cities were incompatible with upsetting the rural social structure. Building a nationwide organization out of thousands of village units was beyond the government's capabilities. Entrenched families bent new structures to old purposes. The revolutionary elite was itself drawn from the middle and upper peasantry, who defended a new status quo after elimination of the large estates. For all of these reasons the state consistently devoted less political backing and fewer material resources to the cooperatives than to the labor unions, even though this support was far more necessary for the survival of new associations in the countryside.[3]

The inherent ambivalence of Nasser's corporatist initiatives was clearly reflected in the differential strength of the new unions and cooperatives. This, in turn, accounts for much of the controversy over Egypt's experience with populist authoritarianism and its impact on subsequent events. Nasser is simultaneously portrayed as the nemesis of capitalist development whose baneful influence continued long after his death and as the unwitting author of a bourgeois counterrevolution that quickly brushed aside many of his halfhearted social reforms. The major corporatist organizations inherited from the Nasserist era are attacked as deeply entrenched centers of power that have frustrated long overdue economic corrections and, at the same time, as feeble appendages of the state that have helped to rescind the socialist gains of the lower classes.

The Labor Movement

The restructuring of the Egyptian labor movement from pluralist to corporatist lines has greatly altered union leaders' relations with the state and with their memberships. The long-term consequence of corporatist policies has been to strengthen and selectively co-opt working-class organizations rather than to smash them and exclude them from the policy-making process. Union leaders have had to pay a high price for their enhanced status and power not only by moderating their political and economic demands but also by insulating themselves from the mounting discontent of the rank and file. Nevertheless, this process of corporatization is by no means irreversible. Indeed, it already has generated new tensions throughout the union hierarchy that may help to promote the reemergence of pluralism both in the labor movement and in the political system as a whole.

The transformation of the labor movement can be examined from four perspectives, each of which highlights a particular dimension of the corporatization process: changes in public policy toward union organization; the growth of union membership and its changing distribution across economic sectors and geographic regions; the evolution of the Egyptian Confederation of Labor, including its increasing interconnections with governmental, legislative, and party structures; and finally, the appearance of several types of cleavage within the confederation and its affiliates that seriously threaten the future of corporatist unionism and the stability of the current regime.

Changes in Union Legislation

The state has sought to promote and control unionization through four major statutes: the trade union laws of 1942, 1952, 1959 (amended in 1964), and 1976 (amended in 1981).[4] Each statute attempted to impose a different type of unionism by spelling out increasingly detailed regulations for the coverage, structure, activities, and leadership selection of working class organizations. The first union law, passed by the Wafdist government during World War II, provided the Egyptian labor movement with its closest approximation to a pluralist model of organization, even though the variety of pluralism selected clearly was intended to be highly restrictive and debilitating for union leaders. Despite the new freedom and recognition accorded to unions, the Wafd was determined to preserve a small, fragmented, and vulnerable labor movement.

Unionization was prohibited among agricultural workers, civil servants, and health workers. Local unions with fewer than fifty members were forbidden. No provision was made for dues checkoffs or union shops, but multiple federations were allowed to organize in identical work branches and regions. Although no reference was made to establishment of a union confederation, this was interpreted by the Wafd and succeeding governments as an implicit prohibition against forming a nationwide organization. Unions were specifically forbidden to engage in political and religious activities or to invest in business and profit-making enterprises. The formation of a new union required approval by the Ministry of Social Affairs, which also was empowered to close down unions accused of illegal activities, even in the absence of a court order.

The 1952 law reflected a similar ambivalence toward organized labor among the Free Officers. This statute was the most "mixed" of all the Egyptian union laws in terms of combining both pluralist and corporatist provisions in an interesting, though short-lived, hybrid formula. On one hand, the law encouraged the rapid proliferation of new unions. Union membership was extended to agricultural workers. Checkoffs were permitted and, in enterprises where three-fifths of the work force was unionized, union shops were required. The establishment of new unions required only registration with, but not approval from, the Ministry of Social Affairs, and the power to close down existing unions was transferred to the judiciary.

On the other hand, it was clear that the new regime intended to amalgamate these groups in the sort of unitary and state-sponsored framework that the monarchy and the Wafd had explicitly rejected for the working class. Thenceforth, no more than one union federation was permitted in each occupational category. At the national level, a single labor confederation was to enjoy a monopoly of representation for the union movement as a whole. The government had not yet specified the categories in which federations were to be organized, and it was deliberately vague about when union leaders would actually be allowed to establish an Egyptian Confederation of Labor. Nevertheless, a monistic, hierarchical, and semi-official model of union organization was set in place less than five months after the July revolution.

The transformation of the unions into full-fledged corporatist structures was completed between 1959 and 1964. The Unified Labor Code of 1959 and the Trade Unions Law of 1964 marked a decisive break with the labor movement's long-standing pluralist traditions. These codes laid down elaborate regulations encompassing all aspects of employment, including sweeping provisions for centralized union organization around a small number of national federations under the supervision of a unitary confederation and the new Ministry of Labor. In 1960 an official list of sixty-four occupational categories was issued, and by 1962 new federations had been established for fifty-nine of these groups. In 1964 the government tightened union centralization once again by cutting the number of federations in half.

Compared to their fragmented and regionally based predecessors, the new industrial federations possessed much larger memberships, vastly expanded finances and authority, and officially guaranteed monopoly status. The size of the labor movement was rapidly increased by permitting the unionization of civil servants and encouraging organization drives among agricultural workers. Federations were empowered to negotiate and ratify all collective work contracts and were responsible for collecting and disbursing the lion's share of union dues according to government-issued guidelines. To facilitate organized labor's contribution to building the new socialist society, the traditional legal bans on union political, religious, and entrepreneurial activities were abolished and never again reinstated.

However, the socialist union laws introduced several new prohibitions, such as bans against inciting class antagonisms, organizing work stoppages, trying to overthrow the political system, and using force to recruit union members. In exchange for such pledges of loyalty and self-restraint, union leaders were provided with unprecedented legal guarantees concerning job security, promotions, and retirement benefits. Thus, the corporatization of the labor movement also involved the selective co-optation of a collaborative, powerful, and handsomely rewarded segment of the noncommunist union leadership.

The Sadat regime tried to transform the top of the union hierarchy into a self-recruiting elite with broad powers of consultation in economic policy-making. Soon after Sadat came to power he purged the leadership of the labor confederation and again reduced the number of federations to only sixteen. By 1976 a newer and smaller cadre of unionists was firmly in power, buttressed by additional delegations of authority that Sadat expected would cement their alliance with the regime. The most recent union laws of 1976 and 1981 substantially strengthened the administrative and financial controls of the Egyptian Confederation of Labor over the federations and of the federations over their local affiliates, producing the largest and most hierarchical corporatist bureaucracy in the nation.

A new system of indirect elections has insured the tenure of top union officials and greatly reduced their accountability to their constituents. Elected positions at all levels of the union hierarchy are filled nearly simultaneously, with higher-echelon leaders being chosen by lower-echelon leaders after a screening of all candidates by the Socialist Prosecutor's Office. The term of elected leaders has been lengthened gradually from two years to three years in 1976, and to four years in 1981. Since 1973 turnover in the federation and confederation leaderships has fallen steadily, and was virtually nil in the union elections of 1983.

As confederation leaders have become more secure, they also have become more prominent political and economic figures. The confederation president is generally an *ex officio* member of the cabinet, serving as head of the new Ministry of Manpower and Vocational Training. Most members of the confederation's executive committee are leaders in the ruling party, three are deputies in the People's Assembly, and three others are representatives in the Majlis al-Shura. Confederation leaders are ubiquitous and often statutorily designated members of countless economic planning councils, parliamentary committees, public sector management boards, and ministerial consultative bodies.[5]

Since 1981 the confederation's powers have been expanded in two important areas. It has been granted exclusive control over the new Workers' University designed to integrate a multitude of union leadership training

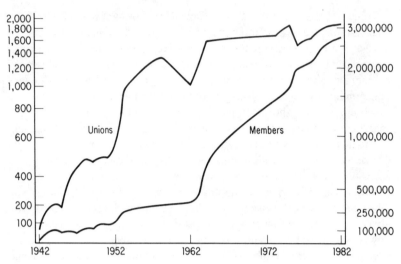

Figure 5.1 Number of Unions and Union Members, 1942–1982 (semilogarithmic scales)

programs formerly run by rival state and party agencies with conflicting goals and programs. In addition, the labor confederation has been allowed to join in the widening movement of syndical capitalism by using pension funds and state subsidies to establish its own economic enterprises. The new Workers' Bank now occupies a prominent area of the confederation's headquarters, symbolizing the expansion of organized labor's economic role beyond the traditional limits of public sector industry.[6]

The Growth and Diffusion of the Union Movement

Long-term changes in the size and composition of union membership provide ample evidence of the decisive role of state intervention in shaping the labor movement during the past four decades. Before the revolution, sharp fluctuations commonly appeared in both the number of unions and the number of union members as governments alternated between encouragement and repression of unionization in the final years of the monarchy (Figure 5-1).[7] Immediately after the revolution a stronger and more continuous increase occurred in both indexes of union growth, reflecting the new regime's effort to present a more favorable environment for working-class organizations.

Initially, however, the Free Officers continued the monarchist and Wafdist practice of promoting the growth of new groups far more rapidly than the growth of new members. After 1958, when labor policy shifted toward a more consistent corporatist strategy, increases in union membership accelerated, whereas increases in unions diminished sharply. State intervention no longer aimed at encouraging the proliferation of small and weak groups but at promoting the merger of existing unions and strengthening them with new members and resources.

The consolidation of union organization since the adoption of the Unified Labor Code of 1959 is observable through dramatic changes in several indexes (Table 5-1). The average size of local union committees has multiplied nearly six times. While total union membership has grown from about 300,000 to nearly 3 million, the number of industrial federations has fallen from well over a hunred to fewer than two dozen. Nine federations currently include over 100,000 workers, and five of these (construction, land transport, textiles, agriculture, and educational services) have enrolled over 200,000 members.

The restructuring of unions has been accompanied by an important change in the composition of their membership (Figure 5-2).[8] The most striking development has been the precipitous decline in the relative importance of manufacturing workers and their replacement by government service and transport workers as the largest component of the labor movement. Although this trend was temporarily reversed during the industrialization drive of the early 1960s, it was resumed and accelerated with adoption of the open door policy. The memberships of the private service

TABLE 5-1. Consolidation of Union Organization, 1958–1983

Year	Average Size of Union Committees	Number of Federations	Average Size of Federations (thousands)	Largest Federation (thousands)	Federations with over 100,000 Members
1958	239	121	2.6	47.4	0
1962	343	59	5.8	113.2	1
1964	467	27	28.3	185.3	1
1971	828	16	87.5	224.3	2
1976	1300	21	93.4	330.8	6
1983	1425	23	118.2	479.0	9

Sources: Wizarat al-Quwa al-ʿAmila wa al-Tadrib al-Mihani, ''al-Nashra al-Sanawiya li-Ihsaʾaat al-Niqabaat ʿAn ʿAm 1983'' (Cairo, December 1983); Willard A. Beling, *Pan-Arabism and Labor* (Cambridge: Harvard University Press, 1961), chap. 2.

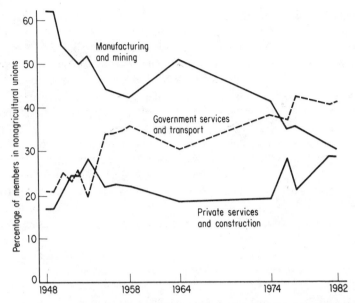

Figure 5.2 Sectoral Distribution of Membership in Nonagricultural Unions, 1948–1982

and construction unions also rose quickly during the late 1970s, reaching near parity with the once-dominant industrial unions.

These changes in union membership undoubtedly reflect the long-term stagnation of Egypt's manufacturing industry and the spurts of employment in the state and private sectors. However, they also reflect the regime's steady effort to diminish the role of traditionally more militant industrial workers by packing the unions with civil servants and public employees who are more dependent on the state and more susceptible to political manipulation. A key aspect of the shift toward corporatist labor policies has been a corresponding reversal in official attitudes toward the participation of civil servants in the union movement. Before 1959 civil servants' unions were prohibited in order to limit the contagion of labor radicalism in the state bureaucracy. But when unionization became a semiofficial enterprise, unions of government employees were regarded as key instruments for penetrating and deradicalizing working-class associations.

It is clear that corporatist unionism has not reduced wide disparities in the sectoral and regional distribution of union membership. Union enroll-

ment among the nonagricultural work force has risen to nearly 40 percent, but aggregate increases during the past decade have been quite modest
compared to those of the Nasser era (Table 5-2). Union membership is
closely correlated with the relative prominence of state employment in
different branches of the economy. Unionization is now virtually universal in public utilities and transport. It has reached the 50 percent mark in
the highly mixed manufacturing and construction sectors, where public
and private firms employ nearly even shares of the work force. However,
union membership remains very low in privately dominated businesses
and services. In fact, unionization has been falling in those sectors that
have benefited the most from the *infitah*, trade and banking. Similarly,
within the manufacturing industry, unionization is highest in the publicly
controlled petrochemical and defense enterprises (about 95 percent), much
lower in the mixed sectors of food processing, textiles, and engineering
industries (40 to 50 percent), and lowest in the almost exclusively private
wood and leather firms (about 15 percent).

There is surprisingly little evidence that union membership has diffused
from more urbanized and economically advanced regions to more remote
and developing regions (Table 5-3). After the 1952 revolution Alexandria's share of total union members declined steadily, but Cairo's already
large share grew even further and did not begin to fall until the late

TABLE 5-2. Density of Union Membership by Economic Sector, 1948–1982

	1948	1958	1964	1976	1982
Union membership as percentage of					
Total population	0.7	1.2	2.8	5.4	6.2
Economically active population	1.1	4.1	8.8	20.1	23.2
Nonagricultural E.A.P.	2.3	9.0	18.7	35.3	36.4
Union members as percentage of E.A.P. employed in					
Agriculture	—	0.5	—	3.0	5.4
Private services	0.4	4.9	10.2	15.0	15.1
Trade and Finance	1.6	4.3	8.9	15.3	12.0
Construction	3.3	8.0	23.8	35.1	43.6
Manufacturing	12.1	17.1	33.9	46.3	50.2
Transportation	12.9	22.9	32.5	70.0	85.2
Public utilities	8.0	14.0	32.6	83.0	95.2

Sources: Wizarat al-Quwa al-'Amila wa al-Tadrib al-Mihani, ''al-Nashra al-Sanawiya li-Ihsa'aat al-Niqabaat 'An 'Am 1983'' (Cairo, December 1983); population censuses of 1946, 1960, 1966, and 1976.

TABLE 5-3.   Regional Distribution of Union Membership, 1943–1982

Percentage of Total Union Members Located in	1943	1952	1958	1976	1982
Cairo	26.8	34.0	34.1	38.5	35.2
Alexandria	16.2	23.6	15.5	14.9	11.0
Canal Zone	7.9	8.9	7.5	2.6	3.8
Nile Delta	44.6	22.7	29.2	24.9	27.5
Upper Egypt	4.3	8.8	11.7	18.4	21.3
Frontier areas	—	1.8	2.0	0.6	1.2

Source: Wizarat al-Quwa al-ʿAmila wa al-Tadrib al-Mihani, ''al-Nashra al-Sanawiya li-Ihsaʾaat al-Niqabaat ʿAn ʿAm 1983'' (Cairo; December 1983), pp. 3, 6.

1970s. The Canal Zone and frontier provinces suffered sharp disruptions in their union structures after the 1967 War and still have not regained their earlier shares of total membership. The only persuasive evidence of diffusion appears in the gradual convergence of membership in the provinces of the Nile Delta and Upper Egypt. Thus, the spread of unionization across economic sectors as well as geographic regions seems to reflect not a cumulative organizational strategy of labor leaders but a number of forces beyond their control. Persistent disparities in union membership have been shaped by recurrent political interference, by abrupt changes in economic policy, and by military conflict rather than by a spontaneous process of organizational growth and diffusion.

Evolution of the Egyptian Confederation of Labor

The Egyptian Confederation of Labor has been a central part of the authoritarian state's efforts to fashion effective corporatist controls over the union movement. Gradually, however, union leaders also have learned to use the confederation as their principal instrument for penetrating administrative, legislative, and party structures in order to carve out a key role for themselves in the shaping of economic policy. The confederation's relations with successive governments have become less unilateral and more reciprocal, indicating that the corporatization of the labor movement has not been a simple matter of subordinating the working class to the authoritarian order. Rather, it appears that corporatism has, in time, provided union leaders with new means for defending workers' interests and, ironically, for limiting the decisional autonomy of the regime in certain critical issues.

During World War II the Wafd claimed that no legal protection had been given for the establishment of a national labor confederation *(ittihad 'amm)*. Nevertheless, the Wafd encouraged public employees to enroll in an interunion "congress" *(mu'tamar)* that was designed to undercut the position of 'Abbas Halim. Soon after the war, the Left sought to consolidate its leadership over the increasingly radical labor movement by coordinating the establishment of a nationwide confederation (Mu'tamar Niqabaat 'Ummal Misr). Leftist labor leaders were on the verge of forming a wide-reaching union alliance in June and July of 1946, but their plans were thwarted by the last-minute defection of the transport workers' unions and by Isma'il Sidqi's mass imprisonment of congress members.[9]

Six more years passed before unionists overcame government repression and internal rivalries to organize another attempt at federation. Twice during 1952 "preparatory committees" *(lijan al-tahdiriya)* scheduled founding conventions for an Egyptian confederation of labor only to see both meetings canceled by frightened governments that had just been jolted by spectacular examples of mass protest. The first founding convention was scheduled for the day after the Great Cairo Fire of January 26, 1952, and the second was to take place within a few weeks of the new revolutionary government's bloody suppression of labor unrest at Kafr al-Dawwar the following August.[10]

The Free Officers feared that a union confederation would be manipulated by partisans of the Wafd, the communists, and the Muslim Brotherhood, yet the new regime also was eager to build a mass constituency for the revolution in the labor movement. Accordingly, the junta soon reached a compromise with noncommunist union leaders that permitted the formation of an unofficial "permanent congress" *(mu'tamar da'im)* in lieu of the unitary confederation that had been endorsed in principle in the trade union law of 1952. This agreement allowed both sides to justify an indefinite postponement of the revolution's promise to build strong national federations.[11]

Meanwhile, daily contact between the junta and the labor movement was channeled through the Workers' Bureau of the Liberation Rally under Major Tu'ayma. It was Tu'ayma who later orchestrated the famous transport workers' demonstrations that strengthened Nasser's hand during the March crisis of 1954. Even after Nasser had consolidated power he was reluctant to permit a national confederation, preferring instead to promote the International Confederation of Arab Trade Unions in order to expand his regional influence during the Suez crisis of 1956. Thus, four years after the revolution, Egyptian unionists were in the anomalous position of forming the vanguard for a pan-Arab labor movement while still possessing no peak association in their own country.[12]

Nasser finally permitted establishment of the Egyptian Confederation of Labor in 1957 and then endorsed the Unified Labor Code's sweeping provisions for corporatist union organization in 1959. It was assumed that these measures would be resisted only in the Syrian region of the United Arab Republic, where autonomous local unions formed a key part of the Ba'th's provincial party organizations. In fact, corporatization was accomplished quite swiftly in Syria, but delayed and nearly abandoned in Egypt when Nasser confronted strong police and military objections to the sudden concentration of union power. The project to reorganize the Egyptian labor movement was deadlocked for two years because of disagreements between Husayn al-Shafi'i, the minister of social affairs and labor, and Zakariya Muhi al-Din, the minister of interior. When Nasser realized how much dissension the proposal had created among his colleagues, he considered scrapping it altogether.[13]

Even after Muhi al-Din's objections were assuaged by assurances that communists would be excluded from the new industrial federations, union leaders were drawn into bureaucratic rivalries with some of the most powerful figures of the Nasser era. On one hand, 'Aziz Sidqi, the minister of industry, led strong technocratic resistance to the new socialist laws requiring the participation of elected worker representatives in the management of industrial enterprises. On the other hand, 'Ali Sabri and the radical Workers' Bureau of the A.S.U. applied great pressure for direct party control of union elections and leadership training programs.

During these power struggles the leaders of the labor confederation relied heavily on the patronage of Kamal Rif'at, who served simultaneously as minister of labor, as director of ideological development in the A.S.U. and the government publishing houses, and as director of the "modernization" program at al-Azhar. Rif'at's support was instrumental in preserving the industrial codetermination schemes against managers' demands for their abolition. He also endorsed union demands for greater autonomy from the A.S.U. directorate, arguing that labor-party relations in a socialist society should be shaped according to the more flexible Yugoslavian model favored by the confederation, not the Soviet model favored by the A.S.U. Workers' Bureau.[14]

Rif'at's opposition to doctrinaire notions of "scientific socialism" and his efforts to reconcile "Arab socialism" with "Islamic socialism" were perfectly in tune with the eclectic and moderate views of the confederation leadership. With his aid, the confederation was able to resist the A.S.U.'s plan to convert union educational programs into party-dominated training centers resembling those of the youth organizations and agricultural cooperatives. Rif'at and his union allies succeeded in preserving a degree of continuity in the labor movement's leadership training institutes that was quite remarkable during the turbulent years of "socialist transformation." These institutes continued to provide an unusual combination of technical knowledge with liberal socialist and Islamic principles. To this day, the programs of the new Workers' University reflect the enduring influence of the directors of the first union institutes, such as Hilmi Murad, 'Abd al-Mughni Sa'id, and Jamal al-Banna', all of whom have descended from what might be termed the "left-wing" of Misr al-Fatat and the Muslim Brotherhood.[15]

During the crisis that followed the military defeat of 1967, it appeared that Nasser was prepared to make important concessions to union leaders in order to ensure their support for the weakened regime. Amid the mass demonstrations of February 1968, Nasser personally went to Halwan to make a direct appeal for industrial workers to disengage from the escalating marches organized by radical university students. Shortly thereafter Nasser also held an unusual series of meetings with the labor confederation's executive committee in which each federation president rose in turn to present a list of long-ignored demands for greater union authority and autonomy. The gradual acquiescence of the labor movement to the promises of reform contained in the Declaration of March 30, 1968, allowed the regime to isolate and suppress the more persistent and violent student movement in the months ahead. Just as during his confrontation with Najib and Khalid Muhi al-Din several years earlier, Nasser had to rely on labor leaders to provide a decisive display of mass support at a time when his power was threatened, but the military was divided and unreliable.[16]

However, just as after the 1954 crisis, Nasser continued in his final years to deny union leaders anything more than a subordinate and symbolic position in the ruling coalition. There were notable increases in the representation of workers and union officials in many party and administrative bodies, but no new elections were allowed at any level of the union hierarchy between the time of the 1967 war and Nasser's death three years later. Nor did Nasser satisfy confederation demands that the unions be allowed to select or at least to screen the elected worker representatives in industrial management committees. Instead, Nasser encouraged still greater organizational rivalry in the factories by forcing both managers and unionists to share authority with independent workers' delegates and local party committees.[17]

Sadat was much more forthcoming in his relations with the leaders of the labor confederation than Nasser had been, even though they commonly regarded Sadat's administration as being antilabor and in some areas potentially counterrevolutionary. By the mid-1970s Sadat had made good on most of the pledges to augment the confederation's powers and resources that his predecessor had given in principle after the 1968 demonstrations but never implemented. Several factors made Sadat far more dependent than Nasser had been on the political support of a strong and reliable union elite. Sadat lacked the broad popular sympathy that would have allowed him to continue Nasser's practice of ignoring the mediation of representative groups and appealing directly to the working class through personal addresses and redistributive reforms.

Furthermore, Sadat's plans for a multiparty system aroused considerable resistance from union officials, who perceived the dismantling of the A.S.U. as an attempt to dilute the influence of the labor movement in the "coalition of popular working forces." Labor leaders displayed little enthusiasm for a multiparty system until the government created new sinecures at the top of the union bureaucracy that were even more attractive than the party posts that were abolished with the A.S.U.

Most important, Sadat's policies of economic liberalization quickly generated working-class discontent by reversing earlier trends toward social equity and exposing the economy to greater international competition. Mounting labor unrest required military intervention on two occasions: against violent strikes in Mahalla al-Kubra in 1975, and during the "bread riots" of January 1977. It was against this backdrop that Sadat endorsed new union reforms designed to strengthen the confederation, to distance its leaders from the rank and file, and to co-opt them more effectively as junior members of the authoritarian elite and privileged partners in the emerging capitalist economic order.

The Mubarak government has tacitly recognized the labor confederation as a veto group whose prior consent is indispensable to the success of any major policy initiative in such key areas as reform of public sector industries, reduction of consumer goods subsidies, and the antiinflationary indexing of wage and price increases. Mubarak has, in effect, agreed to a partial surrender of state autonomy in many areas of economic policy-making in exchange for the cooperation of confederation leaders in implementing necessary but highly unpopular austerity measures. Mubarak has been particularly careful to reassure union leaders that his efforts to promote a mixed economy will not jeopardize their interests in the public sector industries. For example, to quash persistent rumors about the imminent divestiture of the state enterprises, he incorporated a string of the confederation's favorite socialist slogans into his 1983 May Day speech. Then, with uncharacteristic playfulness, he refused to continue the oration until the audience of union leaders rewarded his "conversion" with a standing ovation.[18] Afterward, Mubarak arranged a long series of "surprise" factory inspections during which television viewers frequently saw the president clad in civil servant "fatigues" reminiscent of Nasserist days. To insure that the intended symbolism of these telecasts was not misunderstood, they were often followed by rebroadcasts of nationalist and socialist songs that had not been aired since the industrialization drive of the 1960s.

As the Egyptian Confederation of Labor has acquired more authority and resources, its leaders have become less firmly based upon the independent support of affiliated unions and much less accountable to the general union membership. Confederation presidents, in particular, have assumed the increasingly contradictory role of trying to represent both the government and the union movement at the same time. The tendency of the top union leadership to become more encapsulated by the state bureaucracy and more insulated from rank-and-file pressures can be illustrated by comparing the careers of the men who have occupied the confederation's presidency and by examining long-term changes in the confederation's executive committee.

The first president of the confederation, Anwar Salama (1957–1962), was the leader of the petroleum workers' federation. He had played a key role in organizing the workers' boycott of British installations in the Canal Zone and in aiding the guerilla campaign of the Muslim Brotherhood after the abrogation of the Anglo-Egyptian treaty in 1951. Later he helped to instigate strikes and sabotage by petroleum workers in other Arab countries to protest the tripartite aggression of 1956. In 1962 Salama was appointed minister of labor to preside over the corporatist reorganization of the unions, but he resigned his position as confederation president, insisting that the two offices should not be occupied by the same person.

His successor, Ahmad Fahim (1962–1969), was the president of the textile workers' federation, the largest and best-organized union in the country. He had been one of the major figures urging the Free Officers to sponsor a labor confederation, and he was the principal author of the report on union reorganization that eventually became the basis for the corporatization of the labor movement. As with Salama before him, Fahim also was offered the Ministry of Labor, but he declined the position, preferring to remain as confederation president. His tenure was extended by the suspension of union elections after the 1967 War, and he died in office in 1969.

The third president, ʿAbd al-Latif Bultiya (1969–1971), was a transitional figure who was appointed by the A.S.U. to fill out Fahim's already overdrawn term only to be cashiered in Sadat's purge of the confederation shortly after the Corrective Revolution. Bultiya was notable solely because he was the first confederation president who agreed to serve simultaneously as a member of the cabinet. Union officials who have served in the confederation since its inception point to Bultiya's brief term as a turning point, after which the organization began to lose much of its original independence and vigor.

When Sadat ordered the first union elections in seven years, his candidate for confederation president was Salah Gharib (1971–1976), another leader of the textile workers' federation. However, Gharib was chosen not because he represented a large and powerful faction in the union movement but because of his close association with Mamduh Salim, the Alexandria governor and police chief who provided Sadat with timely support in his coup against the ʿAli Sabri clique and who later became minister of interior and prime minister. In fact, Gharib was quite notorious for his unpopularity among workers in many federations. The strongly pro-Nasserist defense and metal workers in Halwan taunted him as a government stooge and held him captive overnight during one of their factory occupations. Gharib made a serious effort to intervene in such incidents of worker protest, but when it became clear that his presence tended to aggravate rather than soothe unrest, he was retired from the confederation after expiration of his second term.

The fifth and most important president, Saʿd Muhammad Ahmad (1976–1987), was the leader of the food workers' federation. In and out of the confederation's executive committee during the 1960s, he was barred from the elections of 1971, "rehabilitated" and elected Salah Gharib's vice-president in 1973, and then elected to three consecutive terms as president beginning in 1976. Ahmad served longer than any of his predecessors, presiding over a steady expansion of the confederation's political influence and economic activities as well as its linkages with the state bureaucracy and the ruling party. In addition to his role as head of the union movement, Ahmad also directed the Ministry of Manpower and Vocational Training (formerly the Ministry of Labor), the Workers' Bank, the Workers' University, and several interministerial committees concerned with the state economic enterprises, emigrant workers, and economic planning.

TABLE 5-4.   Continuity of Membership in the Executive Committee of the
Egyptian Confederation of Labor, 1957–1987

	1961	1964	1971	1973	1976	1979	1983	1987
Percentage of members with experience in previous executive committees	28	24	14	44	48	76	92	74

Sources: Al-Ittihad al-'Amm li-Niqabaat 'Ummal Misr, *al-Ittihad al-'Amm li-Niqabaat 'Ummal Misr fi 'Ishrina 'Aman* (Cairo: Matabi' al-Ahram al-Tijariya, 1977), pp. 86–91; Muhammad Muhammad 'Ali, "al-Qiyadaat al-Niqabiya li-'Ummal Misr," *al-'Amal:* 247 (December 1983): 36–39; 248 (January 1984): 54–56; al-'Amal: 295 (December 1987) 13: 60–61.

One of the most important characteristics of the confederation presidency is that its now considerable powers are attributable primarily to the nature of the office rather than the personality of the officeholder. Sa'd Muhammad Ahmad was certainly conscientious, affable, and prudent. Yet he was a thorough "organization man" who could have been replaced at any time by several rivals who also rose to prominent positions in the union hierarchy during the Sadat era. In 1986, when Ahmad's staunch opposition to public sector employment cuts antagonized Mubarak's increasingly probusiness cabinets, he was removed from the government and then from the confederation leadership as well. Symbolic of the widening rift between the government and the union movement, the Ministry of Manpower and the confederation presidency were separated for the first time since the days of Ahmad Fahim. The division of offices reflected, at the same time, the government's concern that the confederation presidency had become too powerful and unionists' complaints that it had become indistinguishable from the state bureaucracy.[19]

Turnover of the top union leadership has fallen dramatically since the early 1970s (Table 5-4). Once they have cleared background investigations by the police, federation presidents tend to form a self-perpetuating elite. New faces appear only as a result of death or voluntary retirement and almost never because of electoral challenges or pressures from the shop floor. By the mid-1980s thirteen of the twenty-three federation presidents had been in office ten years or more, and four had managed to survive for at least nineteen years. Nearly two decades after its only real purge, the confederation's executive committee now contains a rather embarrassing surplus of experienced and ambitious union leaders, many of whom feel more than prepared for higher posts.

New Pressures for Pluralism

Growing competition for the presidency is by no means the most important source of conflict within the confederation. As the unions have grown
in size and influence, several lines of cleavage have emerged to crack the
formal facade of corporatism and to generate new pressures for pluralism
both in the labor movement and in the party system. There are at least
five dimensions of conflict within the labor confederation that make the
preservation of corporatist unionism increasingly difficult and unlikely.

First, the enhanced authority and prestige of the confederation presidency has elicited resistance from many federation leaders who are eager
to assert their independence from central union bodies and to demonstrate
their separate lines of political influence. This conflict is most evident
among the several federation presidents who sought to embarrass Sa'd
Muhammad Ahmad by openly defying the confederation's official ban on
unapproved affiliations with international union organizations. Ahmad tried
to impose an official policy of "neutrality" concerning foreign affiliations in order to dampen partisan conflicts over invitations for Egypt to
join the pro-Western International Confederation of Free Trade Unions,
which most Arab unionists regard as biased in favor of Israel. At least
half a dozen federation presidents nevertheless joined I.C.F.T.U. affiliates, not only to display their enthusiastic endorsement of the government's pro-Western foreign policy but also to show that their own political resources allow them to challenge the confederation president with
impunity, especially when he seeks to assuage union factions that are
close to the opposition parties.[20]

Second, as the composition of the union membership has diversified,
it has become more difficult for the conflicting interests of all federations
to be represented adequately by a unitary structure. Pronounced and growing
differences separate Egypt's twenty-three union federations—differences
in size and heterogeneity; in industrial, white-collar, or agricultural membership; and in public, private, or foreign employers. Such interfederation
rivalries are aggravated by the government's arbitrary determination and
frequent reclassification of the occupational categories under each organization's jurisdiction. The number, size, and composition of federations
commonly are reshuffled by bureaucratic fiat in order to promote or in-
hibit the fortunes of particular union leaders. Although confederation leaders
argue that the establishment of a single peak association ended the historical fragmentation of the labor movement, there are growing doubts
within many affiliates that the interests of all workers can be served any
longer by one association. For the first time in three decades, there is
open discussion of secession.

Third, relations between the summit and base of the union movement have become increasingly strained by the widespread intervention of the police in union elections. Candidates excluded from union office by government veto are overwhelmingly young, active in local union committees, and connected with one of the opposition parties. Confederation leaders realize that their ability to contain labor unrest is seriously jeopardized when union elections lose their credibility due to open government interference. They have tried to persuade the government to stop nullifying unacceptable candidates and instead to invest greater resources in the socialization of a younger generation of ''responsible'' union officials in the Workers' University.[21]

In the meantime, however, workers in many enterprises are supporting a dualistic system of union representation in which informal groups arise alongside official union structures. The strength of these extralegal groups is evident in numerous wildcat strikes and factory occupations. The most impressive examples of informal organization are not simple work stoppages, but obviously well-planned schemes to continue and even increase production while regular union officials are barred from entering work sites along with the plant managers.

Fourth, several confederation leaders who belong to the ruling party are openly expressing dissatisfaction with what they perceive as the party's increasing favoritism toward private business interests over the interests of organized labor. Many unionists are members of the government party by default more than by design. They were routinely enrolled by National Democratic Party officials who did not bother to inquire into their real partisan preferences. Many confederation leaders hope that the government eventually will permit the establishment of a separate Labor Party in which unionists would be the dominant force. In the absence of such permission, most of them prudently choose to remain in the N.D.P. to avoid the embarrassment and possible retaliation that would accompany an open break with the government.

In the months preceding the 1984 parliamentary elections, however, several unionists resigned from the N.D.P., protesting the second-rate positions that were offered to labor leaders by the party's slate-makers. These defectors included the heads of two of the most important federations in the country—the engineering, metal, and electrical workers' federation, representing about 100,000 public sector manufacturing workers, and the construction workers' federation, Egypt's largest union, claiming nearly 500,000 members, primarily in the private sector.[22]

Fifth, three of the major opposition parties already have demonstrated their ability to draw off support from the N.D.P., both among top-level union leaders and among voters in working-class constituencies. The New

Wafd, for example, has no members in the confederation's executive committee, yet during the 1984 elections its candidates ran extremely well in many working-class districts, such as Sayida Zaynab (33 percent of all votes cast), Imbaba (35 percent), Bab al-Sharqi (30 percent), Mahalla al-Kubra (29 percent), and Kafr al-Dawwar (30 percent). The Socialist Party received a share of the vote that was more than twice its national average in Damietta (17 percent) and Kafr al-Dawwar (14 percent).[23]

Among the opposition parties, the Socialist Party has the most extensive overlap between its current leaders and the union movement. Hilmi Murad and ʿAbd al-Mughni Saʿid both were directors of the Workers' Cultural Institutes during the 1960s. Hamid Zaydan, former editor of the party newspaper, *al-Shaʿb,* was also the editor of the labor confederation's newspaper, *al-ʿUmmal,* during the early 1970s. Socialist Party members include presidents and vice-presidents of three major unions— the construction, defense, and printing federations. Finally, the Tajammuʿ Party enjoys strong pockets of support in Halwan and Aswan, and among pro-Nasserist factions in the federations of commercial, metal, and petroleum workers.

The political implications of these divisions in the labor movement are not encouraging for the Mubarak regime. Examining the relationship in each province between the strength of the union movement and the degree of electoral support for the ruling party, one finds a persistently negative correlation in the parliamentary elections of 1976, 1984, and 1987. Moveover, the strength of the negative relationship has increased with time and with further advances in unionization. Under Sadat, the vote for the "center platform" of the A.S.U. was already inversely related to union membership ($r = -.44$). During the 1984 elections under Mubarak, the National Democratic Party was less popular among organized workers ($r = -.65$).

As Sadat and Mubarak solidified their alliances with the Egyptian Confederation of Labor, the rank and file have become more dissatisfied with the government's economic policies and more alienated from their own representatives. Growing discontent at the base of the union movement is percolating upward, causing new divisions in the confederation and straining its uneasy partnership with the regime. While union leaders plead for more concessions from the ruling party, their members are finding it easier to cast protest votes for opposition parties than for independent unionists whose candidacies are nullified by the police.

The Cooperative Movement

Corporatist initiatives in agriculture began earlier and developed more gradually than in the union movement, but they were also more cautious and incomplete. Each time the state increased the resources available to cultivators, it also increased its control over the cooperative societies, turning them more and more into mixed commissions regulating local farming techniques and marketing arrangements. The cooperatives were granted greater responsibility for distributing credit, inputs, and after the revolution, land as well. But they were never allowed to create their own banking network outside the state Agricultural Bank. Nor were they permitted to develop an organizational structure at the provincial or national levels that could compete with the multiple government agencies that shaped and administered agricultural policy.

Even during the 1960s, when state sponsorship of the cooperative movement reached its peak, Nasser was reluctant to consolidate its power in a centralized bureaucracy comparable to the Egyptian Confederation of Labor. A vastly expanded network of cooperatives with compulsory and nearly universal membership had helped the revolutionary regime to extend its economic control and to mobilize political support in the villages. Nevertheless, Nasser did not want to encourage a powerful and potentially independent force in the countryside that might eventually try to bridge the traditional gap separating the rural and urban political arenas.

Nasser granted cooperative leaders' demands for a more unified corporatist organization only in the final days of his life, when he at last approved the creation of the Egyptian Confederation of Agricultural Cooperatives. By that time, however, the most radical advocates of agrarian reform had been seriously weakened and cooperatives throughout the country were being torn apart by renewed power struggles between agents of the A.S.U., newly participant peasants, and larger landholders, who were beginning to reestablish their dominance over local politics. Thus, the first tentative efforts to consolidate the cooperative movement at the national level coincided with an increasing fragmentation of its base in the provinces.

During the early years of the Sadat regime these contradictory tendencies appeared to neutralize the confederation, giving the new government a free hand to reintroduce capitalist policies into the agricultural sector. But as soon as the A.S.U. opened the way for quasiparty competition, the political ambitions of the new confederation president, Ahmad Yunis,

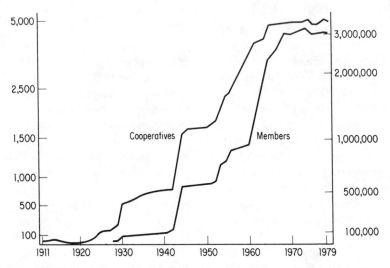

Figure 5.3 Number of Agricultural Cooperatives and Cooperative Members, 1911–1979 (semilogarithmic scales)

confirmed Sadat's fear that the cooperatives might be fashioned into a nationwide electoral machine that would be used by his enemies. Yunis's refusal to join the government's election campaign coupled with his public demands for a stronger and more autonomous confederation had all the markings of a badly timed grab for power. By overplaying his hand at a point when Sadat was prepared to tolerate only the weakest forms of opposition even in the cities, Yunis provoked political retaliation so forceful that it proved to be not only a fatal blow for the confederation but a decisive setback for the entire cooperative movement.

State Intervention in the Cooperatives

Before the 1952 revolution the growth of cooperatives proceeded in a cumulative, steplike manner, with each advance coming as a direct response to major disruptions in the rural economy. Successive peaks in the growth of organizations and members closely paralleled the agricultural crises of 1907, the early 1920s, the Great Depression, and World War II (Figure 5.3).[24] Each period of crisis and development was also accompanied by a corresponding change in the movement's relationship with the state. In time agriculture became a classic example of a sector in which associational development went hand in hand with cyclical economic interventions by the newly independent state.

Initially, the British were quite hostile to the emergence of voluntary associations in the countryside, especially because of their early connection with Muhammad Farid's project to create "agricultural unions" under the leadership of the Hizb al-Watani. During the monarchy, however, a series of special laws and new banks expanded the movement until, on the eve of the revolution, it encompassed about one-fifth of the rural population. With each decade, the nature of state intervention shifted subtly but decisively from sponsorship to regulation and then to direct control. By the end of the monarchy the cooperatives had lost their originally private and voluntary character, operating as little more than semi-official credit agencies whose "representative" bodies were dominated by government appointees.[25]

In 1923 the government formally recognized the movement, establishing a Department of Cooperatives in the Ministry of Agriculture. Four years later Bank Misr provided a special allocation of low-interest loans for small holders who were unable to secure credit from foreign commercial banks and who welcomed the cooperatives as an alternative to local moneylenders. However, with the creation of the Agricultural Credit Bank in 1931, several changes in lending policies undercut the authority of the cooperatives, allowing the state to use rural indebtedness as a powerful lever of both political and economic control during the depression.

Unlike Bank Misr, the Agricultural Credit Bank made the bulk of its loans not to the cooperatives but to individuals, most of whom were not cooperative members. Throughout the 1930s and 1940s the share of credit advanced to cooperatives was only about 15 to 25 percent of the bank's total credits and never exceeded 30 percent. Supplies of credit, seed, and fertilizers were specifically tied to contracts for the compulsory delivery of future production at prices determined by the state. The bank was also empowered to seize crops and land in the event of default. If cooperative societies became insolvent, their members' liability was not limited to their shares in the association but included all personal property. Since interest rates on cooperative loans were only about 2 percent lower than interest on personal loans, there was little incentive for small holders to assume the added burden of collective risk that was now an inherent aspect of cooperative membership.[26]

Peasants began to lose access to cooperative services because of more stringent lending policies, and also because larger landholders were being encouraged to take their place. Although the 1923 cooperatives law had restricted membership to farmers with no more than thirty feddans, the Agricultural Bank steadily increased this ceiling until, by 1937, the definition of "small owners" included cultivators with as much as two hundred feddans. As large landowners used cheap credit to increase their holdings, the state tried to reshape many cooperatives into public welfare agencies for dealing with rural poverty—the very problem the cooperatives were supposed to alleviate until they fell under government and aristocratic control. In a tacit admission of the movement's deviation from its original goal of combating landlessness, the government transferred direction of the cooperatives in 1939 from the Ministry of Agriculture to the new Ministry of Social Affairs.[27]

During World War II the Wafdist government relied heavily on the cooperatives to control food supplies and foreign exchange and to build political capital in the countryside. Between 1942 and 1944 the Wafd stimulated an enormous expansion of cooperative activity: the number of societies doubled, the volume of their assets and transactions tripled, and their membership increased fivefold. This was accompanied by a major reorganization of the cooperative movement, setting up the first nationwide system of representation in agriculture. Just before it was ousted from power in 1944, the Wafd adopted a new cooperatives law that marked the beginning of a clear shift from pluralist to corporatist policies.

The Department of Cooperatives and local societies were linked by a Supreme Advisory Council in the capital that supervised regional advisory councils in each province. Representation on both councils was divided between appointed and elected members, but in each case cooperative leaders were outnumbered two to one by bureaucrats, bank officials, technical advisors, and politicians chosen by the minister of social affairs or the provincial governors. Local cooperative boards remained in the hands of elected members, but they were explicitly forbidden to receive any compensation for their services.[28]

Meanwhile, the advisory councils were given quasi-judicial authority to reverse cooperative decisions and to conduct annual audits. Indeed, ministry officials were required to initial every page of every register and account book used by the local cooperatives at the end of each fiscal year. Although the Wafd claimed that it was trying to breath new life into the cooperatives, the most lasting effect of its reforms was to intensify the bureaucratic assault on what remained of their original voluntarism and independence. On the eve of the revolution a resident foreigner and longtime defender of the cooperatives would note with considerable understatement that "privately, the spirit of the co-operators was healthy, [but] officially, the picture was not satisfactory." [29]

The revolution added an entirely new dimension to the cooperative movement that was organized along corporatist lines from the beginning. Land reform cooperatives were established as a separate compartment for recipients of confiscated and newly settled lands, whom the regime had staked out as a special constituency. Ownership remained private, but it was tied to compulsory membership in a new cooperative system that carefully regulated farming patterns while enforcing a state monopoly over the provision of inputs and the sale of produce. Leadership of local cooperatives was shared by government agronomists and elected peasants who were also encouraged to participate in the elections of village councils and party branches.

The regime had many reasons to be encouraged by the success of the land reform cooperatives. They helped to raise crop yields, they implemented a hidden tax on agriculture that aided the financing of industrialization, and they allowed the controlled mobilization of lower-class supporters who had a vital stake in the revolution. During the second land reform of the early 1960s, the remainder of the cooperative movement was reorganized according to similar principles. Credit and marketing functions were brought together in compulsory associations, which gradually extended the system of administered prices and delivery quotas from wheat and rice to most other export crops as well. By the end of the decade there were more than 5,000 cooperatives encompassing about 3 million farmers on well over 90 percent of the cultivated land.[30]

Although the universalization of the cooperative system was accompanied by a rapid increase in agricultural credit, small holders were still not the major beneficiaries. Over 80 percent of the cooperative borrowers owned less than five feddans, yet they received less than half of the total loans. The other half went mainly to operators owning between five and twenty-five feddans. As late as 1966 about 15 percent of the cooperative loans were being granted to large holders with more than twenty-five feddans. Large holders were able to use this credit for not only cultivation but to finance additional land purchases, private businesses, and money lending.[31]

Many cooperative privileges, including livestock insurance, fodder rations, and special seed, were legally reserved to large operators. Whereas the terms of trade for agriculture as a whole remained stable during the 1960s, they steadily improved for bigger farmers, who were more reliant on heavily subsidized machinery and whose diversified production included larger shares of unregulated commodities such as fruits, vegetables, and livestock. Thus, even at the height of cooperative activity during the socialist transformation, the system once again encouraged redistribution in favor of rich peasants and rural magnates who managed to disguise the true extent of their holdings by deeding them to other family members.[32]

Outside the land reform areas even the vigorous intervention of A.S.U. Leadership Groups could not prevent the new cooperative system from being penetrated and manipulated by local notables and their retainers. Powerful families commonly circumvented the law and diverted cooperative resources to their own advantage. In one district after another government investigations confirmed daily reports of black marketing, evasions of crop deliveries, violations of tenants' rights, and bribery and intimidation of cooperative and party leaders. In 1966 the murder of an A.S.U. activist by the Fiqqi family of Kamshish in Minufiya Province provoked a new campaign to liquidate ''feudalism,'' but the assault was deflected by ʿAli Sabri's rivals in the military and quickly dissipated after the June war.[33]

It was precisely the growing frustration with these discouraging results that prompted A.S.U. leaders and cooperative officials to demand the creation of a unitary cooperative confederation as part of a third land reform toward the end of the decade. Nasser granted this demand in 1970, but only after taking two other steps that guaranteed that a national confederation would not threaten the local power of the rural middle class. In 1969 a new cooperatives law seriously undercut the representation of small peasants on village cooperative boards. The majority of board seats had been reserved for owners of less than five feddans, but now the ceiling was raised to ten feddans and a new literacy requirement was added.[34]

Moreover, in the same year, Nasser made sure that the A.S.U. would not be able to control the elections for parliament. With the party's Leadership Groups severely weakened in the villages and with Anwar Sadat as the chairman of the candidate-screening committee, rural notables increased their representation in parliament and in many local party branches as well. Thus, by the time the piecemeal corporatization of the cooperative movement was finally capped with a unitary confederation, the forces most interested in controlling the new organization were stalemated. The national elections had been a standoff between radical and moderate factions within the A.S.U., and local cooperative boards were slipping more and more out of the hands of the small-scale producers who were supposed to be their principal constituency.[35]

The Demise of the Confederation and Eclipse of the Cooperatives

Immediately after the Corrective Revolution Sadat considered abolishing the cooperative confederation but decided instead to purge its leaders and to put it under the direction of his own candidate, Ahmad Yunis. During the next five years Yunis generated increasing mistrust among Sadat's closest supporters as he appeared to be turning the confederation into precisely the kind of national power base that Nasser had scrupulously tried to prevent. Yunis quickly fleshed out the confederation's internal organization, setting up eighteen provincial branches with over 4,000 employees. The confederation published its own weekly newspaper with wide circulation in the countryside and made large financial contributions to international cooperative groups in Europe and the Arab world.[36]

Yunis also sought to give the confederation a new policy-making voice in the government itself. He became chairman of a 160-member inter-ministerial committee on agriculture and irrigation that included several former cabinet members as well as a large contingent of confederation appointees. At the same time he was gradually building a sizeable bloc of supporters in the People's Assembly by putting deputies on the confederation's payroll as salaried consultants. This parliamentary bloc played a decisive role in organizing rural middle-class opposition to proposals for a direct tax on agricultural land. Before long Sadat was receiving police reports warning that Yunis was able to influence as many as one-third of the votes in the legislature and that he was well on the way to creating an extensive electoral machine to advance his own presidential aspirations.[37]

As the 1976 elections approached, Yunis's public statements provided his enemies with more than enough ammunition to justify a counter-assault against his political manipulation of the confederation. In 1975 he told over 4,000 peasants in Minufiya that the confederation should be able to undertake its own projects of land reclamation without the approval of other government agencies. The confederation's funds, he declared, were the peasants' monies and should be spent by their own representatives, not by government bureaucrats. In the same vein, when Jihan Sadat asked the confederation to contribute £E 250,000 to her campaign to raise scholarship money for needy students, Yunis said he was prepared to give her twice that amount if the confederation could choose the students from among the families of its own members. Early in 1976 Prime Minister Mamduh Salim asked Yunis to instruct the confederation to support the progovernment platform in the coming elections. Although Yunis asserted that the confederation preferred to retain a nonpartisan position, it became clear that he was endorsing Wafdist candidates who were planning to run as independents while his general secretary was openly campaigning for the left-of-center platform.[38]

In February 1976, at a mass rally in Cairo attended by over 7,000 members of cooperatives, Yunis made what he termed a "spontaneous declaration of independence" for the cooperative movement. He outlined a proposal for a new cooperative law that would give the confederation unified control over all cooperative societies, including the land reform cooperatives. He called for an end to "administrative interference" in the confederation's affairs and demanded the freedom to establish "democratic links" between the cooperatives, the labor unions, and the professional syndicates. Yunis also challenged the government's accounting of cooperative debts, saying that the total arrears amounted to less than half of the official figures and that several thousand peasants were actually entitled to refunds of excess payments. Then, attacking perhaps the most onerous aspect of agricultural policy since the revolution, Yunis called for an end to the entire system of compulsory crop deliveries and administered prices.[39]

By the time he finished, Yunis's unilateral declaration appeared to be nothing less than an alternative election manifesto that had been tailor-made to spark an early Wafdist comeback in the provinces. Sadat had encouraged Yunis to use the cooperatives to strengthen the hand of the rural middle class in many ways—by increasing the representation of larger landowners on cooperative boards, by helping to return sequestered lands to their original owners, by transferring the settlement of village disputes from the cooperatives to the courts, and by easing the legal limits on agricultural rents. But all of these economic concessions were intended to secure the gratitude or at least the acquiescence of rural notables, not to whet their appetite for a return to power. As it became clear that Yunis's vision of an independent cooperative movement was about to turn into a front organization for the Wafd, Sadat concluded that the confederation had outlived its usefulness.

During the summer of 1976 *al-Akhbar* ran a series of articles accusing Ahmad Yunis of gross mismanagement and embezzlement, and demanding that he be suspended from the confederation presidency pending the outcome of a special parliamentary investigation.[40] Then, just two months before the national elections, *Akhir Sa'a* published the findings of a binational commission of Egyptian and American experts disclosing evidence of widespread "corruption and anarchy" in the agricultural cooperatives. The 200-page report was prepared in collaboration with the U.S. Agency for International Development after about forty days of local field inspections. It stated that the cooperative bureaucracy had swelled to over 150,000 employees—one for every forty feddans of cultivated land—imposing unnecessary costs on producers and stifling economic freedom. The report was quickly embraced by Sayyid Mar'ai, the former minister of agriculture, and 'Uthman Ahmad 'Uthman, who convinced Sadat to abolish the cooperative confederation on the eve of the October 1976 elections.[41]

The destruction of the cooperatives confederation occurred almost simultaneously with the strengthening of the Egyptian Confederation of Labor. While the corporatist organization of the union movement was being solidified, the cooperatives were being stripped of their only means of leverage at the national level, reducing them once again to an atomized and isolated set of local societies. Whereas Sadat felt it necessary to devolve greater powers to the union hierarchy and to assure them that their interests in public sector industries would not be threatened, he was able to demolish the younger and far weaker agricultural confederation with little more than a publicity campaign and a handful of criminal indictments.

Both cases appeared to confirm the view that Nasser's corporatist experiments had not generated sufficient mass participation and loyalty to prevent continued manipulation by the state. Nevertheless, the stark contrast between the relative strength and prudence of the unionists versus the vulnerability and recklessness of the cooperative leaders indicated that Nasser's corporatist legacy had endowed these two sectors with very unequal organizational resources and political skills. The leaders of the labor movement had to turn their backs on most of their constituents in order to survive a major transformation of the regime, but they were able to defend the core of the socialist reforms while enhancing their ability to fight future battles. The leaders of the cooperative confederation, on the other hand, were so tempted by their new potential for mass mobilization that they badly overplayed a much weaker hand, squandering their political resources before they could be consolidated.

After the abolition of the confederation, the local cooperatives became increasingly marginalized as their economic and representative functions were transferred to newer organizations that Sadat created to strengthen government and ruling-party links with the provincial middle class. The most important of these new groups were the "village banks" that often "rented" the headquarters of local cooperatives for nominal fees and gradually took over most of their credit, supply, and marketing operations. The village banks revived the prerevolutionary practice of lending directly to individual farmers rather than to cooperatives, and of demanding both land and crops as collateral. Cooperative leaders were not represented in the bank boards, which also made loans to municipal governments and private businessmen for nonagricultural projects.[42]

Alongside the village banks, the Ministry of Local Government sponsored the Organization for the Rehabilitation and Development of Egyptian Villages which helped to channel large amounts of foreign economic aid into loans for agribusiness. Local capitalists and party loyalists also benefited from the new program of administrative "decentralization," which encouraged village and municipal councils to fund a host of profit-making enterprises, including animal raising, food processing, clothing and furniture factories, and transportation companies. Each of these agencies actively fostered business partnerships between civil servants, wealthy farmers, and provincial capitalists, helping the regime to cement its alliances with the flourishing private sector under the aegis of the provincial governors and the local branches of the ruling party.[43]

As economic initiative in the countryside shifted to the village banks, O.R.D.E.V., and local governments, the cooperatives became little more than a holding area for the growing number of poor peasants who had to choose between continuing to grow the most highly regulated crops or leaving the land for alternative employment in the cities and the Gulf countries. Sadat decisively ended any possibility that the cooperatives would be used to mobilize a mass opposition and he managed to divert much of the rural middle class into entrepreneurial associations controlled by the state. However, his emasculation of the cooperative movement also eliminated the only symbol of representation that could be identified with the principal victims of rural poverty and depopulation.[44]

Just before his death Sadat prepared to fill this institutional gap with a new corporatist design for the cooperative movement that included the establishment of another national confederation. A new cooperatives law was adopted in 1980 and amended in 1981, but its implementation was delayed after the assassination and the new confederation was not created until 1983. What most distinguishes the reconstituted cooperatives confederation from Egypt's other corporatist associations is its utter lack of authority over regional federations and local branches. The Ministry of Agriculture and the provincial governors retain extensive powers to appoint cooperative leaders, to veto the decisions of elected boards, to supervise their accounts, and to close cooperatives by administrative order.

The president himself is granted similar authority over the confederation. Confederation deliberations must be monitored by government observers, who are to be given no less than ten days' notice before each meeting. The president is explicitly empowered to suspend or abolish the confederation by special decree. Elections at all levels of the cooperative movement are to be held only once every five years. They are supervised not by the confederation but by a special commission selected exclusively from officials of the Ministries of Interior, Justice, and Agriculture. The confederation council is an unwieldy committee of over a hundred members. During the first confederation elections in 1983, the entire council was composed of members of the ruling party, 80 percent of whom were elected by acclamation.[45]

Foreign pressure from European cooperative leaders seems to have encouraged the government's decision to reestablish at least a paper confederation. Several European groups refused to renew international cooperative agreements with the Egyptian government, and the Swedish confederation flatly stated that it would deal only with elected representatives who could speak for the cooperatives themselves.[46] Nevertheless, external influence on the cooperative movement has been quite modest compared to the pressures exerted by the International Labor Organization in local union affairs. The Egyptian Confederation of Labor has a special international relations division that is fully occupied in drafting responses to inquiries about Egypt's implementation of I.L.O. conventions on freedom of association. Similar inquiries regarding the cooperatives are rare and they are treated with considerably less concern and formality.

The belated efforts of Sadat and Mubarak to revive and monopolize corporatist representation in agriculture were countered by simultaneous initiatives from old cooperative leaders and opposition parties to establish an independent and voluntary confederation of Egyptian peasants. Wafdists, Nasserists, and socialists collaborated in resurrecting the memories of the ''martyrs'' of the cooperative movement to rally peasants around a rival association that was portrayed as the authentic successor to the confederation that Sadat had abolished. As soon as Mubarak moved to renew corporatist policies in the countryside, an assortment of party and syndicate leaders rushed to create a pluralist alternative.

Ibrahim Yunis, a journalist and surviving brother of Ahmad, fought a number of court battles to clear the reputations of the purged confederation leaders, demanding payment of financial damages by the Sadat family and several former ministers. These suits were sponsored by forty leading members of the bar association, including Ahmad al-Khawaja and ʿAbd al-ʿAziz Shurbaji. In the spring of 1982, when the courts retroactively dismissed all criminal charges against the former confederation leaders, Ibrahim Shukri of the Socialist Party attended a mass rally in Ahmad Yunis's birthplace to honor the memory of the "oppressed pioneer of independent cooperativism."[47]

The Tajammu' Party tried to maximize its role in the new peasants' federation by reviving the even more bitter memory of the Kamshish affair. One of the leading agitators for the federation was Shahinda Maqlad, the widow of Salah Husayn Maqlad who had been assassinated for defying the "feudalists" during the 1960s. Shahinda was prominently displayed as a founding member of the federation to emphasize that its antecedents rested not merely with Ahmad Yunis and the rural middle class but with the most radical elements of Nasserist populism. The establishment of the peasants' federation was announced and postponed several times during 1982 as rival parties tried to position their followers on the founding committee. However, the Tajammu' faction was able to arrange the federation's first public meeting on April 30, 1983, so that it would coincide with the seventeenth anniversary of Salah Husayn's murder.

The founding convention of the peasants' federation had great difficulty in agreeing on the constituency that it intended to represent. There was a clear division between those who wanted to open membership to owners of ten feddans and those who insisted that the ceiling be placed at five feddans. After heated debate a compromise was reached allowing medium-sized owners to join the association but excluding them from membership on the regional and national boards of directors. This compromise reflected the embarrassing prevalence of the Tajammu' faction in the federation's early activities. Tajammu' leaders wanted to ensure the overrepresentation of small farmers, but they also wished to avoid the impression that the federation was nothing more than an extension of the party's peasants' bureau. Thus, the federation's first elected council was a carefully mixed group of twenty-six peasants, half of whom claimed no affiliation with any of the existing parties. Shahinda Maqlad, who served on the Tajammu''s executive committee, was excluded from the federation council. Instead, she was given a purely symbolic post on a three-member advisory board that had no voting power in the federation's affairs.[48]

The peasants' federation also tried to adopt a conciliatory posture toward the new cooperative confederation. Instead of denouncing the confederation as a creature of the ruling party, the peasants' federation invited all cooperative leaders and opposition parties to participate in a campaign to revive the cooperative movement and to use it in reshaping agricultural policy. The main target of this campaign was not the government-dominated confederation or even the rural middle class but the village banks, which were portrayed as having usurped the rightful functions and resources of the cooperatives to serve partisan interests.[49]

By defining its struggle in political rather than class terms, the peasants' federation is trying to pave the way for a multiparty alliance that might eventually recapture the corporatist confederation from within and turn it into a more authentic representative of private interests. However, by asserting the desirability of at least two separate agricultural associations, the peasants' federation is also highlighting the inherent limitations of corporatism in such an enormous and highly stratified economic sector. The leaders of the peasants' federation believe that the cooperative confederation can become a more effective and independent spokesman for agriculture, but they seem resigned to the fact that it will always serve the strong far more than the weak. Hence, they view a new association of smaller producers as a pressure group within a pressure group. The hegemony of the rural middle class within the cooperative movement is grudgingly conceded, with the hope that it can be tempered somewhat within an expanding context of associational and party pluralism.

6

Hybrid Sectors: Businessmen's Associations and Religious Groups

The business and religious sectors are the most heterogeneous areas of associational life in contemporary Egypt. In both sectors growing discontent with the artificiality and rigidity of corporatist representation has prompted the emergence of new voluntary associations that are rapidly undermining the legitimacy of older, state-sponsored groups. In both sectors representation is now divided among a wide assortment of groups that extend well beyond the spectrum of conventional corporatist and pluralist structures to include a number of illegal, underground organizations as well. In its efforts to isolate and destroy the most threatening of these illegal groups—black marketeers and Muslim revolutionaries—the Mubarak government has allowed nearly all other business and religious organizations greater maneuverability and influence, hoping that this relative freedom will encourage them to cooperate with the state in managing Egypt's economic and cultural crises.

As a result of the proliferation and diversification of organized groups, business and religion have become the most dynamic and conflict-ridden areas of associational activity. Rival spokesmen are not only locked in bitter struggles with one another to represent the business and religious communities as a whole but are also confronting the state with increasingly aggressive demands for far-reaching economic, political, and cultural reforms. Mounting pressures from organized businessmen for a free market economy and from organized Muslims for the ''Islamization'' of the legal system have had a profound influence on the policy agendas and public discourse of all other political actors. To a remarkable extent, the government, the parties, and interest groups in other sectors have been forced to redefine their positions and alliances in order to endorse or resist initiatives advanced by the most independent and assertive representatives of the business community and the Islamic movement.

The recent revival of pluralism has shaken the long-standing edifice of corporatist controls more forcefully in these two sectors than anywhere else in Egyptian society. Nevertheless, business and religious groups have presented the regime with very different kinds of challenges. The specialization and competitiveness of businessmen's associations have made it more difficult than ever for the government to coordinate economic activity. The formulation and implementation of economic policy is no longer the exclusive preserve of the state bureaucracy and its preselected agents but the product of continuous negotiations with multiple factions of the private sector. Each of these factions, in turn, has developed its own lines of influence in the cabinet, in the ruling party, and with foreign investors and creditors.

By cooperating with businessmen's associations in a more formal and visible manner, the Mubarak government has sought to win greater support from private enterprise in general. But this very cooperation has generated resentment among many business groups that continue to feel neglected by the government or that are threatened by its concessions to their more favored rivals. Mubarak's increasing attentiveness to the views of large, internationally connected entrepreneurs in the new Egyptian Businessmen's Association and in the many binational business committees has overshadowed the corporatist chambers of commerce and industry that still represent the vast majority in the private sector.

Each time a particular businessmen's group appears to receive special treatment, alarms signal in several other groups—not just in the business world but in other economic sectors as well—calling for a more inclusive process of consultation and bargaining. As the government tries to manipulate the new pluralism in the private sector to select its preferred interlocutors, it is confronted with repeated accusations of favoritism and with mounting demands for economic summit meetings that will provide some semblance of symmetry and parity among competing interests.

The problem is not that collusive bargaining between the state and associational elites is deplored; indeed, such consultation is often welcomed as a sign of greater government willingness to involve organized interests in decision making. But as the practice becomes more widespread and more open to public scrutiny, it is increasingly difficult for the government to justify the inclusion of some groups and the exclusion of others who also have a stake in the outcome. Although both business leaders and their rivals recognize the state's responsibility for setting the bargaining agenda and for limiting the range of acceptable compromises, they do not wish to see a negotiating process so narrow and contrived that its results will be predetermined by the government's arbitrary choice of participants.

The growing diversity and assertiveness of religious organizations pose a more serious challenge to the regime. Demands from this sector go far beyond pressures for greater access to decision makers and for the reconciliation of competing economic interests. Religious groups with vastly different political programs and social bases are calling for nothing less than a fundamental reform of cultural policies by reshaping the legal system in conformity with the *shari'a.* The Sadat and Mubarak governments have tried to embrace these demands in principle in order to neutralize them in practice. This tactic has bred widespread cynicism concerning the regime's commitment to its own pledges, and this cynicism, in turn, has helped to intensify the campaign for legal reform.

However, as a broader Islamic movement has crystallized on behalf of the codification of the *shari'a,* organized Muslims have come to disagree more and more over the political methods that are appropriate for their cause and that are most likely to achieve their ends. The *'ulama'* of al-Azhar and the leaders of the Sufi orders say that the existing regime offers ample opportunity for changing society through more vigorous preaching and religious education. The older members of the Muslim Brotherhood argue that an Islamic society requires an Islamic government, but they are confident that in time both can be constructed through legal political mobilization and democratic debate.

Younger leaders of many "Islamic associations" insist that changes in behavior must not await long-term changes in formal institutions and public opinion. They have undertaken the ambitious task of creating Islamic communities from the ground up, combining persuasion by example and peer pressure with material inducements and physical intimidation. All of these approaches are denounced by the most radical and desperate secret organizations, who regard armed struggle and revolution as the only realistic means for changing what they view as an unreformable despotism and a hopelessly corrupt society.

These divisions have made Islamic organizations more susceptible to manipulation by the regime and, at the same time, more threatening to it as well. Many governments have tried to bolster al-Azhar's position as the most authoritative interpreter of religious orthodoxy. But as al-Azhar has drawn closer to the state, it has become less capable of reflecting, let alone directing, popular sentiment. The "overco-optation" of the 'ulama' has eroded their prestige and credibility while enhancing the popularity of rival groups that say they represent more independent and authentic interpretations.

As religious organizations have become more polarized between those that are wedded to the regime and those that are sworn to destroy it, governments have sought to cultivate a middle ground by opening contacts with a number of groups they previously ignored or mistrusted. The Sadat and Mubarak governments have carried out a sweeping corporatist reorganization of the Sufi orders. They have subsidized many voluntary associations engaged in religious education, philanthropy, and the construction of private mosques. They have allowed the Muslim Brotherhood to operate as an unofficial opposition party whose candidates have won several seats in syndical councils and in parliament. And they have given wide latitude to many Islamic associations to expand their activities in universities, working class neighborhoods, and provincial capitals.

By identifying itself with the many mass-based groups that are challenging the traditional authority of the 'ulama', the regime hopes to isolate and eventually crush the most radical segments of the Islamic movement. Al-Azhar is being blamed from all sides for its aloofness and pedantry, for its indifference to the corruption of popular religion, and for its failure to prevent the spread of antisocial behavior among the youth. Especially since the assassination of Sadat, the government has regarded the containment and "rehabilitation" of religious fanatics as urgent matters requiring the combined efforts of all Muslim organizations regardless of their formal legal status or their past quarrels with the revolution.

The price of this collaboration is not only more freedom of expression and political maneuver for Islamic groups but more attention to their common demands for implementation of the *shari'a*. The greater the government's willingness to meet this price, the greater the anxiety of secularist and Christian groups, who fear that it will be paid at their expense. The debate over how to Islamize the legal system has helped to set off a chain reaction of organization and counterorganization among Muslims and Christians throughout the country. In many urban quarters and provincial towns these groups have armed themselves in the conviction that the issue may have to be settled privately long before it can be settled in parliament.

Thus, Mubarak's efforts to manage Egypt's cultural crisis are at least as problematic as his efforts to manage its economic crisis. In both cases he has sought to enlist the support of powerful voluntary associations that have arisen to challenge previously dominant corporatist representatives. And in both cases his greater receptivity to the demands of prospective allies has generated apprehension among rival groups, who feel that they are being squeezed out of decisive national debates. Embracing big business's desire for freer competition has prompted the chambers of commerce and industry as well as the labor unions to press for more comprehensive economic summit meetings. Endorsing the Islamic movement's call for legal reform has spurred secular intellectuals and Coptic groups to seek more explicit protection for the rights of religious minorities.

In trying to manipulate the new associational pluralism to compensate for its own economic and political weaknesses, the regime has been forced to make concessions that are heightening the country's already serious class and communal tensions. The resurgence of pluralism among business and religious groups may be advancing certain notions of economic and political liberalism, but this does not necessarily mean that it is advancing democracy. Instead, economic liberalization is becoming more closely identified with a narrow segment of the business world, and political liberalization is seen as paving the way for the tyranny of a self-righteous majority.

Businessmen's Associations

The interests of the private sector are represented through three types of association that encompass distinct segments of the business community despite their overlapping memberships. The most inclusive groups are the older corporatist associations that emerged during the prerevolutionary period: the chambers of commerce and the chambers of industry. During the Nasser era both of these groups operated more as agents of state regulation than as representatives of private interests. Although the open door policy granted individual entrepreneurs much greater freedom in the marketplace, it did not include reforms to increase the independence and flexibility of their traditional associations. Business leaders have made several attempts to persuade the Sadat and Mubarak governments to reorganize the chambers, but all of their proposals have been buried in party and parliamentary committees. Finding themselves saddled with the same kind of bureaucratic restrictions that typified the socialist period, many businessmen have begun to bypass the chambers and seek other forms of collective action.

For a time it appeared that some of the newer professional syndicates would become the major alternatives to the chambers. The entrepreneurial corporatism of the engineers' and commercial employees' syndicates provided a particularly attractive meeting ground for the specialized interests of construction, consulting, banking, and foreign trade. However, by the end of the 1970s businessmen realized that the syndical formula exposed them to new problems that could be even worse than the paternalism and red tape of the chambers. As the commercial successes of the professional associations became eclipsed by scandals and factional struggles, the would-be businessmen's syndicates were drawn more and more into the personal quarrels of former ministers who were battling for position within the ruling party.

Moreover, the polyglot memberships of the syndicates did not constitute reliable probusiness constituencies. They included large contingents of civil servants and private sector employees, forcing businessmen to share power on syndical councils with candidates who reflected the views of various government agencies and opposition parties. The advancement of private sector demands through the syndicates required constant politicking and embarrassing publicity that many businessmen wished to avoid. The engineers' and commercial employees' associations might appeal to business leaders who aspired to become political entrepreneurs but not to the growing number of managers and owners who preferred more prudent and predictable means for defending their economic interests.

With the uncertainty that followed Sadat's assassination and Mubarak's procrastination over how to reform the *infitah,* businessmen began to turn away from the chambers and the syndicates in favor of more specialized and autonomous voluntary associations. In quick succession a number of new groups appeared that represented private banks, Islamic banks, exporters, managers, and local agents of American, European, and Japanese enterprises. As the Mubarak government scrambled to define its new economic policies, the private sector rapidly reorganized itself along more pluralist lines. As various segments of the business community came under pressure to renegotiate the terms of the *infitah,* they prepared to exert more effective counterpressures to insure that their earlier gains would not be jeopardized.

During 1984 and 1985 two new groups played a particularly important role in changing the government's relations with the private sector: the Egyptian Businessmen's Association and the illegal ring of black market currency smugglers. These groups displayed the most determined and vigorous opposition to Mubarak's plans to reintroduce strict government controls over banking and foreign trade. They were the leading forces that prompted Mubarak's sudden annulment of the new regulations in March 1985 and his subsequent appointment of probusiness ministers and economic advisors.

Once it abandoned proposals for a radical assault on the *infitah*, the Mubarak government began to sort out its relations with the wide assortment of organizations that were competing for leadership of the private sector. Its main goal was to crush the underground network of the money changers while establishing more formal and regular consultations with the legal businessmen's groups. By 1986 the black market in foreign exchange had been wiped out. Instead of throttling private financial institutions with more Central Bank controls, the government gave them greater freedom to implement flexible exchange rates that brought foreign currency back into the banking system.

The rapprochement between the government and the banks was a direct result of the economic warfare that the black market leaders orchestrated from their jail cells throughout 1984 and 1985. By raising the real price of the dollar as much as 10 percent per week, the currency smugglers thought they could force Mubarak to halt their trials and return their sequestered assets. This tactic merely strengthened Mubarak's resolve to break their power once and for all even if it meant dropping his long resistance to devaluation and openly embracing a number of business lobbies.[1]

While the black marketeers were being put behind bars, the members of the Egyptian Businessmen's Association were being courted as the preeminent spokesmen for private enterprise. The association's meetings with cabinet ministers are no longer limited to working lunches and private banquets. Since December 1985, they have been formalized in a permanent joint commission where government and business representatives discuss all policies affecting the private sector from import quotas and investment strategy to energy prices and labor relations. The government's delegation includes the prime minister, who serves as chairman, and the five heads of the major economic ministries. The private sector delegation includes fourteen representatives, eleven of whom are selected from the Egyptian Businessmen's Association.[2]

Thus, after several years of associational diversification and experimentation in the business world, the government has tried to reconsolidate the representation of private sector interests around a handful of groups that are eager to negotiate demands instead of trying to dictate them and that can be trusted to help in implementing economic policies instead of subverting them. Mubarak and his advisers have focused their attention on three very different organizations: the chambers of commerce and chambers of industry, which remain locked into the same corporatist mold that was inherited from Nasserist days; and the Egyptian Businessmen's Association, which has been selected as the semiofficial spokesman for *infitah* entrepreneurs, who have insisted on developing more independent forms of collective action.

The Chambers of Commerce

The chambers of commerce are provincial organizations with a total membership of about 3 million. Their constituency is nearly equal in size to the labor movement and the agricultural cooperatives, and about three times as large as all of the professional syndicates combined. Each chamber is divided into several branches grouping various categories of trade, small manufacturing, and transportation. The largest chambers, Cairo and Alexandria, contain over twenty branches, each of which implements a myriad of regulations on different commodities and services issued by the Ministries of Trade, Finance, and Economy.

Although membership has been compulsory since World War II, the Cairo chamber estimates that its current enrollment of 250,000 includes only about 70 percent of the business establishments operating in the capital city. Chamber leaders in other provinces report even higher levels of nonparticipation, arguing that many small businessmen see no benefit in supporting associations that have so little influence over local government. The chambers are able to fine unregistered businesses, but the amount of the fines (like nearly all other chamber powers) is fixed by an outdated statute that has been virtually unchanged since 1951. These now-token penalties are much smaller than the fines that chambers often are required to impose on behalf of the state. Hence, ignoring the chambers is a relatively inexpensive form of protest for shopkeepers and craftsmen who see them as serving only businessmen with powerful political connections.[3]

Since World War II state control over the chambers has been insured through government appointment of a large portion of their boards of directors. In 1955 the number of appointed officials was increased from one-fourth to one-half. The main function of the chambers is to regulate competition by issuing licenses and franchises, enforcing price controls, and gathering information on local market conditions. Occasionally, they have also shared responsibility for allocating import licenses, but they have never had much influence in determining the volume and categories of imports. Their delegated authorities are quite narrow, and even these are commonly duplicated or overridden by parent ministries, state banks, and local police forces. They are encouraged to offer advice on policy implementation, but unlike most other corporatist bodies, they have no clear right to draft or review legislation.[4]

The most important innovation in chamber organization after the revolution was the creation of the Egyptian Confederation of Chambers of Commerce in 1955. The confederation's directorate is a mixed committee of thirty-two members, including the presidents of the twenty-six provincial chambers and six delegates appointed by the state. Under the Sadat and Mubarak governments, the confederation has become an important instrument of the ruling party, allowing it to screen nominees in chamber elections and to balance the influence of the Cairo and Alexandria organizations with groups in the Canal Zone and the Nile valley.[5]

Twenty of the twenty-six current chamber presidents are leaders of provincial branches of the National Democratic Party. Several are also members of parliament or the Majlis al-Shura. The electoral lists for local chambers are generally prepared by the confederation president and the Ministry of Trade in consultation with the businessmen's committee of the ruling party. Since 1978 the confederation has been headed by 'Izzat Ghidan, the longtime president of the Bani Swayf chamber who has also accumulated a number of key posts in the party and the legislature. Ghidan serves simultaneously as party secretary for his home province, as head of the party's committee on commerce and industry, and as a member of the economic committee of the Majlis al-Shura. During his presidency, leadership positions in the confederation have been shared with a number of merchants from other regions, especially those from Port Sa'id, Sharqiya, and Gharbiya.[6]

By buttressing older corporatist restrictions with multiple ties to the ruling party, Sadat and Mubarak were able to smooth out a few of the many disagreements that divided the chambers and the government during the *infitah*. In 1977 and 1978, when Sadat tried to impose limits on the profit margins of many imported goods, he faced strong objections from the Cairo chamber, which insisted that the measures were unenforceable. At first the government tried to remove the head of the Cairo chamber, Mustafa Kamal Murad, who was trying to build a private sector following for his opposition Liberal Party. When the confederation intervened in the dispute, it tried to play a mediating role by objecting to the manner in which the regulations were promulgated instead of attacking the decision itself.

When Murad's presidential term expired, he was replaced by Muhammad al-Balidi, a member of the ruling party with strong connections to importers in the duty-free zone of Port Sa'id. With al-Balidi heading the Cairo chamber and Ghidan leading the confederation, both the importers and the government were persuaded to accept a quiet stalemate. It was agreed that the profit ceilings would remain on the books, but that they would not be enforced until parliament reviewed several confederation proposals for a new chamber law.[7]

Between 1978 and 1983 the National Democratic Party discussed several conflicting reorganization plans submitted by the confederation and the Ministry of Trade. The confederation's proposals called for the removal of government appointees from all chamber bodies in favor of representation based exclusively on election. Other demands included forming new branches for exporters and foreign investors, giving the confederation a voice in setting import quotas, and empowering the chambers to license and supervise all foreign commercial activities. Hence, the confederation not only sought greater self-governance and participation in policy making but also wanted broader authority over foreign capitalists and their local agents.[8]

The Ministry of Trade consistently blocked the confederation's initiatives with counterproposals designed to increase bureaucratic controls over the chambers. Each year the confederation was forced to submit new and watered-down drafts that compromised one demand after another. After 1985 the Mubarak government became more willing to liberalize foreign trade, but it continued to resist the confederation's pleas for a more flexible and autonomous brand of corporatism. In 1986 the government finally abolished profit restrictions on imports along with the "guidance committees" *(lijan al-tarshid)* that had kept import licenses in the hands of the Ministry of Economy. Although these were important concessions to the private sector as a whole, they were by no means a victory for the chambers of commerce. Unable to renegotiate relations with their parent ministries or to assert stronger controls over foreign trade, the chambers have been outflanked by newer voluntary associations that are providing big business direct access to economic decision makers over the heads of both confederation leaders and party patrons.

As the chambers of commerce became more specialized preserves of small business, they also became more divided by conflicts between the few who enjoy close connections to the ruling party and the many who do not. The uneven impact of government regulation and foreign competition on different branches and regions has made political influence more important than ever in the scramble to exploit or escape the consequences of economic liberalization. Interchamber relations are increasingly dominated by quarrels over local market shares, over the differential effects of price and quality controls on particular commodities and provinces, over rapidly changing foreign trade protocols, and over taxes, users' fees, energy costs, and quotas on raw materials.[9]

In the heightened struggle for exemptions and concessions, licenses and subsidies, the chambers and the confederation have become incapable of aggregating the interests they seek to represent. For many businessmen, survival now depends on developing political resources outside the chambers rather than through them. For smaller operators in the provinces, this generally means falling in line with the local branch of the ruling party in order to seek redress and loans from municipal authorities. For wealthier entrepreneurs in the capital, it has meant creating their own private associations to bargain more effectively with the cabinet and with potential foreign partners.

The Federation of Egyptian Industries

Compared to the chambers of commerce, the chambers of industry are more cohesive, more centralized, and more influential representatives of the managers of manufacturing establishments in both the public and private sectors. Whereas the chambers of commerce have changed little since the revolution, the structure and composition of the chambers of industry were seriously altered, first by the economic nationalizations of the 1950s and 1960s, and then by the shift toward economic liberalization during the 1970s and 1980s. Under Nasser, the Federation of Egyptian Industries was transformed from a steering committee of the big bourgeoisie into an agency of the Ministry of Industry. Under Sadat and Mubarak, the federation has become a more effective spokesman for native manufacturers, including public sector managers seeking greater operational independence as well as the smaller and more numerous private entrepreneurs who favor a renewed emphasis on protectionism and import substitution.

Shortly after World War II, industrialists took the first steps in converting the chambers from voluntary associations to semipublic bodies, hoping that the government of Isma'il Sidqi would endorse their campaign for state subsidies and for the further Egyptianization of industrial management. However, after the revolution, the initiative for additional corporatist measures passed to the Free Officers' regime. In 1953 compulsory membership was adopted for all manufacturing firms with a capitalization of £E 10,000 or more. In 1958 membership was expanded to include all firms that had at least £E 5,000 of fixed investment or that employed at least twenty-five workers. The Ministry of Industry, created in 1956, was granted extensive supervisory powers over the chambers, including the authority to veto all of their decisions. Technically, the chambers can override government vetoes if three-fourths of their directors concur, but this right has little practical value because the ministry also appoints one-third of all chamber board members, including the president of the federation.[10]

When Nasser nationalized foreign enterprises and large private firms, the Federation of Industries was reorganized around a smaller number of chambers. On the eve of the revolution, the federation possessed a diversified set of national affiliates representing twenty-four branches of manufacturing. As the state consolidated its control over large-scale industry, it tightened the already highly centralized associations that had been inherited from the private cartels. The number of chambers was reduced to twenty in 1958, to thirteen in 1967, and then to twelve in 1972.[11]

The reorganization of the chambers was accompanied by adoption of a complex formula of proportional representation for the federation's board of directors. Supposedly, this system was designed to balance public and private sector interests with a blend of appointed and elected members. However, over the past thirty years, all of the federation's presidents have been managers of large state enterprises in textiles, tobacco, chemicals, and steel. Two presidents were former ministers of industry, and one was promoted to that post while serving as head of the federation.[12]

Since 1972 the federation has tried to give greater prominence to private sector spokesmen. The board of directors is now composed of twenty members: the president and six others are government appointees, and the remaining thirteen are elected by chamber affiliates. Five of the appointed members are public officials, including the deputy ministers of industry and trade, the head of the Industrial Development Bank, and directors of two special investment funds for state industries. Appointees also include two representatives of the private sector, generally one industrialist along with the president of the Confederation of Chambers of Commerce.

Only two of the elected members represent the public sector, the heads of the steel and petroleum chambers. Eleven others are private industrialists chosen from the specialized affiliates: metallurgy, engineering, textiles and clothing, chemicals, printing, wood and furniture, leather products, food processing, grain milling, construction materials, and film making. Each of these chambers enjoys equal voting strength in the federation despite vast differences in their relative contributions to total industrial employment and production. Furthermore, each chamber is represented by a private businessman even though state enterprises account for most of the investment and output in every sector except wood and leather products.[13]

Thus, during the *infitah* continued government control over the federation's presidency and decision-making process has been balanced somewhat by the overrepresentation of private owners against state managers and of small operators against large ones. Sadat and Mubarak have tried to give a greater voice to the nearly 7,000 private firms enrolled in the federation while preserving the pivotal position of the 300 public sector establishments that dominated the chambers during the 1960s. With two-thirds of the seats on the federation council, private industrialists possess a voting weight that represents a crude compromise between their growing numerical strength and their continued economic weakness.

The compromise has caused a good deal of dissension among the professional staff that directs the federation's daily operations. Some of the federation's top administrators feel that the tilt toward small industry has gone too far, while others argue that it has not gone far enough. Although both sides agree that private sector interests deserve greater attention, they have very different visions of the federation's future constituency. One group would like to raise the current capital requirement for chamber membership from £E 5,000 to £E 25,000 or even £E 50,000, but an equally influential group would like to lower the ceiling to only £E 2,000. The former strategy seeks to increase the federation's leverage in policy-making by explicitly identifying the association with the most powerful firms in the private sector. The latter strategy aims at broadening the chambers' control over small workshops so that the federation can gradually replace the Ministry of Industry as the principal regulator of all private manufacturing.

Even though there have been no formal changes in its jurisdiction and functions, the federation has adopted an increasingly dualistic role vis-à-vis the private sector, operating as a more outspoken advocate for the strong and as a more intrusive regulator of the weak. Concerning the larger and more capital-intensive firms in engineering, chemicals, and textiles, the federation vigorously demands greater market sharing with foreign and state enterprises as well as guaranteed access to raw materials at subsidized prices. However, concerning the smaller, labor-intensive producers of leather, wood, and metal goods, the federation has allied with the government to expand the list of "essential commodities" that are subject to price and quality controls.[14]

The swift reemergence of private business influence in a corporatist association that Nasser had redesigned to represent the technocratic and managerial elite of the public sector is largely attributable to the political vulnerability and economic opportunism of the managers themselves. Between 1973 and 1975 Sadat purged hundreds of managers who were sympathetic to greater decentralization and efficiency but who would have opposed attacks on the principle of public ownership of large industry. Their successors continued to portray themselves as stewards of the public sector, but they showed an alarming penchant for steering their enterprises into controversial joint ventures with foreign firms and then popping up on the local boards of those same corporations.[15]

When Sadat encouraged debate over the reorganization of state enterprises, the Federation of Egyptian Industries advanced proposals that went far beyond the technocrats' earlier demands for administrative autonomy and greater reliance on market forces. The federation wanted to limit or abolish such socialist reforms as worker participation in management, profit sharing, and job security. It endorsed plans to permit private and foreign investors to acquire equity in profitable state industries, acknowledging that this could be the first step toward the gradual divestiture of public enterprises. The federation also prepared detailed demands for state subsidies and incentives for private industry, hoping to promote a decisive shift in the balance of investment and power in favor of private manufacturing.

Thus, during the *infitah* the federation provided the business community with a ready-made mixed commission for reshaping industrial policy in close consultation with the state's key bankers, planners, and economic ministers. The federation's system of proportional representation aided private manufacturers not only in recapturing their original associations but also in penetrating government agencies that had become indifferent or hostile to their interests.

Particularly under the Mubarak government, the federation has tried to formulate a common industrial policy that could accommodate the demands of both public managers and private entrepreneurs. This has led to important adjustments of the federation's positions concerning collective bargaining and protectionism. Industrialists in both sectors are demanding a freer hand in negotiating collective contracts with organized labor. The federation is calling on the state to make a clear distinction between production workers and civil servants in order to circumvent the minimum wages, bonuses, and job guarantees that pad labor costs in manufacturing. Federation leaders argue that when working conditions are freed from extensive government regulation, they will be able to accept union proposals to conclude more industrywide agreements. Managers clearly assume that because of organized labor's weak bargaining position, the chambers of industry will be able to control employment levels and to withhold wage increases until there are corresponding increases in productivity.[16]

While the federation is demanding less state intervention in industrial relations, it is urging much greater assistance against foreign competition. One of the most important developments in the federation during the Mubarak period is the growing insistence of both public and private industrialists that the liberalization of the *infitah* is perfectly consistent with the continued protection of native manufacturing. The federation's leaders do not defend import-substitution in principle. Indeed, they frequently criticize the country's existing enterprises for their low productivity, inferior quality, and high costs. But they assert that precisely because of Egypt's past mistakes, the state must adopt a long-term strategy of carefully encouraging more competitive enterprises over the next fifteen to twenty years. During this period of transition, they argue, the degree of protection must be continually adjusted on a commodity-by-commodity basis to insure that as competition increases, it will always be "reasonable, acceptable, and planned."[17]

The federation's effort to develop a common platform for native manufacturers has been highly compatible with Mubarak's desire to "correct" the *infitah* with a new form of guided capitalism in which the state attempts to harmonize the interests of public and private industry while gradually exposing both to the pressures of the international marketplace. By more effectively coordinating the demands of its diverse constituency, the federation has aided Mubarak in smoothing out some of the conflicts between state, private, and foreign enterprises that seemed to be developing into irreconcilable contradictions during Sadat's presidency. However, many of Egypt's most powerful private entrepreneurs are quite impatient with the federation's corporatist structures and its gradualist policies. Businessmen with greater access to foreign capital and technology have a far more ambitious timetable and they have developed a more specialized and independent association for implementing it.

The Egyptian Businessmen's Association

Between 1978 and 1982 a combination of factors convinced the most prominent *infitah* businessmen that they needed to devise novel forms of collective action. First, the government and the ruling party refused to negotiate a more flexible relationship with the chambers of commerce that would allow special representation for the binational businessmen's committees that were trying to broaden ties with American, European, and Japanese investors. Second, a new corporations law, adopted in 1981, helped to strengthen the position of local entrepreneurs by granting them most of the exemptions that were originally intended to attract foreign capital and by requiring overseas investors to enter into more partnerships with Egyptian firms. Third, the uncertainty surrounding Mubarak's intention to replace "consumptive liberalization" with "productive liberalization" suggested that the new government and the business community would be locked in a lengthy and complex renegotiation of the private sector's role in the economy.

The Egyptian Businessmen's Association formed as a by-product of meetings that the Mubarak government arranged with the Egyptian-American Businessmen's Committee during 1982.[18] The association began with a small loan from the binational committee, shared a common headquarters, and gradually established its own staff and specialized branches for dealing with government agencies and with foreign investors from a dozen countries. From its inception the association was designed as a small and exclusive assemblage of Egypt's most powerful business leaders. Membership is reserved to "owners, chief executive officers, and holders of ultimate decisional authority" who have no fewer than ten years of managerial experience. Applicants must be sponsored by at least two existing members. They must pay initiation fees and annual dues of £E 500 (increased to £E 1,000 after 1985) in addition to separate enrollment fees for each of the association's special policy committees.[19]

By 1983 the association included about two hundred members who constituted a broad coalition of foreign trade, manufacturing, construction, banking, and consulting (Table 6–1). In reporting their primary fields of economic activity, members are particularly eager to identify themselves as agents of industrialization and as importers of advanced technology. One-half of those engaged in foreign trade say they specialize in intermediate and capital goods instead of the finished goods and consumer products that dominated the early years of the *infitah*. One-half of the manufacturers are concentrated in the traditional areas of food processing and textiles, but the other half are producing construction materials, metal products, chemicals, pesticides, plastics, and transportation equipment.

The association's emphasis on local industry is also evident from the large number of members who have joined functional and geographic committees designed to attract Arab capital and European technology (Table 6–2). The committees on industry and foreign investment contain two to four times as many members as most other committees. Overseas contacts are strongest with the Gulf countries, growing with Canada and Western Europe, and just beginning with Brazil, Argentina, and Mexico.

TABLE 6-1.   Principal Fields of Economic
Activity of Members of Egyptian
Businessmen's Association

Import-export	59
Manufacturing	40
Construction	30
Banking	25
Consulting	19
Accounting	7
Agribusiness	6
Insurance	4
Law	3
Tourism	3
Advertising	3
Petroleum	3
Retail trade	2
Sea transport	1
Total	205

Source: Jam'iyat Rijal al-A'mal al-Misriyin, *Al-Taqrir al-Sanawi wa Dalil al-A'da' lil-Jam'iyat Rijal al-A'mal al-Misriyin*
(Cairo, Dar al-'Alam al-'Arabi, 1983), pp. 6–31.

The effort to encourage collaboration among capitalists representing different economic sectors and nationalities is most evident in the large and
eclectic contingent of investment bankers. The association has enrolled
twenty-five bank managers, including the heads of twelve foreign banks,
six private sector banks, four Islamic banks, and three state banks. Association leaders have begun to recruit more managers from the state
economic enterprises, but public sector representatives still constitute only
about 5 percent of the total membership.

During 1983 and 1984 the Businessmen's Association quickly emerged
as the leading private sector negotiator with the new Mubarak government. Seeking the business community's support for his economic reforms, Mubarak instructed one minister after another to speak at the association's monthly dinners and to chair special commissions that would
discuss businessmen's objections to each agency's policies and operations. With the minister of planning, association leaders insisted that renewed government intervention in the economy must not revive the controls of the 1960s. Instead, they argued, Egypt required a voluntary type
of ''indicative planning'' that would stimulate greater private investment
in industry while shielding it from ''unfair competition'' from both the

state and the multinational corporations. Planning officials agreed in principle to establish new industrial zones in which private firms would be provided with improved land, low-interest credit, subsidized energy, and duty-free raw materials.[20]

With the minister of finance, the association pleaded for top-level bargaining and dispute settlement to circumvent the army of corrupt tax collectors and customs officials who were siphoning off revenues from both the state and the business world. Both sides admitted that they were caught up in a hopeless game of "cat and mouse" in which 100 percent of the import declarations were falsified and 70 percent of the customs levies were illegal. They also agreed that native businessmen often faced unfair treatment in tax and customs matters because poorly trained bureaucrats did not yet realize that many Egyptian companies were now entitled to the same exemptions that once had been reserved to foreign and joint venture firms.[21]

One of the association's most successful meetings was with the minister of energy. The government was proposing an across-the-board increase in the price of electricity of 20 percent each year so that local costs would eventually equal the world price. When the association objected that a flat rate was incompatible with the government's desire to promote native manufacturing, the ministry agreed to negotiate a complex rate schedule that preserved large energy subsidies for three categories of

TABLE 6-2. Membership in Functional and Geographic Committees of Egyptian Businessmen's Association

Functional Committees		*Geographic Committees*	
Industry	62	Gulf countries	61
Foreign investment	60	Canada	53
Importing	42	France	48
Agriculture	32	Italy	42
Exporting	30	West Germany	32
Taxes and customs	22	Total	236
Construction	15		
Petroleum	15		
Legislation	12		
Tourism	12		
Total	302		

Source: Jam'iyat Rijal al-A'mal al-Misriyin, *Al-Taqrir al-Sanawi wa Dalil al-A'da' lil-Jam'iyat Rijal al-A'mal al-Misriyin* (Cairo, Dar al-'Alam al-'Arabi, 1983), pp. 6–31.

private industry: firms that produced for export; firms that produced for the local market while developing an exporting potential; and firms that produced exclusively for the local market but received a special dispensation from the Ministry of Investment.[22]

With the minister of economy and foreign trade, association leaders urged the adoption of several incentives that governments had used to spur exporting in Turkey, India, and the Netherlands. Discussions focused on the relative merits of each country's strategy and on determining the particular mix of incentives that would be most suitable to Egypt's conditions. Intense bargaining resulted in preliminary agreements on a number of proposals: paying direct cash bonuses to exporters; allowing exporters to retain their foreign exchange earnings; reducing price and quality controls for direct transactions between local manufacturers and foreign buyers; and establishing an exporters' insurance fund against sudden currency devaluations and market fluctuations.[23]

During 1985 and 1986, when Mubarak appointed more openly pro-business governments, these private and informal meetings were gradually replaced by a joint economic council that included six cabinet ministers and eleven members of the association's executive committee. Although the council was supposed to represent the views of the private sector as a whole, all other business groups were allotted only three seats. The government's open embrace quickly proved to be a mixed blessing for the Businessmen's Association. On one hand, such rapid success seemed to vindicate the view that entrepreneurs could exert greater influence over public policy by ignoring the state-sponsored chambers and professional syndicates and by relying on their own resources to build more independent and homogeneous voluntary organizations. By underlining the association's primacy over all of the traditional corporatist groups of the private sector, the state itself provided dramatic confirmation of its respect for the new autonomy of big business.

On the other hand, the government's solicitude for such a small and privileged segment of the business world seriously compromised the whole process of consultation, making it seem more like collusion than power sharing. The association had always boasted that it comprised "a select group of the Egyptian business elite" (*majmu'a mukhtara min safwa rijal al-a'mal bi misr*),[24] yet the very exclusiveness that provided the group with much of its strength and cohesion also made it more vulnerable to political attacks as its activities became more publicized.

As soon as the government formed its joint committee with the Businessmen's Association, the Confederation of Chambers of Commerce demanded that the committee be reconstituted in order to restore the leadership of the "legitimate" representatives of the private sector.[25] A rival group of entrepreneurs and managers arose in Alexandria, declaring that its alliances with the chambers of commerce and the state economic enterprises continued to outweigh its connections with foreign capital.[26] The Egyptian Confederation of Labor denounced the Businessmen's Association for mounting a "vicious campaign" of influence seeking and called upon the government to establish additional joint committees that would provide unions and cooperatives with the same kind of access that was being granted to private business.[27] Articles began to appear in both state- and party-owned newspapers declaring that the association was asking the U.S. embassy and the I.M.F. to withhold foreign aid and credit until the Mubarak government agreed to its demands for budget cuts, freer importing, and devaluation.[28]

As the association attracted more and more unfavorable publicity, its leaders were forced to devote greater attention to self-defense. Previously, members had been asked to contribute to special funds that were earmarked for building a new headquarters in Giza and for establishing a holding company to promote joint ventures in agribusiness. Since 1984, however, the association's vice-president, 'Ali Jamal al-Nazir, has been urging that a portion of these funds be set aside for publication of a weekly magazine that would counter the growing assaults on the private sector in the party press. Al-Nazir asserts that opposition journalists commonly publish false rumors about the association's activities and then privately tell the group that they are prepared to print rebuttals in the form of paid advertisements if the businessmen are willing to pay higher rates than all other advertisers. In al-Nazir's view, this amounts to a deliberate campaign of disinformation aimed at forcing the Businessmen's Association to finance its political enemies.[29]

The rapid rise of the Egyptian Businessmen's Association has helped to redirect public debate about representative government from an earlier fixation on the party and electoral systems toward a more serious consideration of functional associations and their role in shaping economic policy. Long-standing dissatisfaction with the disparity between government and opposition parties in parliament is giving way to a growing concern over the "lost balance" between organized groups representing competing social and economic interests. Politicians and association leaders as well as scholars and journalists are portraying Mubarak's rapprochement with big business as a direct challenge to all other groups to develop more effective and independent means of collective action.[30]

The debate over group imbalance sharpened considerably toward the end of 1986 when the head of the Confederation of Labor, Sa'd Muhammad Ahmad, was suddenly dropped from the cabinet after a decade of service as minister of manpower and vocational training. Ahmad had been quarreling for several months with Fu'ad Sultan, the minister of tourism, over new proposals for employment cuts in public sector industries. Sultan was one of the founding members of the Egyptian Businessmen's Association and the longtime director of the Misr-Iran Bank, one of the leading sources of investment capital for private manufacturers. Ahmad's dismissal deepened the labor movement's alienation from the ruling party and highlighted the possibilities for new alliances between opposition parties and disaffected interest groups.[31]

Opposition leaders continue to demand a freer and more representative party system, but they no longer suggest that the parties alone are adequate guarantors of social justice for workers and peasants, shopkeepers and craftsmen, tenants and consumers. More than ever before, Egypt's politicians are beginning to distinguish between the *freedom* of association and the *art* of association. Even as they struggle for equal political rights, they realize that their partial victories are already paving the way for new inequalities in which well-organized minorities can continue to prevail over poorly organized majorities.[32]

By favoring the Businessmen's Association over larger constituencies in the private sector, Mubarak has tried to reconsolidate representation in Egypt's increasingly pluralist business world. But the government has chosen its favored interlocutor in an arbitrary and discriminatory manner, prompting rival groups to press for a more inclusive and equitable process of consultation. Mubarak is groping toward some form of economic summitry that can provide a measure of support and legitimacy for unpopular policies of austerity. His first steps in that direction already indicate that economic summitry will have to be combined with a greater concern for social symmetry if he wishes to persuade his countrymen that he prefers voluntary sacrifices that are shared by all instead of imposed sacrifices that benefit the privileged few.

Religious Groups

Religious organizations constitute the most important sector of associational life in which pluralism remains the predominant mode of representation. Yet religious institutions also display a striking and growing structural heterogeneity because of the coexistence and competition of a wide variety of groups that span the broad continuum of pluralist, corporatist, and hybrid types. The persistence of spontaneous, privatist traditions among religious associations and the increasing conflict between differentially organized religious groups are interrelated phenomena. Indeed, the former has contributed to the latter. The survival and self-renewal of pluralist residues in the highly sensitive area of religious activity has prompted recurring corporatist initiatives from the state designed to co-opt, fragment, or repress specific segments of a traditionally autonomous and recalcitrant sector of Egyptian society. Yet the very success of corporatist policies has served to radicalize those who reject the right of state-appointed religious leaders to bend Islam to the needs of a secularizing regime.

An appreciation of the heterogeneity of Egypt's leading Muslim organizations is important for several reasons. It clearly contradicts the conventional Orientalist argument that Islam discourages the art of association and promotes shapeless, "unincorporated society." It encourages far greater caution in generalizing about the likely consequences of collective action among Muslims than has been evident in so many anxious accounts of Egypt's "Islamic awakening" *(al-sahwa al-Islamiya)*. And it also reminds us of the highly malleable nature of organized Muslims' relations with political authorities, exemplified by their unusual aptitude for mixing pluralist and corporatist institutional forms in changing proportions.

These points can be illustrated in a comparative overview of five types of Muslim organizations that vary widely in terms of their internal structures and relations with the state: the bureaucratic complex of al-Azhar; the newly corporatized Sufi orders; the voluntary yet state-supported philanthropic associations and private mosques *(al-jam'iyaat al-khayriya* and *al-jawami' al-ahliya)*; the extralegal "Islamic associations" *(al-jama'aat al-Islamiya)*; and the illegal societies of Islamic "militants."

Al-Azhar and the 'Ulama'

Most clearly at the corporatist end of the scale is the semiofficial complex of al-Azhar with its attendant institutions of education and research, publication and preaching, and its management of government-owned mosques and pious foundations from within the state bureaucracy. From a sociological viewpoint, al-Azhar's "century of reform" can be seen as a leading case of religious institutionalization and adaptation in an increasingly secular environment. From a political viewpoint, however, these reforms are a classic example of co-optation.

A long series of government-imposed reorganizations has provided al-Azhar with a more bureaucratic and hierarchical administration, a more specialized and secular curriculum, and a quasi-public monopoly in religious censorship and interpretation. The Azharis have tried to delay and obstruct all outside initiatives for reform since the 1870s, forcing succeeding regimes to adopt increasingly ambitious and intrusive reorganization laws in 1896, 1911, 1930, and 1961. Over time, however, resistance to pedagogical innovation has been accompanied by acceptance of administrative centralization that has greatly enhanced the political prestige and economic resources of the leading 'ulama', especially the Shaykh al-Azhar.[33]

Although state-sponsored reform diminished the traditional autonomy and informality of al-Azhar, it bolstered the position of al-Azhar vis-à-vis rival representatives of Islam and of the Shaykh al-Azhar vis-à-vis multiple centers of power within his own institution. Even as the spread of secular education and law undercut the value of religious training, al-Azhar acquired an unprecedented preeminence over other religious leaders, such as the head of the sharifian families (naqib al-ashraf), the chief of the Sufi orders (shaykh mashayikh al-turuq al-sufiya), and the judges of the shari'a courts (quda al-mahakim al-shar'ia).[34] Around the turn of the century, when the state sought to tighten control over the endowments and rites of the mystical orders, Azharis were given leading positions on the new Sufi Council, sharing authority to appoint successors to the turuq, to manage their finances and shrines, and to enforce new regulations concerning their public processions. Many local madrasas and mosques traditionally run by independent Sufi orders were transformed into institutes (ma'ahid) of al-Azhar and gradually incorporated into a single, nationwide framework.[35]

After World War I al-Azhar was also able to absorb its two most troublesome competitors in the field of religious education—the Teachers' Training College (Dar al-'Ulum) and the School for Religious Law (Madrasat al-Qada'). Both institutions had been sponsored by secular bureaucrats and religious reformers who sought to bypass the Azharis and to inject new blood into public instruction and the religious courts. After recurrent protests, al-Azhar managed to narrow the curricula of these schools and to challenge the credentials of their graduates for government appointments. By the mid-1920s both schools were placed under al-Azhar's control and they were quickly abolished during the next major reorganization in 1930. Azharis had to accept a number of reforms consolidating their faculties into the three colleges of Theology, Shari'a, and Arabic, and bringing primary and secondary education into line with the state system. But they managed to restore their monopoly over religious education and to eliminate a major source of competition to their claims on teaching positions and judgeships.[36]

Centralization and standardization also strengthened the rector's hand over the personal, sectarian, and national groupings that for centuries had divided the *madrasa* into self-contained and feuding compartments, each defending its distinctive privileges and curriculum. At the head of the expanded Administrative Council and a system of specialized colleges, the Shaykh al-Azhar was able to exert greater control over examinations, salaries and promotions, and pious endowments. This growing authority allowed succeeding rectors to impose greater discipline over a student body that was becoming increasingly dependent upon government employment, to assert the primacy of the official Hanafi *madhhab* over the rival Shafiʿi and Maliki schools, and to resolve disputes between the various provincial dormitories *(arwiqa)* over the allocation of space and finances.[37]

Al-Azhar's survival and expansion have come at the price of growing reliance on state budgetary support and of sharing power with administrators and faculty appointed from outside the ranks of the ʿulama'. As the authority of the rector increased, he also became more vulnerable to political manipulation. During the constitutional monarchy rectors were replaced with increasing frequency as they were forced into open alliances with the palace or the Liberal Constitutionalists and then suffered reprisals when their Wafdist opponents took power. After the revolution a sweeping secularization of the curriculum was accompanied by an awkward system of dual control in which government bureaucrats and lay experts were placed alongside *shuyukh* in one department and committee after another.[38]

Even while curbing al-Azhar's autonomy, each regime has tried to reaffirm its status as the ultimate arbiter of correct Islamic teaching. Semiofficial views on current religious issues have been sanctioned through the Committee of High ʿUlama' (Hay'at Kibar al-ʿUlama') and more recently through the Academy of Islamic Research (Majmaʿ al-Buhuth al-Islamiya). By and large, however, Azharis have been extremely reluctant either to issue final pronouncements on "true Islam" or to modify accepted interpretations in line with the supposed requirements of "modernity." Especially since the revolution, they have preferred circumlocution and accommodation over doctrinal consistency. Determined to preserve their shrinking yet substantial niches, they have tended to rationalize or at least acquiesce in the views of the government while expressing their misgivings in guarded and often convoluted language.

This combination of collaboration and caution has earned the 'ulama' the mistrust of the secular regime as well as the contempt of its religious opponents. With the spread of public education and the mass media, the moral authority of the 'ulama' has been challenged on several fronts by pious laymen who constantly remind their coreligionists that Islam possesses no priesthood mediating between God's word and individual believers and no infallible human authority whose judgment can bind the rest of the community. From the salafiya movement at the turn of the century to the Muslim Brotherhood to many of today's most popular religious writers and television personalities, Egyptians have been told that an authentic understanding of God's will is available to anyone who can undertake the direct study of the Qur'an and the Sunna. The "official" 'ulama' are commonly portrayed as an isolated and corrupted elite—as "parrots of the pulpit" who condone injustice, forcing Muslims to exercise independent judgment and initiative in fulfilling their obligation to "order what is good and prohibit what is forbidden" (al-amr bil-ma'ruf wa al-nahi 'an al-munkar).[39]

Ironically, in the 1970s when attacks on the 'ulama' turned from verbal abuse to physical assaults, even the Sadat government seemed to agree that al-Azhar had become too discredited to stem the rise of religious radicalism. After Shaykh Muhammad al-Dhahabi, a former minister of awqaf, was kidnapped and slain by the al-Takfir wa al-Hijra group, the murderers were turned over to a special military tribunal where the Azharis were denied the right to testify for the prosecution.[40] Four years later, when Sadat himself was assassinated, the Mubarak government exerted great pressure on al-Azhar to denounce the killers as heretics. This demand caused considerable resentment and dissension among many of the leading shuyukh because several cabinet members were simultaneously declaring that al-Azhar was to blame for the spread of extremism among the younger generation. Eventually, the Shaykh al-Azhar issued a lengthy refutation of the assassins' theological positions, but many 'ulama' complained bitterly that the state could not expect them to win over misguided young people while al-Azhar was being forced to imitate the assassins' error of arrogating the right to declare who was and who was not a "real" Muslim.[41]

The gulf separating the Azharis from the religious radicals was painfully revealed during their "prison dialogues" arranged by the Ministry of Interior in the Liman Tura penitentiary. The 'ulama' asserted that the police had denied them prior, private contact with the inmates. They were visibly embarrassed to see the prisoners rise, one by one, before the television news cameras, asserting their complete acceptance of the Azharis' admonitions and asking to be set free as a result of their sudden spiritual "rehabilitation." The *'ulama'* quickly ended the charade, complaining that the militants were practicing dissimulation *(taqiya)*, that their true opinions were disturbingly idiosyncratic, and that their reeducation would be a long and arduous process.[42]

Before long, the government realized that it was pointless to expose hard-core militants to the *'ulama'*. Instead, it turned to the older and chastened generation of radicals represented by 'Umar al-Tilmisani and the Muslim Brotherhood. Having themselves just been released after imprisonment by Sadat, they were now invited to reenter the jail cells as government-sponsored mediators who could be expected to demonstrate greater tact and credibility than the infuriated Azharis.[43]

Thereafter the *'ulama'* did their best to turn their obvious weaknesses to good advantage. Tacitly admitting that it had become alienated from the masses and superseded by more popular and independent religious organizations, al-Azhar began to plead for still greater government subsidies. According to the *'ulama'*, Egypt was suffering from a genuine crisis of morality and authority that could be reversed only by improving religious training at all levels of education, placing qualified preachers in every mosque, and increasing religious publishing and broadcasting. The remedy, in short, was to increase the number of Azhar graduates, to enhance their living standards and job opportunities, and to organize them into a new professional syndicate. More than ever, al-Azhar was prepared to serve the state provided the state was willing to hand over a greater share of the budget and public employment.[44]

The Mubarak government has responded to these demands with great reserve, giving the Azharis no reason to expect that Egypt's growing religious tensions will redound to their benefit. Speaking to the *'ulama'* on the thousandth anniversary of al-Azhar's founding, Mubarak coupled praise for the institution with criticism of its leadership. Explaining that all Egyptians had a vital interest in the sound understanding and practice of religion, the president insisted that matters of faith were too important to be left to the *'ulama'* alone.[45]

The Sufi Orders

A newer and less consolidated corporatist arrangement appears among the recently reorganized Sufi orders. Since 1976 Sufi leaders have accepted a state chartered confederation of sixty-seven officially recognized groups under the guidance of the Higher Council of Sufi Orders. The council, which includes several government appointees and Azhari *shuyukh,* has

broad powers to license mystical fraternities, to settle disputes over jurisdiction and leadership succession, to inspect their finances, and to regulate their celebrations and public processions. In exchange for their acceptance of this more bureaucratic and hierarchical structure, Sufi leaders
have received annual government subsidies and token recognition of their
claim to represent an important social link between the state and their
followings in the provinces.[46]

Sufi and government leaders began negotiating the transformation of
the orders from pluralist to corporatist lines soon after the 1967 War.
Nasser hoped that refashioned and officially sanctioned groups would be
able to absorb some of the postwar rise in popular religiosity and deflect
it from political action. By reviving a more controlled version of the
"religion of the streets," the weakened regime hoped to promote a pliable and quietist alternative to the Muslim Brotherhood, which had recently been suppressed for the second time since the revolution. For their
part, many Sufi leaders saw in corporatism a possible remedy to the steady
deterioration of their fragmented, amorphous, and squabbling organizations.

Through most of the nineteenth century the orders had enjoyed a flexible and effective authority structure around the descendants of the al-
Bakri family that was based on a concessive *firman* from Muhammad
ʿAli and a pledge of noninterference from al-Azhar. In return for their
recognition of the al-Bakris' suzerainty, Sufi *shuyukh* received confirmation of their lines of succession, the right to revenues from their shrines
and *awqaf*, and protection against secessionist threats from ambitious
subordinates in local *zawiyas*. During the system's heyday before the
British occupation, the al-Bakris were even able to uphold the principle
of *qadam*, a quasi-monopolistic grant of jurisdiction that prohibited any
tariqa from conducting processions where another *tariqa* was already established.[47]

Between 1881 and 1905 this voluntary network of fealty gradually broke
apart as the state and al-Azhar became determined to convert it into a
centralized bureaucracy capable of regulating the internal affairs of the
turuq and abolishing the more heterodox aspects of their public ceremonies and private worship. Faced with a new and more intrusive Sufi Council
that was forced to placate the government's demands for reform, the *turuq* began to disassociate themselves from the al-Bakris and split into
self-contained units. Attempting to increase centralization, the government had instead provoked a new wave of secessions; hoping to impose
standardization and control, it had merely encouraged concealment and
evasion.[48]

In their struggle to cling to leadership, the al-Bakris themselves hastened the process of fragmentation by recognizing the independence of
dozens of small, local orders and abandoning the principle of *qadam*
altogether. Whereas previously the *turuq* had accepted al-Bakri authority
in order to secure their privileges, now the al-Bakris were compelled to
accept multiple claims of tenure in order to shore up what little remained
of their crumbling authority.[49]

During their subsequent decline the Sufi orders suffered a particularly
severe form of the problems that plagued associational life in the period
of "palace pluralism": recurrent fissions, organizational weakness, intense rivalries, and overlapping memberships. Under simultaneous attacks from secularists, orthodox *'ulama'*, and the reformers of the *salafiya* movement, the mystical fraternities were eclipsed by new religious
associations such as al-Shubban al-Muslimin and the Muslim Brotherhood, which appealed to educated urbanites less tied to the authority of
traditional notables and more prone toward political mobilization.[50]

In attempting to rebuild the orders during the past two decades, Sufi
leaders have been more dependent than ever on the support of the state
and the guidance of al-Azhar. Accordingly, the partial revival of the Sufi
movement has occurred in an explicitly corporatist framework emphasizing administrative centralization, government control, and doctrinal orthodoxy. These restrictions have diminished the autonomy and charis-
matic appeal that provided the *turuq* with much of their traditional flexibility
and popularity. Nevertheless, Sufi leaders have been willing to accept
external direction as the unavoidable price for overcoming their chronic
weakness and disorganization.

Since 1976 a modified version of the principle of *qadam* has been
reintroduced through a state-controlled licensing process that strictly limits the number and jurisdiction of officially recognized orders. The Higher
Council of Sufi Orders receives regular government financing for its public processions, highlighted by a well-managed celebration of the Prophet's birthday that draws large contingents from all of the major *turuq* to
the capital city once a year. The council also receives a generous subsidy
for its monthly magazine, *al-Tasawwuf al-Islami*, which devotes great
attention to its periodic meetings with the president of the republic, where
the agenda commonly includes requests for greater public works projects
in the provinces. The council's publications strongly reflect the "respect-
able" brand of mysticism endorsed by the leading *shuyukh* of al-Azhar,
who constantly portray Sufism as an authentic aspect of indigenous culture capable of deterring the spread of ideological contamination from
abroad.[51]

Although Sufi leaders have been responsive to the government's desire to promote a more orthodox and ideologically congenial form of popular religion, they have not been willing to turn their refurbished organizations into an electoral machine for the ruling party. When Mamduh Salim asked the Higher Council of Sufi Orders to endorse the progovernment platform in the 1976 elections, the council's president, Muhammad Mahmud al-Sutuhi of the al-Sutuhiya al-Ahmadiya, responded that the orders did not wish to become directly involved in partisan politics. Satisfied that it would not face a potential threat in the countryside comparable to the agricultural cooperatives under Ahmad Yunis, the government did not press the issue. When al-Sutuhi died in 1982, he was succeeded by Abu al-Wafa al-Taftazani, a professor of philosophy at Cairo University, who steered the council closer to the conservative teachings of al-Azhar while preserving its formal neutrality in day-to-day politics.[52]

Corporatism has not only encouraged important changes in the organization of the Sufi fraternities and their relations with the state; in some cases it has helped to alter their brand of piety and their social bases as well. As early as the 1960s momentum within the Sufi movement already had shifted toward newer orders that placed an unusual emphasis on bureaucracy, conformity with the *shari'a*, the avoidance of magic and superstition, and the leadership of civil servants and businessmen.

One of the prototypes of this sanitized Sufism was the al-Hamidiya al-Shadhiliya order, founded in the early twentieth century and formally recognized only in the 1920s. Michael Gilsenan argues that the distinctive characteristics that previously had limited this order's popular following were precisely the factors that made the group attractive to the state after the 1967 War and throughout the Sadat era. These characteristics included an elaborate hierarchy of officials who insulated the *shaykh* from personal contact with his followers, a detailed set of internal regulations that explicitly emphasized the Qur'an and Sunna over ecstatic and emotional rituals, a unique prohibition against membership in any other religious organization, and the preeminence of a new middle-class elite more closely connected with the state than with the petite bourgeoisie and the working class.[53]

By the end of the 1970s the al-Hamidiya al-Shadhiliya appeared to be flourishing as a leading example of what the government considered a "true and proper" form of Sufism, but its artificially imposed order and conformity were breeding serious internal divisions. With funds and land provided by the state, the commercial and professional elite moved the *tariqa*'s headquarters from the popular quarter of Bulaq to a new site in Zamalak directly across from the Gazira Club. When the *shaykh* of the order died, the organization quickly split between the middle-class leaders who transported his remains to the new mosque and the impoverished majority who rallied around the *shaykh's* younger brother, demonstrating their determination to retain the *tariqa's* center of gravity in Bulaq.[54]

The al-Hamidiya al-Shadhiliya provides an instructive example of the inherent limitations of the state's attempt to manipulate the Sufi orders through corporatist initiatives. Because its early development had involved a relatively high degree of administrative centralization and spiritual restraint, the *tariqa* seemed particularly amenable to the more formal methods of cooptation and regulation that were adopted during the 1970s. However, when corporatist controls were combined with the ascendence of privileged strata benefiting from the government's capitalist economic policies, an important showcase of the "new Sufism" began to break apart. By endorsing leaders who appeared to supersede rather than mediate the powerful links between the *shaykh's* family and its mass following, the government unwittingly stimulated exactly the tendencies it had hoped to discourage: a succession crisis that ended in schism and a revival of popular religious sentiment focusing on saint worship, miracles, and *baraka*.[55]

Philanthropic Associations and Private Mosques

By far the most numerically significant type of religious group is composed of philanthropic and mosque-building associations. Most of these are small groups that began as private, voluntary organizations and then gradually became enmeshed in such an extensive net of state regulation and sponsorship that they now constitute a hybrid category combining both pluralist and corporatist characteristics. The leaders of philanthropic associations have been fairly successful in preserving a delicate balance between their voluntarist origins and the generally uninvited embrace of the state. Many of these groups have been able to retain formal ownership of their clinics, schools, and orphanages despite steady government intrusion into financing and management. When these facilities have been appropriated by expansionist ministries, the associations have been able to regenerate similar projects, sometimes on an even more ambitious scale than their predecessors.[56]

In the area of mosque construction and administration, however, the coexistence of public and private initiative has been more conflictual and unstable. Collective worship has become increasingly divided between "government mosques" *(al-jawami' al-hukumiya),* owned and managed by the state, and "private mosques" *(al-jawami' al-ahliya),* owned and managed by individuals or associations of local subscribers. Unlike other voluntary organizations, private mosques that accept state subsidies are not likely to settle down in the twilight of semicorporatist arrangements but tend to be transformed sooner or later through outright annexation into incontestably public entities.[57]

When the broad category of religious associations is disaggregated into Christian and Muslim varieties, striking differences are evident in the levels, structures, and social correlates of collective action in the two religious communities. The rate of association formation among Christians is approximately five times the rate among Muslims. In 1982 there were about 1,600 Muslim groups and about 600 Christian groups. If Christians are slightly more than 6 percent of the total population, then on a nationwide basis the Christian community contains twenty-six associations per 100,000 people compared to five groups per 100,000 Muslims.[58]

Several factors contribute to this unusually high level of associational pluralism among Egyptian Christians. Sectarian diversity encourages organizational proliferation with numerous confessional subgroups seeking to affirm and preserve their distinctive identities. The common sense of insecurity in the relatively small Christian minorities promotes a desire to increase communal self-reliance and to fashion associational bridges that can reduce deep class and regional divisions between coreligionists. Such divisions are particularly evident between the relatively prosperous business and professional elements in the major cities and their brethren in the provincial towns and villages of Upper Egypt. Furthermore, continuing legal restrictions on church building tend to divert Christians' collective action into the less rigidly controlled channel of voluntary organizations, many of which have been accused of operating unauthorized places of worship.[59]

Christian and Muslim groups also differ in terms of their predominant types of legal status and formal organization. Most Christian associations are registered specifically as religious groups and are required to limit their activities to a single, clearly defined goal. Most Muslim groups, on the other hand, are registered as multifunctional organizations, which are allowed to engage in a variety of activities, such as education, philanthropy, and construction. This contrast in formal, structural characteristics reflects an implicit distinction in public policy concerning the regulation of associational life in the two religious communities. In the case of Christian groups, the scope of activity is narrowly circumscribed by the state, but associational autonomy is otherwise preserved. In the case of Muslim groups, a broader range of action is permitted, but government

TABLE 6-3.   Correlates of Associability among Muslims and Christians

	Christian Associations	Percentage Muslim	Percentage Christian	Literacy
Muslim associations	.47	− .56	.55	.22
Christian associations		− .37	.36	.52

intervention is more extensive, including both tighter bureaucratic controls and more generous subsidization.

Finally, there are striking differences in the social correlates of collective action among Christians and Muslims (Table 6–3). Christian associability is closely related to the percentage of Christians in the local population, with the notable exception of three metropolitan areas and three Upper Egyptian provinces. Port Saʿid, Suez, and Cairo have very high rates of associability and only moderate proportions of Christians, whereas Minya, Assyut, and Sohag have moderate rates of associability and very high proportions of Christians. These six provinces provide the clearest evidence of the regional gap in the art of association between the Christian communities of the big cities and Upper Egypt. Accordingly, the level of socioeconomic development is a much better predictor of Christian organizations than the size of the Christian community.

Muslim associations, however, have a very weak relation to development and a surprisingly strong *negative* relation to the percentage of Muslims in the local population. Ironically, the main correlates of Muslim associability are the size of the local Christian minority and the propensity of that minority to engage in collective action. These findings suggest highly competitive and mutually reinforcing processes of association formation that both reflect and heighten the country's communal antagonisms. While this is a nationwide phenomenon, it is particularly serious in the six Upper Egyptian provinces between Fayyum and Qena that contain over half of Egypt's Christian population.[60]

Another example of rivalry between differentially structured religious groups is the increasing tension between private and government efforts to organize collective worship among Muslims. Between 1962 and 1982 the total number of mosques in Egypt nearly doubled (Table 6–4).[61] In the nation as a whole, private mosques continued to outnumber government mosques by a ratio of roughly four to one. Within the category of private mosques, however, there was a relative decline of independently financed mosques and a sharp increase in state-assisted establishments.

TABLE 6-4. Trends in Government and Private Mosque Building, 1962–1982

	1962			1982		
	Number	Percentage	Mosques per 100,000 Population	Number	Percentage	Mosques per 100,000 Population
Government	3,006	17.4	11.0	6,071	18.6	14.0
Private	14,212	82.6	51.8	26,622	81.4	61.4
(with state aid)	(999)	(5.8)	(3.6)	(7,160)	(21.9)	(16.5)
(without aid)	(13,213)	(76.8)	(48.2)	(19,462)	(59.5)	(44.9)
Total	17,218	100.0	63.1	32,693	100.0	75.5

Source: Morroe Berger, *Islam in Egypt Today: Social and Political Aspects of Popular Religion* (Cambridge: Cambridge University Press, 1970), p. 18; Wizarat al-Awqaf.

The growth of independent private mosques did not keep up with the increase in population, and it lagged far behind the growth of establishments owned or subsidized by the state.

When trends in mosque building are examined at the provincial level, we find clear evidence of long-term government efforts to alter the ratio of private and state mosques in nearly every locality. In each region the state employed a particular combination of techniques to shift the relative balance of public and private mosques in the desired direction—accelerating or freezing government mosque building, granting or withholding financial subsidies and building permits for private mosques, and annexing private mosques that had become dependent on government aid. Where government mosques had been relatively overbuilt, there was a transfer of resources to support private efforts. Where private mosques had enjoyed a virtual monopoly, their proliferation was slowed and they were challenged by new government-supported rivals. In a few areas the state stimulated both public and private construction in a particularly competitive manner.

After more than twenty years of increased state intervention, there was a steady erosion of the once clear distinction between local initiatives to organize collective worship from below and official initiatives toward organization from above. With mosques, as with many other facilities connected to voluntary associations, much of what is formally private is in fact promoted and eventually appropriated by the state. Alternatively, much of what is formally public was originally created by private, voluntary initiative and has been attached to a bureaucratic apparatus in which regulatory ambition far exceeds managerial and financial resources. Although the government says that it annexes private mosques only when their patrons are unable to keep them in good repair, officials in the Ministry of Awqaf quietly admit that the most prosperous establishments are the most likely to fall under state control.

Sadat's audacious order of September 1981 that all private mosques be nationalized was not an abrupt break with preceding policy. Rather it was an intensification of long-term government efforts to dominate a key dimension of religious associability. Sadat declared that his objective was to make state regulation of collective worship more direct and comprehensive, to implement a uniform, nationwide policy instead of providing a different combination of inducements and constraints for public and private mosques in each region. Nevertheless, when we compare trends in mosque building before and after the annexations of September 1981, we observe three divergent policy patterns each of which encompasses a different group of provinces. These inconsistencies suggest that the nationalization campaign was motivated by Sadat's desire for political revenge and limited by the bureaucracy's inability to implement his hasty and ill-conceived commands.

First, in Upper Egypt the initiative in mosque building shifted from the private sector to the state sector in a clear and continuous manner throughout the period from 1962 to 1982. Increasing state aid to private organizations and eventual annexation were key instruments for tightening government regulation. In 1962 the proportion of private mosques in these provinces receiving government subsidies ranged between 3 percent and 13 percent; by 1982 the rate had risen to 70 percent in Minya, 60 percent in Assyut, 40 percent in Giza, and 25 percent in Bani Swayf and Aswan. In Sohag and, above all, in Assyut there was unusually intense competition between public and private mosque building. By 1982 these two provinces were among the nation's leaders in both categories of mosques. Upper Egypt provinces were among the leading targets of the 1981 nationalizations. In Minya, Assyut, and Giza between one-third and one-half of all private mosques were annexed by the state. Hence, it is in Upper Egypt that one finds greatest support for the argument that Sadat was trying to rein in a burgeoning religious movement that was largely his own creation.

Second, in the largest metropolitan areas, private mosques grew at a much more rapid pace than government mosques until 1981. Then the Sadat government halted this trend with cuts in state subsidies and with annexations that occasionally approached the magnitude of those in Upper Egypt. In Cairo the government was able to stem the rise in private mosque building with relatively little resort to nationalization because a large portion of these establishments had been created with state funds in the first place. In Alexandria, however, the growth of private mosques was almost entirely the result of an independent movement by local organizations. Accordingly, the government's crackdown on Alexandrian mosques was more severe and much more likely to involve nationalization than was the case in Cairo. By far the most abrupt reversal of policy occurred in the cities of the Canal Zone. In Port Saʿid and Suez the state promoted private mosque building on an extraordinary scale, especially during the resettlement and reconstruction of the 1970s, and then suddenly appropriated most of these establishments in the final days of Sadat's reign.

Imams in the private mosques of Alexandria and Suez had combined in strong associations that were led by two of Sadat's most caustic critics—Shaykh Ahmad al-Mahalawi and Shaykh Hafiz al-Salama. During the same speech in which Sadat announced the annexation campaign, he made a particularly tasteless reference to the arrest of the frail *shaykh* from Alexandria, boasting that he had been "thrown into prison like a dog." This sort of invective seriously discredited the nationalization policy, prompting Mubarak to return most of the jailed imams to their posts after he assumed power.[62]

Finally, in the frontier provinces and the more urban-industrial areas of the Delta, the growth of private mosques continued to exceed the growth of government mosques even after 1981. In the frontier provinces (Sinai, the Red Sea, Matruh, and the New Valley) the newly emergent network of private mosques is, like most aspects of associational life in these regions, largely a creation of the state. Similarly, in the Delta provinces of Damietta, Gharbiya, Qalubiya, and Kafr al-Shaykh mosque building has relied heavily on large government subsidies. These regions were the areas that were least affected by the annexations of private mosques in 1981. Outside the capital city, they were also the regions in which religious associations were most closely tied to the state.

Thus, regarding both philanthropic and mosque-building groups, greater state intervention has failed to fashion a more coherent organizational structure out of preexisting associations. During the past two decades there has been a gradual diversification of religious groups and a steady increase in the conflict generated by their growing competition. More than any other sector of associational life in contemporary Egypt, religious groups have become a catalyst for polarization along several dimensions at the same time: between semiofficial groups and purely voluntary associations; between organized Muslims and organized Christians; and between communities that actively solicit state subsidies versus those that prefer to avoid outside aid in order to preserve their traditions of local independence.

The Islamic Associations

A fourth type of religious group, more clearly pluralist in nature, is composed of the so-called Islamic associations *(al-jama'aat al-Islamiya),* which have attracted great attention since the mid-1970s because of their rapid spread among working-class neighborhoods in the big cities and their domination of student politics in many of the major universities. To maintain their private, voluntary character, these groups have chosen to remain on the margins of legitimacy occupied by those extralegal organizations that refuse to register with the Ministry of Social Affairs. Nevertheless, in view of their extensive social welfare activities, the formal autonomy of these groups is seldom taken at face value.

Islamic associations commonly have been accused of accepting covert contributions from the state as part of a campaign to undercut the Left in its traditional strongholds, or of receiving subsidies from other Arab countries that sought to curb the Sadat regime's cosmopolitan and pro-Western excesses, or of providing funds and safe houses for members of underground revolutionary societies. In all probability most of the Islamic associations have done none of these things. Rather, their ability to combine autonomy and voluntarism with effective collective action can be considered an example of the intimate connection between nongovernmental Islam and the art of association that has impressed observers of Egypt for several decades.[63]

The leaders of the Islamic associations trace the origin of their groups to the Qasr al-'Aini hospital, where, in 1970, young doctors and interns first encountered imprisoned members of the Muslim Brotherhood who were receiving medical treatment. Influenced by their discussions with the prisoners and by the heated debates they observed between rival factions of the Ikhwan, the doctors began to organize study groups in which they read the works of several Ikhwan authors that had been published outside Egypt. These groups spread to the medical faculties of Cairo University, 'Ain Shams University, and al-Azhar, and then also to universities in Alexandria, Mansura, Minya, and Assyut.[64]

The doctors acknowledge that their early efforts received important guidance and support from a number of senior *shuyukh* at al-Azhar, such as Muhammad al-Ghazali, Hasan al-Baquri, and Sayyid Sabiq, who in their youth had developed ''in the school of the Muslim Brotherhood.'' The leaders of these groups commonly emphasize that their thinking has always centered on the writing and example of Hasan al-Banna', not on the works of Sayyid Qutb. Indeed, they characterize Qutb's followers as forming "isolationist and terrorist societies" *(jama'aat in'izaliya wa ir-habiya)* that have no connection with the Islamic associations and that denounce them as infidels.[65]

In response to assertions that the Sadat government's support was responsible for their success, the leaders of the Islamic associations insist that, in fact, Sadat fought them every step of the way. They declare that in the early 1970s university administrators repeatedly turned down their requests to organize welcoming ceremonies for entering students. In 1972 and 1973, they say, Sufi Abu Talib, then rector of Cairo University, tried to recruit them to fight against Nasserist and Marxist students, but they told him they were not "a stick in the hands of the authorities." From 1973 onward student unions permitted the Islamic associations to organize "cultural camps" on campuses in several cities. According to the association leaders, the government allowed these activities only because one of Sadat's cronies, Muhammad 'Uthman Isma'il, thought he could use them to infiltrate the new groups with his own sympathizers and agents. Although association leaders argue that Isma'il had very little success in Cairo and the Delta, they admit that he became a constant thorn in their side in Upper Egypt during his long hold on the governorship of Assyut from 1973 until 1982.[66]

Between 1975 and 1977 the Islamic associations became the leading force in student politics. Expanding from one faculty to another and from one city to another, they soon controlled the country's only nationwide student organization, the Confederation of Egyptian Students. Although Nasserists and Marxists contend that Sadat paved the way for the victories of Muslim students, the Islamic associations note that university and police officials tried to disqualify many of their candidates and that only court intervention prevented the government from rigging the elections. Moreover, the Islamic associations state that after taking over the student confederation, they regularly provided legal defense for leftist students who were being harassed by the government and helped to finance the independent publications of both leftist and Christian groups on several campuses.[67]

The Islamic associations attribute their popularity not only to their political independence but, above all, to their imagination in addressing the needs and grievances of students who were struggling for survival in overcrowded classrooms and in an inflationary economy. The associations used the funds and authority of the student confederation to supply a number of widely appreciated services. Expensive textbooks and lecture notes were published and sold at about one-fifth of their market price. Study halls were arranged in local mosques for those who found it impossible to work in noisy dormitories. A special bus service was established for female students who had become fed up with the daily indignities of public transportation. When the managers of the cafeterias at Cairo University were accused of selling drugs on campus and of drawing female students into prostitution rings, the Islamic associations persuaded the university to find other concessionaires. When the new operators continued the same illegal activities, the associations asked the university to shut them down and, then, tried to drive them out of business by opening their own student run cafeterias.[68]

Gradually, the Islamic associations began to devote more and more student resources to the special needs of their religiously motivated constituents. These efforts focused on organizing exhibitions of religious books, providing various types of ''Islamic costumes'' at discount prices, and arranging group fares for annual pilgrimages. Emboldened by their considerable power and popularity, the associations sometimes sought to impose their private views on the entire university community even when their leaders candidly admitted that such demands had no basis in the *shari'a*. These demands began with the relatively modest and widely endorsed suggestion that male and female students sit in separate rows while attending public lectures. Before long, however, the associations were opposing jazz concerts, dancing, ''indecent'' films, chaperoned trips, and virtually any appearance of public ''courtship.''[69]

Almost immediately after Sadat's trip to Jerusalem, it was obvious that the Islamic associations were on a collision course with the government. Throughout 1978 the associations clashed with supporters of the ruling party in several student unions. In some provinces police closed the associations' cultural camps; in others the camps were allowed to convene but the government prohibited the student confederation from paying for them with its own funds. In 1979 Sadat abolished the Confederation of Egyptian Students and froze its assets. Thenceforth student associations could form only in individual faculties, not at the university or national levels. Appointed professors rather than elected students held the majority of votes in the councils of these associations, and university deans were allowed to veto all council decisions.[70]

The confrontation with the government enhanced the popularity of the Islamic associations but weakened their more moderate leaders. Facing new restrictions in the universities, the associations were forced to improve their alliances with nonstudent groups. They began to increase their activities in working-class neighborhoods and to organize mass public prayers on religious holidays, especially 'Id al-Fitr and 'Id al-Adha. They cooperated with members of the Muslim Brotherhood to bolster the Islamic factions in several professional organizations, such as the doctors', pharmacists', and journalists' syndicates. By early 1981 they formed the Federation of Islamic Associations, which joined the Muslim Brotherhood and a number of Azhari *shuyukh* in organizing the Permanent Congress for Islamic Preaching (al-Mu'tamar al-Da'im lil-Da'wa al-Islamiya).[71]

On the other hand, Sadat's growing hostility toward the associations tended to radicalize many of their members and to undercut the position of their original leadership. The government began to blame numerous assaults and sectarian clashes on the Islamic associations, eventually accusing them of trying to provoke a religious civil war *(fitna ta'ifiya)* between Muslims and Christians. The leaders of the associations countered that many of these incidents never occurred and that the police were encouraged to make them up. They described other incidents as isolated quarrels with no political overtones or as the work of renegade members who were trying to drag others into personal vendettas.[72]

On two important occasions—during sectarian fighting in the Minya village of Jad al-Sayyid in 1980 and in the Cairene neighborhood of al-Zawiya al-Hamra' in 1981—the Islamic associations accused the government of instigating the bloodshed and then using it as a pretext for cracking down on their members. In the Minya incident, a large crowd of Muslims gathered in a mosque after two of them allegedly had been fired upon while walking through the local Christian district. Members of an Islamic association supposedly had quieted the crowd when police stormed the mosque with tear gas, arresting several innocent bystanders. When angry residents besieged the police headquarters, the minister of interior, Nabawi Isma'il, carried on an all-night negotiating session by telephone with Dr. Hilmi al-Jazzar, the titular head of all of the Islamic associations, finally agreeing to release the prisoners if the crowd would disperse. However, the very next day, as soon as Sadat returned from a trip to the United States, he not only rejected the compromise but ordered mass arrests of association members in both Minya and Assyut.[73]

According to the leaders of the Islamic associations, the al-Zawiya al-Hamra' incident the following year began when the local branch of the ruling party prodded Muslims to seize a plot of land on which Christians already had been given permission to build a church. When the police lost control of the situation, the minister of interior once again invited the associations to intervene and ask the Muslims to lay down their arms. The associations quickly formed a committee of reconciliation that included 'Umar al-Tilmisani and several *'ulama'* who were sympathetic to the Muslim Brotherhood. The Islamic associations say they mobilized 10,000 youths in support of the committee, allowing it to end overnight the violence that police and ruling party officials had failed to quell for several days.[74]

As after the earlier incident in Minya, the willingness of the Islamic associations to cooperate with the government in a local crisis earned them not gratitude or legitimacy but renewed repression. The display of strength that helped to contain both situations merely deepened Sadat's determination to crush the groups once and for all. After the mass arrests of September 1981 the associations' leaders became convinced that the episode at al-Zawiya al-Hamra' had been fabricated by the security forces so that Sadat could begin to tighten the noose around all of his political opponents in the name of "national unity."

The rebuilding of the Islamic associations under the Mubarak government has involved renewed efforts to diversify their constituency and to emphasize a gradualist strategy of social change. They have not only resumed their leading position in the student unions but made new inroads into many faculty clubs as well. However, their most important gains have been outside the university campuses. They have nominated more candidates in the elections of professional syndicates. They have equipped and staffed a number of low-cost clinics in working-class neighborhoods. They have opened several private schools that combine religious instruction with foreign language training, providing middle-class families with attractive alternatives to both the poorer public system and the Western-dominated private schools. And they have helped to increase the amount of personal savings invested in Islamic banks and development companies.[75]

By spelling out more explicitly their views of social reform, the associations' leaders hoped to distinguish themselves from both their allies and rivals in the Islamic movement. Given the early and continuing importance of al-Azhar's medical school as a recruiting ground for the Islamic associations, it is not surprising that they would try to clarify their relationship with the *'ulama'*. The *'ulama'*, they argue, have the "largest share" of responsibility for Islamic preaching *(al-da'wa al-islamiya)*, but it is an error to assume that this special role constitutes anything approaching a monopoly of authority. On the contrary, in their judgment, it is the responsibility of all Muslims to propagate their religion and to reshape society according to its ideals.[76]

The associations have been equally concerned to establish a separate identity from the Muslim Brotherhood. The Ikhwan were the original model for the intellectual and organizational development of the Islamic associations. The older leaders of the Ikhwan have provided them with frequent counsel and guidance, mediating many of their quarrels with the Sadat and Mubarak governments and generally trying to discourage the younger generation from emphasizing political activity over religious and philanthropic work.

The Islamic associations have come to differ markedly from the Ikhwan in placing the need to change society ahead of the need to change the state. Since Sadat's assassination, the Ikhwan have become an informal political party and a sizeable block in parliament, whereas the Islamic associations have evolved into a series of increasingly self-sufficient local communities. Recently, the associations' emphasis on building an Islamic society from the bottom up has found greater resonance among the Muslim Brotherhood as well. Softening their earlier demands for the rapid implementation of the *shari'a,* many of the Ikhwan have begun to embrace the associations' view that the Islamization of Egypt's legal and political systems must await further advances in the Islamization of the people.[77]

Most of all, however, the Islamic associations have been eager to divorce themselves from the revolutionary societies of religious militants seeking the immediate establishment of an Islamic state via guerilla warfare. While the associations' leaders condemn all forms of terrorism (including "intellectual terrorism," "political terrorism," and "police terrorism"), they insist that "religious terrorism is the most reprehensible of all because it misuses the name of Islam."[78] Instead, they advocate a "step-by-step" process of social change through persuasion and example, beginning with the individual *(al-fard),* expanding to the family *(al-usra),* and then to many "small societies" *(mujtama'aat saghira)* that will ultimately "stand shoulder to shoulder" *(tatakatif)* in constituting the "great society" *(al-mujtama' al-kabir).*[79]

The heads of the Islamic associations have tried to elaborate an ideal image of religious leadership that represents both a call for greater restraint among their followers and a clear criticism of all they think is lacking in the Muslim revolutionaries. Describing the "essential personal characteristics" of an Islamic leader, they emphasize knowledge of the Qur'an, honesty *(sidq),* compassion *(rahma),* modesty *(tawadu'),* flexibility *(lin),* and patience *(sabr).* In describing the means by which their cause is to be carried to the masses, the Islamic associations are so eager to portray themselves as legitimist that they have begun to appear conventional and unimaginative. Reform through "practical action" is cited last after reform through "speech" and through "writing." When association leaders specify the types of action they regard as most appropriate, they most commonly mention supplying material benefits to the poor (particularly through clinics, hospitals, charity, and business enterprises) as well as providing a personal model through exemplary behavior *(al-qudwa al-hasana)*.[80]

The Revolutionary Societies

The postassassination efforts of the *jama'aat* toward a rapprochement with the new government reflected their appreciation of some critical differences between Sadat and Mubarak in dealing with the diversity of religious organizations. In his public statements, Sadat did his best to blur distinctions between the Muslim Brotherhood, the Islamic associations, and the revolutionary societies. Sadat was well aware of the rivalries between these groups, particularly of the radicals' contempt for the "collaborationism" of the Ikhwan and the "reformism" of the *jama'aat*. Nevertheless, he thought it useful to portray fanatical fringe groups such as al-Takfir wa al-Hijra as making up the "secret army" of the Muslim Brotherhood.[81]

As the Mubarak government consolidated power, however, it became increasingly clear that the evidence contradicted Sadat's declarations. The testimony of the assassins, the statements of Ikhwan and *jama'aat* leaders, and the findings of independent scholars all pointed in the same direction: the armed extremists were a small and isolated fringe of the Islamic movement who were as hostile to other Muslim organizations as they were to the regime. Accordingly, the Mubarak government began to discard Sadat's indiscriminate hostility toward his religious critics, trying instead to take advantage of their mutual differences in order to discredit and crush the remaining pockets of armed resistance.

Mubarak has permitted the Muslim Brotherhood a greater voice as a legitimate parliamentary opposition while allowing the Islamic associations to reach out to a larger constituency among both middle-class and working-class Egyptians. By tolerating more open debate and organization among those advocating peaceful and liberal paths to Islamic reform, he has tried to free the security forces for the urgent task of hunting down the most desperate and militant groups who see no hope of creating an Islamic society until the "infidel" state is overthrown.

As Mubarak gradually adopted a more flexible attitude toward Muslim associations, several divergent explanations were offered for the appearance of the revolutionary societies. Immediately after Sadat's assassination the government asserted that such groups were "alien" to Egypt, implying that they had no firm roots in Egyptian society and that they must have been directed from abroad. Amid the tension and uncertainty following the assassination, so many members of parliament interpreted the government's statements literally that Mubarak was forced to reveal more details of the murder plot in order to head off an incipient war party that was demanding swift "reprisals" against Libya.

In contrast, the older leaders of the Ikhwan argued that the state itself had paved the way for religious fanaticism by depriving political opponents not only of their civil rights but of their dignity as human beings. In their view the brutality of Nasser's prison camps had embittered an entire generation of young Muslims, driving them to embrace the increasingly deviant interpretations of the role of *jihad* that were articulated by Sayyid Qutb, Shukri Mustafa, and ʿAbd al-Salam Faraj.[82]

Perhaps the most persuasive explanations came from a number of investigators who tried to identify the sociological origins of the three most important revolutionary societies: the members of the Military Academy group who were arrested in 1974; the al-Takfir wa al-Hijra group, who were captured in 1977; and the Tanzim al-Jihad, who murdered Sadat in 1981. Each of these studies traced the Islamic militants' support to specific socioeconomic, regional, and generational cleavages within Egyptian society—cleavages that the state has exacerbated through its own policies of rapid and uneven social change. Together, the studies concluded that the major breeding grounds of the revolutionary societies have been the newer and less stable centers of urban migration in Greater Cairo and Giza; the provincial capitals of Upper Egypt, where erratic growth based on petro-dollars has helped to inflame long-standing sectarian antagonisms; and university students from modest families and small-town backgrounds who have seen their hopes for advancement cut short by diminishing employment opportunities.[83]

As it gradually recognized the internal roots of religious extremism, the Mubarak government was able to pursue a strategy of selective tolerance that helped to neutralize the most dangerous segments of the Islamic opposition. By distinguishing between types of religious groups, by encouraging many of them to compete more openly in public debate and private enterprise, and by tacitly admitting that the regime's past mistakes had contributed to some of its current problems, the government was able to isolate the militants more and more from other Islamic organizations. In time, however, this very success prompted the underground groups to launch a new wave of political violence. During the spring of 1987, after the parliamentary elections that paved the way for Mubarak's second term in office, Islamic revolutionaries carried out a series of armed assaults against Hasan Abu Basha, a former minister of interior, Makram Muhammad Ahmad, the director of the Dar al-Hilal publishing house, and members of the U.S. embassy staff.

In response to these attacks, the security forces closed off entire neighborhoods, conducting house-to-house searches and arresting thousands of young men in the hunt for the suspected gunmen. At the same time the government made a number of unusually open and direct appeals for the support of liberal Muslim opinion. The state-controlled media produced a steady stream of broadcasts and articles denouncing "terrorism" and political violence, but their tone was clearly intended to win over the bulk of the Islamic opposition, not to discredit it.

Although they did not mention the leaders of the Muslim Brotherhood by name, several commentators and writers began to express views that were strikingly reminiscent of arguments that had been made many times before by Hasan al-Banna', Hasan Hudaybi, and 'Umar al-Tilmisani in attacking radical factions and splinter groups that advocated the creation of an Islamic state through force. In effect, the Mubarak government was tapping into a crucial debate that had divided the Muslim Brotherhood for half a century, implicitly endorsing moderate positions that the Ikhwan leadership had never been able to enforce among many of its own members and sympathizers.[84]

Most of this debate was conducted not by *'ulama'* but by lay experts in Islamic law who were less likely to be perceived as semiofficial spokesmen. A key issue was the proper interpretation of a popular Prophetic tradition that had served for decades as a slogan of religious militants seeking scriptural justification for violent political action: "He among you who sees an abomination *[munkaran]* must correct it with his hand; if he is unable, then with his tongue; if he is unable, then with his heart. And the last of these is the weakest of faith."[85]

Already in the late 1930s Hasan al-Banna' rejected the contention of dissident Ikhwan that this tradition sanctioned violent social change "with the hand." He consistently tried to contradict this tradition by appealing to more authoritative Qur'anic verses that urged believers to correct injustice through debate *(jadal),* self-discipline *(taqwa),* and patience *(sabr).* The inability of al-Banna' and subsequent Ikhwan leaders to discredit radical interpretations of this tradition was a major factor contributing to recurrent schisms and power struggles within the Muslim Brotherhood and to its periodic repression by the state.[86]

As the Mubarak government tightened its dragnet around the underground societies, several commentators revived discussion of this tradition, seeking not to refute it but to subject it to increasingly quiescent interpretations. One view held that the tradition actually recommended protest through speech when effective action was impossible and silent forbearance when neither action nor free speech were possible. Those who preferred to change society "with the tongue" or "with the heart" might be considered weaker in faith, but under unfavorable circumstances they had no other choice.

Another view read the tradition as outlining a division of labor between social groups with different aptitudes and responsiblilties. Change "with the hand" was reserved for those who held the reins of government and their expert advisers. Change "with the tongue" was the duty of those who were well instructed in the understanding of the *shari'a*—a category including but not restricted to the *'ulama'*. Change "with the heart" was the proper role of the pious citizens who must do their best to live exemplary lives despite difficult conditions. Both of these views already enjoyed considerable support among older members of the Ikhwan and they were frequently repeated by lay scholars who appeared on Friday evening television discussions of religious questions.

In July 1987 a particularly lengthy and serious treatment of the tradition appeared in *al-Hilal,* a popular monthly magazine whose editor had been one of the chief targets of the armed attacks by religious extremists just a few weeks earlier. The author, Dr. Muhammad Salim al-'Awwa, agreed in principle that all Muslims had a duty to "order what is right and eliminate what is prohibited," but he complained that historically they had tended to oscillate between the extreme positions of ignoring that duty *(tafrit)* and trying to fulfill it with excessive zeal *(ifrat)*. Hence, Muslims were still unable to break out of an endless cycle of despotism and anarchy. Parodying the militants' condemnation of Egyptian society as languishing in a state of spiritual ignorance *(jahaliya),* he explained that Egypt's current crisis stemmed from the ignorance of those who believed that they had the right to impose their will unilaterally. In his opinion, this ignorance could be dispelled only by spelling out the specific conditions under which Muslims have the right to change society "with the hand." [87]

First of all, change must occur in stages and by degrees. He acknowledged that the disputed tradition sanctioned three methods for effecting change, but he insisted that extremists had reversed the proper sequence in which these methods were to be employed. Muslims' efforts to correct abuses must begin "with the heart," proceeding to change "with the tongue" if milder measures are ineffective, and advancing to change "with the hand" only as a last resort. Furthermore, a believer should consider change "with the hand" only when it is certain that failure to do so will result in civil strife *(fitna)* that is greater than the evil he is trying to eliminate.

Second, the right to effect change is reserved to particular individuals who possess adequate knowledge of what Islam commands and what it forbids. In a nation where anyone can change what he regards as contrary to Islam, the result is anarchy, which destroys the rights of the individual as well as the rights of society as a whole. What is required is knowledge based on independent judgment *(al-'ilm al-ijtihadi)* that is backed by solid evidence. This provides Muslims with greater latitude than the "imitative knowledge" *(al-'ilm al-taqlidi)* of the state-appointed *'ulama'*, but it does not endorse the "dictated knowledge" *(al-'ilm al-talqini)* of self-appointed preachers who advance idiosyncratic views on well-accepted matters of scripture and law.

Finally, change "with the hand" is appropriate only in those matters where the community has developed a broad consensus that current practice clearly violates the *shari'a*. The "genius" of an Islamic society is that it requires the entire citizenry to define morality in terms of the public interest, not merely as a set of personal obligations. But this genius also requires that both the state and its opponents respect inevitable differences of opinion and agree to protect everyone's right to express and defend his point of view. Muslims cannot equate change "with the hand" and change "with the revolver" because their mission is to preach and advise, not to punish and exact retribution. Similarly, the state cannot respond to the violence that stems from deviant thinking with violence of its own because force alone can never destroy ideas or correct misguided people.[88]

The same issue of *al-Hilal* carried several other articles that argued that despite outbreaks of "religious terrorism," there are signs of a more tolerant competition between the government and its Islamic opponents that is compatible with further advances toward democracy. Addressing "those who are afraid of Islam and those who are afraid for it," Dr. Ahmad Kamal Abu al-Majd asserted that the regime's confrontation with religious revolutionaries is, in fact, yielding an unanticipated but highly desirable side effect, the strengthening of Islamic liberalism. In his view the most lasting achievement of the revolutionaries has been to highlight the gap separating them from the vast majority of organized Muslims who value civility and moderation. "The deviant behavior of marginal and extremist tributaries has given birth to a greater vigilance and consciousness among large groups of religious and political activists engaging in social action within the reformist mainstream of Islam."[89]

Like many other Muslim commentators, however, Dr. al-Majd coupled his censure of the radicals with a clear warning to the government not to repeat Sadat's blunder of attacking the entire Islamic movement for the crimes of a small minority. "Tens of millions of Muslims have dedicated themselves to a living interpretation of Islam and its principles which transcends the traditional religious views that are still repeated by many official and governmental pulpits. . . . Whoever lacks reason also lacks religion, [but] whoever lacks liberty cannot be condemned for his behavior."[90]

Apparently taking such warnings to heart, the government press began to distinguish more explicitly than ever between the Islamic associations and extremist vigilante groups that tried to take the law into their own hands. *Al-Musawwar,* the most popular publication of Dar al-Hilal, carried interviews with the leaders of a radical society in Minya that was summarily dispensing its own version of "Islamic justice." They admitted raiding a video store that was distributing "obscene" foreign movies, seizing a truckload of beer and destroying the cargo, and disrupting an open-air celebration that featured popular music. In justifying these measures, the "philosopher" of the group identified himself with the same radical interpretation of change "with the hand" that government and liberal Muslim spokesmen had been refuting for months.[91]

Al-Musawwar carefully avoided exaggerating the group's popularity and its ties with mainstream Islamic associations. Instead, the editors noted that many in the group had already served prison terms for instigating the uprising in Assyut that followed Sadat's assassination. Indeed, *al-Musawwar* acknowledged that Islamic associations in Upper Egypt were among the leading victims of attacks by such groups. The magazine gave prominent attention to assaults on the imams of private mosques that were being managed by Islamic associations in the towns of Manfalut and Abu Tij. In both cases, local townspeople had come to the defense of the imams, fighting off radical intruders who tried to take over the mosques and helping the police to apprehend them. Instead of authorizing the routine arrests of members of Islamic associations, the police chief praised them for their energetic cooperation in combating "terrorism." Instead of using the incidents as an excuse to nationalize more private mosques, the Ministry of Awqaf dispatched a committee of leading *shuyukh* from al-Azhar to congratulate "the pious people of Assyut" for upholding "the sanctity of public worship and the dignity of the *'ulama'*."[92]

7

Unruly Corporatism in the Third World

Mubarak's presidency has been marked by a gradual revival of statecraft in dealing with civil society that is a welcome departure from his predecessor's fatal penchant for brinkmanship and repression. Instead of deploring the growing diversity and vitality of Egypt's associational life, Mubarak has tolerated a more heterogeneous group universe that can be manipulated by the regime's supporters and opponents alike.

Sadat tended to view wide disparities in the structure and influence of organized interests as a threat to his monopoly of power; his solution was to impose a more centralized and uniform version of corporatism that would strengthen and enrich his associational allies, who could then more effectively stifle and crush dissent among their constituents. Mubarak, however, has carefully avoided all efforts to refashion group life into a coherent system of representation, rejecting proposals for a more cohesive corporatism as well as demands for an unfettered pluralism. Instead, he has opted for the continued separation of differentially organized interests in the multiple arenas of ''corporatist,'' ''corporatized,'' and ''hybrid'' sectors.

The persistent heterogeneity of organized interests has had mixed consequences for state autonomy. On one hand, groups possessing very different resources have been able to carve out important niches in the state bureaucracy and the economy while broadening their alliances through

205

the parties and the press. This has made it more necessary for the authoritarian elite to engage in bargaining and compromise, including some embarrassing reversals and retreats over economic policy.

On the other hand, the continued segmentation of associational life places formidable barriers in the path of regime critics who might wish to recreate the sort of powerful countercoalition that rose against Sadat. Under Mubarak's presidency all three arenas of group politics have become more effective channels for pressing the demands of specialized interests, but they also have become less capable of coordinating broad programs of political and economic reform. The new freedom of partisan competition and associational capitalism has divided the professional syndicates more than ever into squabbling factions. The increased powers of the union and cooperative confederations have only heightened the alienation of ordinary workers and farmers from their privileged leaders. Even the burgeoning power of the business community and the Islamic movement has been dissipated by the regime's ability to appropriate their slogans while manipulating their deep functional and ideological differences.

By tolerating criticism and recognizing the limits of his own power, Mubarak has been able to tame many of his loyal opponents while isolating and hunting down his most dangerous enemies. The bitter experience of Sadat's drive toward autocracy seems to have made Egypt's rulers more willing to accept Tocqueville's optimistic conclusion that ''Freedom of association in political matters is not so dangerous to public tranquillity as is supposed, and . . . possibly, after having agitated society for some time, it may strengthen the state in the end.'' [1] But the contrast between the associational policies of Sadat and Mubarak suggests a modern ''Egyptian corollary'' to Tocqueville that also has been demonstrated by authoritarian rulers elsewhere in the Third World: ''Beware of corporatism as a false remedy for the ills of 'unruly' society; the 'purer' its form, the more likely it is that the cure will be worse than the disease.''

The broader relevance of the ''Egyptian corollary'' can be illustrated with examples of unstable and self-defeating corporatist experiments in three other authoritarian regimes in the Middle East and Asia, the experiments of Muhammad Reza Shah Pahlavi in Iran, Park Chung Hee in South Korea, and Indira Gandhi's emergency regime in India. These countries are all quite different from Egypt in terms of both degree and type of interest group organization. India's associational life is at least as advanced and heterogeneous as Egypt's, but it has developed in a predominantly pluralist mode in contrast to the increasing prevalence of corporatism in Egypt.

Associability has been substantially more repressed in Iran and South

Korea, yet both countries possess extensive corporatist structures in some key sectors. In Iran merchants and religious leaders preserved unique and powerful forms of traditional corporatism capable of checking and ultimately helping to smash the power of the modern state. In South Korea soldiers and technocrats staked their hopes for rapid industrialization and political survival on their ability to fashion new forms of corporatist control for a working class whose numbers multiplied five times in less than two decades.

Despite these differences, however, each country shared some critical aspects of Egypt's experience under Anwar Sadat—efforts to establish a "new authoritarianism" through the abrupt introduction or intensification of corporatist policies produced not a Third World replica of "bureaucratic authoritarianism" but a more powerful political opposition containing many newly strengthened elements of pluralism. In each case the corporatization of associational life was perceived as a key to tightening political control and accelerating industrialization. Yet, in each case corporatism helped to galvanize a countercoalition of disaffected groups that challenged both authoritarianism and dependent development.

Iran: The Corporatism of the Shah versus the Corporatism of the Bazaar

For more than twenty years after the U.S.-sponsored coup d'etat that overthrew Musaddiq and the National Front, the shah was extremely reluctant to permit any system of interest representation in Iran, pluralist or corporatist. The shah's hostility to pluralism is easily understood. The rapid upsurge of voluntary associability between 1941 and 1953 among workers, farmers, students, intellectuals, and professionals had been so decisively dominated by the Tudeh Party that even limited tolerance of pluralism must have seemed incompatible with the preservation of the monarchy, particularly in the earlier years of the "restoration."

The shah's aversion to corporatism, however, was more complex and less enduring. He evidently feared that any new representative institutions created from above eventually could be infiltrated by his enemies and used against him. Even during the 1960s, when his regime was on much firmer footing, the shah did not attempt to revive the collection of state-sponsored occupational groups that the aristocratic prime minister, Ahmad Qavam, had promoted in the late 1940s to draw off support from the Left's more extensive forces.[2] Perhaps the shah's hesitance to experiment with corporatist techniques of control can be explained by two important factors: one regional and ideological, the other national and historical.

Until the beginning of the 1970s the leading prototype of authoritarian corporatism in the Middle East was, of course, Nasserism. This, in turn, was synonymous with all of the forces that the shah dreaded most: anti-imperialism, socialism, revolution, and naturally, republicanism. Such an alien, menacing, and rhetorically charged variety of corporatism could only have confirmed the shah's suspicion that even a highly contrived form of associational life would not help to sustain the throne, thereby reinforcing his tendency to rely on symbol manipulation, material rewards, and systematic terror.

Moreover, Iranian society already possessed the nucleus of an indigenous, traditional corporatism in the informal but extensive organizational networks of the bazaar and the 'ulama'. The shah reasonably might have concluded that there was no need for the state to create modern corporatist structures when fortune already had provided such enduring and potentially useful institutions to the very segments of the traditional middle class whose political support he viewed as indispensable. Thus, one of the shah's most important associational policies was his decision to tolerate the unique autonomy and power of these two corporatist groups even while gradually trimming their spheres of activity with other policies of industrialization and secularization.

But in 1975 the shah abruptly reversed this policy by trying to build a one-party state around the new Resurgence Party (Hizb-i Rastakhiz) and its collection of government-controlled occupational branches.[3] With the aid of S.A.V.A.K. the party took control of the major economic ministries and launched a direct assault on the half-million craftsmen and merchants in bazaars throughout the country. Asserting that the cause of rapid inflation was *bazaari* "profiteering" rather than government mismanagement of the oil boom, the party enforced a series of measures during 1975 and 1976 that sought to wrest control of the economy from the bazaars and place it firmly in the hands of the state.

The party organization opened new branches in the bazaars and began to extort "donations" from businessmen. It also recruited thousands of people into vigilante "inspectorate teams" with summary powers to fine hoarders and profiteers. Government ministries carried out a partial nationalization of foreign trade by setting up state corporations to import and distribute foodstuffs. Labor and welfare agencies began harassing small workshops with new regulations for minimum wages, social security, medical insurance, and registration of temporary employees.[4]

Municipal authorities imposed higher sales taxes and prohibited construction or repairs in existing marketplaces. In Tehran, the city government even threatened to route a planned superhighway through the center of the main bazaar. Finally, the government abolished the traditional guild system and replaced it with new Chambers of Guilds controlled in the provinces by local governors and in Tehran by government functionaries and nonbazaar entrepreneurs from the ''oil bourgeoisie.'' These structures were responsible primarily for imposing price controls and referring offenders to special Guild Courts, where in less than a year over a quarter of a million shopkeepers were fined or closed down and another 30,000 were deported or imprisoned.[5]

These measures quickly radicalized the bazaar, drove it into alliance with the more militant leaders of the *'ulama'*, and provided Ayatullah Khumayni with his key base of support in what eventually became the Islamic Revolution. In the ensuing confrontation with the government, the traditional corporatist organizations of the *bazaaris* proved to be far superior to the shah's hastily constructed version of state corporatism. The bazaar was particularly well suited to become the focal point of the revolution because of its strong ties with the provinces, with urban migrants, and with the *'ulama'*.

Leading *bazaari* families for generations tended to intermarry not only with other merchant families but also with families having the same provincial origins. This, together with constant commercial interchange, provided a nationwide chain of communication connecting Iran's historically isolated provincial capitals and towns.

Links with urban migrants were based on creditor and patronage relations, and also on the bazaar's financing and leadership of a wide assortment of popular religious groups that regularly organized neighborhood worship outside the mosque. *Bazaaris* were the major sponsors of the Shi'i passion plays *(taziyas)* and religious festivals during the holy months of Ramadan and Muharram. In Tehran alone they were able to mobilize 5,000 procession leaders in the southern and eastern districts. The bazaar organized religious ''missions'' *(heyats)*, some of which administered hundreds of meeting places for mourning, religious instruction, and Qur'an recital. These missions also provided thousands of pilgrimage leaders who guided groups to the holy places in Iraq and Saudi Arabia.[6]

Finally, the bazaar was closely tied to the *'ulama'* by both family and financial relations. Many of the leading *'ulama'* originated from or married into *bazaari* families. Merchants financed the religious schools, seminaries, and charities run by the *'ulama'* and were reported to have contributed as much as 80 percent of all private religious donations and taxes *(zakat* and *khums)*. Although the shah had been trying since the early

1960s to cut back the authority and resources of the religious institution, the prosperity and generosity of the bazaar allowed the ʿulama' to expand their activities so that by the mid-1970s they had penetrated the urban shantytowns and, for the first time, many of the remote areas of the countryside.

In alliance, the bazaar and the ʿulama' were a political force far greater than the sum of its parts. Together, they mobilized a mass opposition that was much more powerful than anything each could have accomplished separately. The Shiʿi ʿulama' of Iran retained a political prominence that was unparalleled anywhere in the Muslim world.[7] Compared to their Sunni counterparts in other countries, they enjoyed greater doctrinal authority and unity, more cohesive and hierarchical organization, a much stronger tradition of independence from the state, and greater ability to act as an effective pressure group in influencing public policy. They were, in other words, the closest thing in Islam to a "clergy" or, more accurately, the most corporatized and self-sufficient group of spiritual leaders in a religious tradition that for centuries has been characterized by pluralist factionalism and recurrent appeals for state assistance in eliminating rivals.

Nevertheless, by themselves the ʿulama' could have mounted no more than a rearguard action against the shah's growing determination to subordinate their informal and unique institutions to his more "rationalized" and comprehensive version of authoritarian corporatism. It was the simultaneous assault on both *bazaari* and religious organizations that antagonized the traditional middle class in general and destroyed the few remaining bridges connecting the regime to Iranian society. By endorsing the reckless campaigns of the Resurgence Party, the shah was not laying the foundation of a more modern authoritarianism but alienating and radicalizing traditional supports he had never before dared to abandon.

Of course, the Iranian Revolution was not simply the product of a "corporatist coalition" of traditional middle-class groups led by the ʿulama' and supported by the bazaar. Nor is it likely that such groups alone could have mobilized a following of revolutionary proportions. But during 1977 the shah sought to check this growing opposition by introducing yet another shift in associational policy, this time in the direction of pluralism. The shah was willing to consider a slight relaxation of police controls to allow the reemergence of voluntary organizations under what he hoped would be more moderate and reformist secular leadership. Old groups were permitted to revive and new ones to form among several segments of the modern middle class: lawyers and judges, writers and intellectuals, university students, white-collar employees, and even guerilla fighters.[8]

But after a quarter-century of repression, secular-nationalist politicians did not possess and could not construct alternative pluralist associations capable of restraining mass emotions or of supporting a liberal compromise with the monarchy. "Liberalization" did not calm or divide the shah's opponents, especially as it coincided with a protracted recession brought on by tight-money policies designed to "fine tune" Iran's boom economy. In the final months of 1977 the shah sought to end the new groups' growing street demonstrations by returning to repression, but this merely drove the burgeoning pluralist opposition of the modern middle class into stronger alliance with the more entrenched corporatist opposition of the traditional middle class.

By terminating his timid experiment with pluralism, the shah alienated the newly activated voluntary groups just as certainly as his hasty conversion to state corporatism earlier had alienated the guilds. Thus, he made possible the coalescence of groups that were far more diverse in organizational structure, class composition, and ideological orientation than any movement the radical *'ulama'* could have hoped to mobilize unilaterally.

Early in 1978, Khumayni and the leaders of the National Front issued their first joint call for a general strike in the Tehran bazaar, initiating the series of massive and remarkably nonviolent demonstrations that drove the shah from his throne within a year.[9] Khumayni skillfully nurtured the formation of this coalition with assurances of his democratic intentions, his commitment to social justice, and his friendliness to the followers of 'Ali Shari'ati. Yet the "Imam" had no more valuable assistance than the erratic and seemingly self-destructive associational policies of the shah himself.

South Korea: Corporatism as the Midwife of Radical Unionism

The construction of a corporatist system of labor control was essential to South Korea's spectacular industrial advance under the regime of Park Chung Hee during the 1960s and 1970s. The gradual dissolution of that corporatist system was equally central to the political crisis that led to Park's assassination in 1979. Ironically, it was the Korean Central Intelligence Agency that was most directly responsible for both creating and operating the corporatist unions and, then, for murdering the president when he insisted on preserving them despite their destabilizing impact on the authoritarian order.

Park's ambitious strategy of export-oriented industrialization was predicated upon mobilizing a new generation of manufacturing workers to supply cheap, docile, and high-performance labor.[10] Korean planners viewed the potential of the work force, not the domestic market or natural resources, as the major source of the country's comparative advantage and as the most attractive lure for foreign investment. Accordingly, agricultural policy was geared not to raising local production but to creating a huge surplus of low-wage labor. By holding down farm investment and relying on imported foodstuffs, the government encouraged a massive depopulation of the countryside and swelled the urban labor market. During the eighteen years of Park's rule, over 7 million peasants—about one-fifth of the total population—migrated to the cities and the number of manufacturing workers swelled from 600,000 to 3 million. The organization, control, and motivation of this new industrial work force was one of the greatest challenges facing the authoritarian regime. Thus, from its inception, Park's combination of mercantilism and militarism—his quest to revive in Korea the Meiji formula of "rich nation, strong army"— entailed an important corporatist dimension as well, particularly toward workers in key exporting industries.

Shortly after its creation by the new junta in 1961, one of the first assignments of the K.C.I.A. was to carry out a purge and thorough reorganization of the labor movement.[11] Older union leaders were removed, ending the long dominance of the party bosses tied to Syngman Rhee and cutting off the brief reemergence of the leftist unionism that followed the 1960 student revolts. These leaders were replaced by a younger cadre of thirty unionists who were handpicked and trained by the K.C.I.A. Using this group as a nucleus, the K.C.I.A. quickly transformed the union movement from a multitude of small, enterprise organizations grouped in rival confederations into about a dozen large industrial federations tied to a single peak association, the Federation of Korean Trade Unions. When militant unionists attempted to establish a rival confederation, a new labor code was enacted in 1963 to formalize the transition from pluralism to corporatism.

Thenceforth changes in labor and union policy were connected closely with, and occasionally anticipated, steady increases in the level of repression in the political system as a whole. In 1969 a special system of compulsory arbitration was created for the new free exporting zones that were established to attract foreign direct investment, especially from Japanese multinational corporations.[12] In 1971 compulsory arbitration was extended to all firms and a state of emergency was imposed primarily to quash new signs of independence and protest from the first generation of industrial workers.

Having subdued the labor movement, Park launched the second and more coercive phase of authoritarianism, the Yushin (Revitalizing) System, designed to tighten and perpetuate his personal rule. Then in 1973 and 1974, when ambitious plans to shift investment from light to heavy industry were jeopardized by the oil crisis, new labor laws removed collective bargaining from the industrial union federations and placed it in the hands of government-sponsored labor-management councils in individual enterprises.

Although corporatist unionism provided Korea's authoritarian modernizers with nearly a decade of relative industrial peace, the system rapidly broke apart with the entry of multitudes of new workers during the 1970s. Many young Korean workers developed a militant union consciousness in an amazingly short time—in some cases as rapidly as they learned the routine of factory work itself.[13] Naturally, this was promoted by exploitative characteristics of employment that are common in many industrializing countries. However, radicalization was encouraged more directly by three other factors that sharply distinguished the experiences of Korean workers: their unusually high rate of literacy, their receptivity to female leadership, and their broad exposure to liberation theology through the Christian missions.

The nearly universal literacy of new workers was a mixed blessing for their employers. It speeded adaptation to modern industry and allowed Korea to enhance the reputation for diligent, high-quality labor that was so critical to its international competitiveness. Yet it also hastened workers' realization that they possessed legal rights that generally were violated in practice and that could be redeemed only through energetic collective action. Korean workers became quite adept at devising legal means of pressure and protest that dramatized daily injustices in the work site and highlighted their connections with the larger context of exploitation and repression.

The high concentration of young women workers in exporting manufacturing industries was a similarly double-edged phenomenon. Unmarried females often were preferred and, indeed, actively recruited through personal networks in the countryside on the assumption that they would be low-cost temporary employees and, above all, with the expectation that they would be timid and tractable vis-à-vis male supervisors and union officials. Yet, in numerous firms in the important textiles and electronics sectors, new majorities of female workers threw out company-sponsored male unionists, spontaneously organized the first independent locals, and provided the cutting edge of new labor militancy. Indeed, it has been argued that in Korea young women were the most committed and altruistic union leaders, that their defiance of male intimidation earned broad public admiration, and that their organizations were considerably more outspoken critics of the regime than opposition parties.[14]

External support for radical unionism came from several student groups, labor research institutes, and most important, from about twenty Protestant and Catholic church organizations, the largest of which was the Urban Industrial Mission. During the late 1960s these church groups, influenced by the example of Latin America's liberal bishops, began to focus their campaigns for human rights on the struggling union movement. At first they supported the official labor confederation, thinking that unionization could be promoted most effectively by working downward through existing organizations. However, after the imposition of the Yushin System, the corporatist confederation became increasingly integrated into the authoritarian order and the U.I.M. shifted its efforts to the new generation of independent unionists emerging at the plant level. The success of the industrial missions was by no means an isolated phenomenon. Rather, it was part of an explosive growth of Christianity—from about 4.5 million to over 10 million in less than ten years—that coincided with the gradual loss of political freedom and economic security during the second decade of Park's rule.[15]

By the mid-1970s the Korean labor movement had divided into two bitterly opposed segments—the corporatist apex with its network of yellow (yeoyong) unionists supported by employers and the K.C.I.A. versus a growing pluralist base of militant locals aided by internationally funded church groups and aligned with the political opposition. The radical groups included about one-fourth of all manufacturing unions and as much as one-fifth of the industrial workers in large plants dependent on foreign investment and export markets.[16]

Faced with mounting pressures from below, corporatist union leaders tried to place a higher price on their cooperation with business and government. They urged the government to grant them wider powers to suppress rank-and-file dissent and argued that their loyalty had earned them a more prominent role in economic policy-making. Through most of the 1970s Park rejected official unionists' efforts to negotiate this sort of quid pro quo and preferred to rely on an assortment of newer techniques of labor control. At first he collaborated with employers in promoting new groups to rival and weaken unions at the enterprise level. Then, after he realized that such measures often stimulated further radicalization, Park belatedly and halfheartedly permitted tentative efforts to create a Korean variety of tripartism.

Labor-management councils originally were welcomed by union leaders, who thought they might evolve into something like the Japanese "quality circles" or even a rudimentary form of codetermination. Instead, they gradually became clear competitors of the unions, taking over discussion of grievances in a "family-like" manner and enforcing new "ethical codes" for workers. In expanding the authority of these councils at the expense of the official unions, the government appeared to recognize that conventional corporatist techniques could no longer preserve the motivation and commitment required for a high-performance work force. Corporatism, it was believed, had to be supplemented with more emphasis on normative and ideological controls.

The clearest expression of this shift in strategy was Park's enthusiastic campaign on behalf of the Factory Samaul (New Community) Movement. Samaul groups had originated in the agricultural sector, where they attempted to reverse the steady decline in rural income by encouraging cooperatives and off-season employment. In extending the movement into industrial workplaces, Park made the Samaul groups the centerpiece of his effort to shore up the Yushin System through popular mobilization in the spirit of "diligence, self-help, and cooperation." His objective was to recover some of the support that had been lost in the countryside after long years of neglect, while applying new pressures on factory workers to make additional sacrifices so that the energy crisis would not jeopardize Korea's new phase of heavy industrialization.

The "Samaul spirit" promoted highly romanticized images of agrarian collectivism and family harmony and held them up as models for ordering relations in the modern factory and in the nation as a whole. This was part of a larger effort to revive aspects of traditional culture that the regime perceived as most compatible with capitalist development and authoritarian rule. A parallel campaign, the New Spirit Movement, stressed more clearly the continued importance of such Confucian values as filial piety and social hierarchy. This movement portrayed Park as the paterfamilias of Korean society and was led, appropriately enough, by the president's daughter.[17]

The insertion of these new groups into industrial enterprises tended to sharpen tensions between the corporatist unionists at the top and their more militant rivals at the base. The official labor confederation assumed more and more responsibility for training and directing groups whose major activities were discouraging the formation of new local unions, reviving the practice of unpaid overtime, and wiping out earlier gains achieved through local union bargaining and protest. As the corporatist union structure broke apart and spawned still greater radicalism among the rank and file, Park became more willing to consider some of the proposals for interest group consultation and "concertation" that he had rejected earlier.

Interest in tripartism grew out of mounting alarm among employers over the rise in industrial disputes and protective labor regulations. In 1970 the Korean Employers' Association was established by small and medium-sized firms, which were particularly sensitive to increasing labor costs and union activity. By 1975 their overtures for dialogue with the union confederation were translated into the Labor-Management Friendly Meeting, which convened with government labor administrators for semi-monthly talks. In 1978 it was the labor confederation that took the initia-tive in organizing a second tripartite forum, the Workers' Welfare Policy Deliberation Committee. The following year government technocrats ad-vanced their own proposal for yet another, more comprehensive body, the Social and Economic Council, which they said was inspired by West German and Dutch practices.[18]

In fact, none of these multiple commissions ever amounted to much. While the employers pursued the unionists to negotiate a "social con-tract," the unionists were pursuing the government to grant them, at last, the powers and material concessions they would need to enforce such an agreement in the face of nearly certain revolt from below. Many of Park's advisers seemed to support this course, realizing that existing corporatist arrangements needed much more than a gloss of neo-Confucianism in order to restore industrial peace. Korea's corporatist unions simply were too weak to control and too contrived to represent. They had become at the same time the catalyst and the target of an alternative union move-ment that continued to gain force in spite of an endless series of counter-measures from the government. Nevertheless, Park rejected any substan-tial change, allowing each group to advance its favored project for a new, more consensual variety of corporatism and lending his support to none of them.

When Park decided that the surest remedy for labor unrest was greater coercion, he touched off a nationwide political crisis that rapidly split his regime and ultimately ended his life.[19] The trigger for the crisis was a long and bitter protest of female textile workers who were demanding that the state salvage their jobs in one of the many private firms that had gone bankrupt during the 1978–1979 recession. Evicted from their dor-mitories, the women occupied the headquarters of the opposition New Democratic Party, thereby encouraging the rise of new militant leaders who were critical of their party's long indifference to labor issues. After riot police attacked the demonstrators, causing many casualties, the dis-turbances quickly spread to the universities. What began as an isolated industrial dispute soon developed into a broad protest movement encompassing the church groups, the radical unions, the newly emboldened opposition party, and the students.

The breakdown of Park's regime was a direct result of divisions among his top aides over how to confront this sudden and vigorous upsurge of pluralism. The president himself ordered an attack on the Urban Industrial Mission, a reinforcement of the Factory Samaul groups, and a firm show of force through the K.C.I.A. However, both current and retired directors of the K.C.I.A.—those most responsible for the creation and supervision of the union organization—urged the president to make concessions to worker and student demands. They argued that some sort of political accommodation was unavoidable in view of the deteriorating economic situation and U.S. objections to the repression of human rights. When Park criticized the K.C.I.A.'s tentativeness in putting down the demonstrations and his security chief prepared paratroopers for the approaching confrontation in the capital, both men were assassinated by the head of the K.C.I.A.[20]

During the temporary paralysis of the security apparatus that followed, Korea experienced an unbridled wave of wildcat strikes that startled the state, the employers, and the official union leadership. After several months a new junta of younger officers consolidated power, but they substantially raised the level of repression against workers and imposed new union legislation that was far more restrictive than any of the Yushin measures. Corporatism had been one of the keys to creating South Korea's principal advantage in the international marketplace: a high-performance work force that remained compliant despite low rewards. But in post-Yushin Korea the authoritarian elite and its industrialist allies have been forced to accept a serious erosion of that advantage, which is unlikely to be reversed unless they are willing to accommodate the growing pluralist tendencies in the union movement and in the nation as a whole.

India: Corporatism as the Captive of Uneven Pluralism

India is widely acknowledged as one of the oldest and most vigorous pluralist systems in the Third World. That reputation was enhanced considerably by the stunning and decisive electoral rejection of Indira Gandhi's effort to extend her ''emergency government'' of 1975–1977 into a more lasting experiment with state corporatism. Yet it is clear that Gandhi's corporatist policies were largely an attempt to build upon and to consolidate a preexisting base of corporatism that had developed within the fabric of India's more dominant pluralist traditions, especially since her assumption of the prime ministership in 1966. Moreover, Gandhi ultimately was deterred from her authoritarian enterprise not so much by the strength of popular commitment to democracy as by her own sober assessment of the endless and insurmountable problems of penetrating and restructuring India's vast, multilayered associational universe and of bending it to her own purposes.[21]

Gandhi soon discovered that corporatizing initiatives were most successful where modern pluralist structures were most developed, and that corporatization was particularly futile where associational life remained elusive and mercurial because of its persistently amorphous, personalistic, transient, and informal character.[22] In this sense the very weakness and unevenness of Indian pluralism proved to be its best defense against the corporatist strategy of a determined but overambitious centralizer. Similarly, by accentuating and making more manifest the corporatist features of the Indian polity, Gandhi indirectly contributed to the invigoration and greater consolidation of some of the country's most fragmented and impotent pluralist associations, the national union confederations.

The emergency regime culminated nearly a full decade of steady erosion in India's democratic institutions that accompanied Gandhi's centralization and personalization of power and the growing bitterness of her attacks on the "selfish, divisive, and undisciplined" nature of pluralism. By the time the Allahabad court tried to ban her from political activity, she had weakened virtually all of the formal, institutional checks on her authority, including the cabinet, the traditional leadership of the Congress Party, the federal system, and, of course, the very judiciary that vainly sought to terminate her rule. Gandhi's decision to confront and subdue her remaining opponents undoubtedly was facilitated by public despair over the lingering effects of a costly war, the oil crisis, and poor harvests, as well as by her evident appeal to antidemocratic quarters that were otherwise antagonistic to one another, such as Hindu nationalists and revolutionary socialists.[23]

However, the deeper basis of Gandhi's assault on pluralism lay in her expectation (or more accurately, her gamble) that the combined organizational resources of the state and the ruling party had reached at last a level that would permit effective control over economic and associational life.[24] Such an objective may not have appeared at all beyond reach, given the extensive network of corporatist arrangements that already had been fashioned with many organized interests by a nationwide party apparatus enjoying nearly three decades of uninterrupted incumbency and by a central government apparatus that had become the principal planner, investor, and employer in the modern sector of the economy. In many cases, it must have seemed that a transition to state corporatism would require not the demolition and thorough recasting of existing representative structures but merely their appropriation, unification, and subordination.

In fact, the impact of the emergency measures on Indian society was highly differentiated and uneven. To a surprising extent the contours of the new corporatism formed a mirror image of the old pluralism: most solid among the urban middle class of civil servants, professionals and businessmen; substantially less coherent and effective in the labor movement; hopelessly decentralized and uncontrollable in the agricultural sector; and nearly incapable of reaching the poor and unemployed for whose benefit the experiment supposedly was intended in the first place.

The greatest conversion of multiple voluntary associations into a party-guild complex of nominated bodies and "national forums" occurred among the modern professions, especially those that had come to depend heavily on government employment and regulation. Journalism was particularly affected as competing news agencies were merged into a single state-run organization supervising a new system of collective self-censorship. Universities were forced to adopt new "codes of conduct" that restricted publication and travel. Even the free professions that still retained large portions of their memberships in the private sector were highly susceptible to the Congress Party's herding strategy and the state's drive for tighter regulation.[25]

Equally strong though far more reciprocal ties were formed quickly with businessmen's associations. Although merchants commonly complained about new price controls, private industrialists were delighted by freer credit and licensing, lower taxes, and government intervention in labor relations. Gandhi's promotion of joint enterprises between state and private investors consolidated ties between the dominant actors in India's mixed economy and put important new public resources at the disposal of private capitalists.[26] Indeed, the new system of corporatist representation involved a growing intimacy with and generosity toward big business that clearly belied the redistributive rhetoric that the prime minister so consistently invoked to justify her declaration of an emergency regime. This swing to the right was eloquent testimony to Gandhi's rapid adaptation to the limitations inherent in any effort to transform the highly skewed distribution of associational resources that had been inherited from the preceding pluralist era.

The obstacles to corporatization were most formidable in the country-side, where associability continued to be structured primarily in traditional forms or where it lacked permanent and formal organization altogether. Local landholders tolerated Congress Party "observers" from Delhi who took over the official bodies of local government to establish new groups and programs with mild redistributive overtones. But when the central government attempted to remove control of farm policy from the states, as it had done in other fields such as education, the proposal was easily defeated by agricultural interests fearing new tax increases. The personal and clientelistic hierarchies of landed notables were not challenged by new externally sponsored groups. Yet, by retaining a powerful presence in elected assemblies and party organizations at both state and national levels, the larger landholders could challenge any initiative threatening the agricultural sector or their privileged position within it.[27]

Among the rural poor a great deal of associational activity was channeled through informal, ephemeral, or illegal groups, such as caste associations, language communities, land-grab movements, and moral revivals. These kinds of amorphous structures were undoubtedly well suited to protest and agitation, but they did not possess the sort of organization that could be annexed and manipulated (or in many cases, even identified) by the state.[28] In view of Gandhi's reluctance to provide the poor with any new associational alternatives and her increasing tendency to seek accommodation with already entrenched interests, it is hardly surprising that rural voters overwhelmingly supported terminating the emergency regime and restoring pluralist autonomy.

In the case of the labor movement, the impact of corporatism was more interesting. Although it was not as successful here as with middle-class and business groups, neither was it as irrelevant as with rural and agrarian groups. The government established bipartite councils in large industrial firms, supposedly to encourage worker participation in management but more immediately to help implement longer work weeks, layoffs, and wage freezes. These councils then were organized in National Apex Bodies, where employers met for industrywide talks with representatives of the competing union confederations.[29] Even though these rudimentary efforts at economic summitry occurred within a larger context of union repression, they provided a rare opportunity and incentive for labor leaders to collaborate with one another and to lessen their traditional dependence on brokers and intermediaries in rival political parties.

For decades Congress Party politicians had pursued a fragmenting and disorganizing strategy toward the labor movement, designed to weaken an important sector in which their opponents' strength consistently equaled or surpassed their own.[30] Before independence Congress had been unable to displace the communist leadership of the All-India Trades Union Congress, and so in 1947 it created a competing organization that gradually acquired privileged and at times semiofficial status. Soon another major confederation arose under socialist leadership. Then in 1970, after Gandhi split the Congress Party and allied with the communists, a fourth union group was formed by left-wing communists who rejected the coalition. Intense rivalry between these and several smaller groups was fostered by labor legislation that preserved multiple union representation in individual enterprises while discouraging collective bargaining in broader sectoral or regional units. This resulted in a persistent inability of unions to defend workers' interests and a long-term stagnation of real wages that, of course, were perfectly compatible with the dominant forces in the Congress Party's regional organizations.

Given this long history of debilitating pluralism, the temporary introduction of corporatist measures was not at all inconsistent with labor leaders' efforts to shape a more cohesive union movement with a greater voice in economic policy-making. After Gandhi's solid electoral defeat in 1977, her successors retained the National Apex Bodies even while reviving earlier tripartite commissions that had fallen into disuse.[31] Thus, the labor movement can be seen as a specific instance of the broader national pattern in which Gandhi's experiments with state corporatism, limited and frustrated by the incoherence of Indian pluralism, also contributed to pluralism's consolidation and revitalization.

Conclusions and Speculations

In conclusion, we can try to identify some common themes concerning the most likely motivations and consequences of these ill-fated experiments with "unruly corporatism." Regarding the question of causation, certain "Latin American" paradigms are relevant, especially those connecting state corporatism with crises arising at various stages in dependent capitalist development and during major attempts either to co-opt or to smash organizations of the working class. There is an undeniable resonance throughout the Middle East and Asia of such common "semiperipheral" themes as strengthening the state, suppressing conflicts of interest between organized socioeconomic groups, fashioning new alliances with foreign sources of capital and technology, and making the big push toward economic growth the primary goal if not the exclusive definition of modernization. Nevertheless, while these "world system" and political economy factors must form a part of any explanation, they are only a part and by no means a determinative one.

Outside Latin America it is difficult to point to incidents of state corporatism as authoritarian responses to the threat of a powerful and radicalized "popular sector," or to the irresistible demands of a hegemonic national bourgeoisie, or to the extreme polarization and imminent collision of the two. Apart from Turkey and the Philippines, there are very few prospective Argentinas or Chiles in the Middle East and Asia. In most other Third World countries, industrialization is less advanced and privately controlled, modern class structures are less crystallized and rigidified, and foreign economic commitments are less sizeable and irreversible. Accordingly, state corporatism appears to be more a choice and initiative of fairly autonomous elites than a necessary or reluctant response to forces beyond their control.

Indeed, it may be the notion of the "autonomy of the state"—so celebrated in both the neo-Marxian and neoconservative writings that currently dominate the field of political development, and so trivialized in earlier liberal writings—that is at the heart of the matter. Why are so many authoritarian modernizers willing to exchange previously acceptable and often quite effective forms of political domination for riskier and unreliable alternatives when they are under no clear compulsion to do so? More specifically, why are they so eager to abandon the hegemony afforded by flexible heterogeneous associational systems that tolerate a certain maneuverability for weak opponents and to pursue instead the phantom of modernized despotism by investing scarce resources in the repressive construction of more comprehensive and coherent state corporatist systems?

The cases examined here suggest three interrelated factors, each of which has promoted exaggerated (one is tempted to say obsessive) efforts to enhance the autonomy of the state vis-à-vis civil society: (1) unbounded personal ambition; (2) infatuation with new foreign models in which corporatism is seen as part of an instant recipe combining "economic miracles" with "social peace"; and (3) the misfortune of relying on the unwise counsel of many in the discipline of political science, where corporatism has been vastly oversold whether as an analytical concept or as an associational policy.

Anwar Sadat, Muhammad Reza Shah Pahlevi, Park Chung Hee, and Indira Gandhi provided particularly vivid examples of political autonomy feeding upon itself. All were animated by an inexplicable certainty and fatal conviction that they could bend society to their own wills. All were prone to enterprises of such extravagance and misjudgments of such magnitude that it was their intimates more often than their distant enemies who pointed to signs of mental imbalance.

None of these regimes was much inspired by the "classical" models of capitalist or socialist development. No matter how much the United States and the Soviet Union have succeeded in reviving and universalizing the Cold War, they have not been able to reestablish credible images of themselves as products of alternative historical processes that are relevant and accessible to modernizing elites today. The most attractive and seriously regarded models of development in the Third World now are not the nations at the top of the heap but those *near* the top, especially if they achieved that position despite considerable resistance and hostility from their more powerful forerunners.

Japan and Brazil, West Germany and Italy, OPEC and the "gang of four" are much more likely to be cited as achievable precedents in the economic plans and patriotic rhetoric of the Middle East and Asia. As elites in these countries have looked more to the "late developers" of Europe and Latin America and, naturally, to one another, they have been more likely to (mis)perceive the modernization of authoritarianism as the key to modernization in general. This has paved the way for a proliferation of state corporatist experiments as authoritarians in more and more countries "rediscover" or simply invent political beliefs and institutions they regard as instrumental in replicating earlier success stories.

Highly ambitious and often unattainable projects to reshape associational life from above also have been encouraged by the more frequent reading and misreading in the Third World of the burgeoning social science literature on corporatism. In Egypt, for example, a spirited debate over the reform of representative institutions tends to crystallize around competing pluralist versus corporatist positions, each of which seeks to justify itself not only by appealing to particular native traditions and social constituencies but also by invoking foreign scholarly opinion. Bemused television audiences were treated to more than one seminar in which President Sadat himself explained to the People's Assembly that modern political science had established beyond doubt the need for strict limitations on the number of parties and interest groups if developing democracies were to become "institutionalized." Similarly, in Iran, the role of this sort of diffusion in promoting an attempted overhaul of the authoritarian regime is well known. Was the shah so wrong when, observing Nasser, he instinctively equated corporatism with political upheaval? Was he better guided by the expert opinion of his U.S.-trained advisers who, newly returned with their doctorates in political science, inspired the escapades of the Resurgence Party?

Finally, regarding the consequences of these unsuccessful state corporatist experiments, two recurrent outcomes are particularly noticeable:

(1) an initial rise in political opposition, causing greater instability, and (2) a gradual strengthening of pluralist forms of representation. Instability appears to be considerably more severe and protracted where associational life historically was repressed and retarded, as in South Korea and especially Iran. Alternatively, the prospects for a more vigorous pluralism are most evident where the art of association was widely cultivated in previous historical periods, regardless of whether this occurred through primarily pluralist means, as in India, or through primarily corporatist means, as in Egypt.

This suggests that if we want some idea of what to expect after an unruly corporatist system has been deeply shaken or overturned, we need to look carefully at what happened before it was created. In Egypt and India, where associability was stronger historically, elites responded to crises of unruly corporatism by fashioning more flexible and heterogeneous systems that combined both corporatist and pluralist elements. Mubarak preserved corporatist authoritarianism but developed a new tolerance (indeed, some say weakness) for interest group bargaining and partisan competition. The Janata government restored pluralist democracy but retained some of Gandhi's innovations to reduce fragmentation in the labor movement and to strengthen the state's ties with big business. Contrastingly, in South Korea and Iran, where associability in general had far weaker roots, crises of unruly corporatism were followed by even more intense elite hostility toward opposition groups whatever their organizational form.

Notes

Chapter 1

1. Yusuf al-Qa'id, "Misr: al-Nizam al-Masrafi fi Khatar" [Egypt: The banking system in danger], *al-Mustaqbal,* November 3, 1984; "Tadil Wizari Wasiʿ wa Tarajuʿ Shamil ʿan al-Islah al-Iqtisadi" [A broad cabinet change and a sweeping retreat from economic reform], *al-Ahali,* April 3, 1985.

2. Hassan ʿAshur, "Tarh 12,000 Thalaja wa 135,000 Butagaz wa 35,000 Sakhkhan min al-Nawʿ al-Shaʿbi Intaj al-Masaniʿ al-Harbiya" [Marketing of 12,000 refrigerators, 135,000 stoves and 35,000 space heaters for low-income civilian use as production of the military factories], *al-Ahram,* August 30, 1984; Hasanayn Tawfiq Ibrahim, "al-Wazifa al-Qitaliya wa al-Wazifa al-Tanmawiya lil-Jaysh al-Misri" [The combat duty and the developmental duty of the Egyptian army], *al-Ahram al-Iqtisadi,* April 4, 1983.

3. Fadwa Gundi, "The Emerging Islamic Order: The Case of Egypt's Contemporary Islamic Movement," *Journal of Arab Affairs* 1 (April 1982); Andrea B. Rugh, *Reveal and Conceal: Dress in Contemporary Egypt* (Syracuse: Syracuse University Press, 1986).

4. For an English translation and critique of *al-Farida al-Ga'iba,* see Johannes J. G. Jansen, *The Neglected Duty: The Creed of Sadat's Assassins and the Islamic Resurgence in the Middle East* (New York: Macmillan, 1986).

5. F. H. Cardoso and Enzo Faletto, *Dependency and Development in Latin America* (Berkeley: University of California Press, 1979); Peter Evans, *Dependent Development: The Alliance of Multinational, State, and Local Capital in Brazil* (Princeton: Princeton University Press, 1979).

6. Marvin Weinbaum, "Politics and Development in Foreign Aid: U.S. Economic Assistance to Egypt, 1975–1982," *Middle East Journal* 37 (Autumn 1983).

7. Heba Ahmad Handoussa, "Conflicting Objectives in the Egyptian-American Aid Relationship," in *The Impact of Development Assistance in Egypt,* ed. Earl L. Sullivan (Cairo: American University in Cairo Press, 1984).

225

8. Kate Gillespie, *The Tripartite Relationship: Government, Foreign Investors, and Local Investors during Egypt's Economic Opening* (New York: Praeger, 1984).

9. Omar Saad el-Din, "The Role of State, Private, and Foreign Capital in Law 43 of 1974 Projects" (Master's thesis, Department of Economics and Political Science, American University in Cairo, 1984); Jeswald W. Salacuse, "Arab Capital and Trilateral Ventures in the Middle East: Is Three a Crowd?" in *Rich and Poor States in the Middle East,* ed. Malcolm H. Kerr and El Sayed Yassin (Boulder, Colo: Westview Press, 1982), pp. 129–63.

10. Some leading examples of the Egyptian literature on dependent development are Fu'ad Mursi, *Hadha al-Infitah al-Iqtisadi* (Cairo: Dar al-Wahda, 1980); Mahmud ʿAbd al-Fadil, *Taʿammulaat fi al-Masʿala al-Iqtisadi al-Misriya* (Cairo: Dar al-Mustaqbal al-ʿArabi, 1983); Galal Amin, *al-Tanmiya Am al-Tabaʿiya al-Iqtisadiya wa al-Thaqafiya?* (Cairo: al-Maktab al-Misri al-Hadith, n.d.); ʿAdal Husayn, *al-Iqtisad al-Misri min al-Istiqlal ila al-Tabaʿiya, 1974–1979,* 2 vols. (Beirut: Dar al-Wahda, 1981).

11. Paul Baran, *The Political Economy of Growth* (New York: Monthly Review Press, 1968); André Gundar Frank, *Capitalism and Underdevelopment in Latin America* (New York: Monthly Review Press, 1967); Samir Amin, *Unequal Development: An Essay on the Social Formations of Peripheral Capitalism* (New York: Monthly Review Press, 1976).

12. Galal Amin, "Hawl al-Buhuth al-ʿIlmiya al-Mushtaraka bayn al-Misriyin wa al-Hay'aat al-Ajnabiya" [On joint scientific research between Egyptians and foreign agencies], *al-Ahram al-Iqtisadi,* October 18, 1982.

13. The emphasis on the cultural aspects of dependent development is particularly notable in the writings of Galal Amin.

14. For definitions of corporatism and pluralism, see Philippe C. Schmitter, "Still the Century of Corporatism?" *Review of Politics* 36 (January 1974). "Corporatism can be defined as a system of interest representation in which the constituent units are organized into a limited number of singular, compulsory, non-competitive, hierarchically ordered and functionally differentiated categories, recognized or licensed (if not created) by the state and granted a deliberate representational monopoly within their respective categories in exchange for observing certain controls on their selection of leaders and articulation of demands and supports."

15. For other examples of heterogeneous systems of interest representation, combining features of both pluralism and corporatism, see Robert Bianchi, *Interest Groups and Political Development in Turkey* (Princeton: Princeton University Press, 1984).

16. For an overview of the political crisis leading up to Sadat's assassination, see Muhamed Heikal, *Autumn of Fury: The Assassination of Sadat* (New York: Random House, 1983).

17. This analysis is developed more fully in Robert Bianchi, "Interest Group Politics in the Third World," *Third World Quarterly* 8 (April 1986).

18. For example, see Philippe C. Schmitter, "Interest Intermediation and Regime Governability in Contemporary Western Europe and North America," in *Organizing Interests in Western Europe: Pluralism, Corporatism, and the Transformation of Politics,* ed. Suzanne D. Berger (Cambridge: Cambridge University Press, 1981); Gerhard Lehmbruch, "Liberal Corporatism and Party Government," *Comparative Political Studies* 10 (April 1977).

19. Guillermo O'Donnell, *Modernization and Bureaucratic-Authoritarianism: Studies in South American Politics* (Berkeley: Institute of International Studies, University of California, 1973).

20. Alfred Stepan, *State and Society: Peru in Comparative Perspective* (Princeton: Princeton

University Press, 1978); David Collier, ed., *The New Authoritarianism in Latin America* (Princeton: Princeton University Press, 1979); David Collier and Ruth Berens Collier, "Inducements Versus Constraints: Disaggregating 'Corporatism,' " *American Political Science Review* 73 (December 1979).

21. Guillermo O'Donnell, "Corporatism and the Question of the State," in *Authoritarianism and Corporatism in Latin America,* ed. James Malloy (Pittsburgh: University of Pittsburgh Press, 1977).

22. ʿAbd al-Mughni Saʿid describes the Free Officers' early interest in Peronism and their efforts to replicate its corporatist reorganization of the labor movement. ʿAbd al-Mughni Saʿid, "Safahaat Majhula min Tarikh al-Haraka al-Niqabiya" [Unknown pages from the history of the union movement], *al-ʿAmal* 236 (January 1983): 11–13. During an international congress of economists held in Lima in 1984 a former Peruvian ambassador to Egypt noted that Velasco's programs of land reform and industrial codetermination were strongly influenced by Nasserist prototypes. Personal communication from Heba Handoussa, who attended the congress.

23. For critical views of Nasserism and Peronism that examine the paradoxical legacies of both traditions, see Louis ʿAwad, *Aqniʿa al-Nasiriya al-Sabʿa* (Beirut: Dar al-Qadaya, 1975); Frederick C. Turner and José Enrique Miguens, eds., *Juan Peron and the Reshaping of Argentina* (Pittsburgh: University of Pittsburgh Press, 1983).

24. Clement Moore Henry and Leonard Binder have described Egypt's current regime as bureaucratic authoritarianism. John Waterbury applies the term to the Nasser era as well. Raymond Hinnebusch, Jr., however, refers to the Sadat era as a "post-populist" authoritarian state, implying a regime that falls between O'Donnell's two ideal types. Clement Moore Henry, "Financial 'Deepening' and Political Mediation: Counterpart to Bureaucratic-Authoritarianism?" (Paper presented at the annual meeting of the American Political Science Association, Washington, D.C., August 1986); Leonard Binder, *Islamic Liberalism: A Critique of Development Ideologies* (Chicago: University of Chicago Press, 1988), pp. 14, 16, 268; John Waterbury, *The Egypt of Nasser and Sadat: The Political Economy of Two Regimes* (Princeton: Princeton University Press, 1983), chap. 1; Raymond Hinnebusch, Jr., *Egyptian Politics under Sadat: The Post-Populist Development of an Authoritarian-Modernizing State* (Cambridge: Cambridge University Press, 1985).

25. Demands for the curtailment of workers' economic privileges have become a regular theme in the president's May Day address to Egyptian union officials. Even former Nasserists have taken up the same argument. For example, see Ahmad Baha' al-Din, "Fi Yawm Awwal Mayo" [On May Day], *al-Ahram,* May 1, 1983; Hamid Zaydan, "Madha . . . Wa ʿId al-ʿUmmal Qadam?" [What now . . . as Labor Day approaches?], *al-Ahram al-Iqtisadi,* April 5, 1982. Concerning the new powers granted to the Egyptian Confederation of Labor by the Sadat and Mubarak governments, see Robert Bianchi, "The Corporatization of the Egyptian Labor Movement," *Middle East Journal* 40 (Summer 1986).

26. ʿAdal al-Mashad, "al-Ghazw al-Istithmari lil-Niqabaat al-Mihniya wa al-ʿUmmaliya" [The entrepreneurial invasion of professional and labor syndicates], *al-Shaʿb,* January 25, 1983.

27. For a discussion of the conditions for "political exchange" between governmental and associational elites, see Wolfgang Streeck and Philippe C. Schmitter, "Community, Market, State—and Associations? The Prospective Contribution of Interest Governance to Social Order," in *Private Interest Government: Beyond Market and State,* ed. Wolfgang Streeck and Philippe C. Schmitter (Beverly Hills, Calif.: Sage, 1985); Philippe C. Schmitter, "Neo-Corporatism and the State," in *The Political Economy of Corporatism,* ed. Wyn Grant (London: Macmillan, 1986).

Chapter 2

1. "Rapport de la Commission du Commerce et de l'Industrie," in *The Economic History of the Middle East, 1800–1914,* ed. Charles Issawi (Chicago: University of Chicago Press, 1966), pp. 452–60; Eric Davis, *Challenging Colonialism: Bank Misr and Egyptian Industrialization, 1920–1941* (Princeton: Princeton University Press, 1983); Robert Tignor, *State, Private Enterprise, and Economic Change in Egypt, 1918–1952* (Princeton: Princeton University Press, 1984); Galal Ahmad Amin, "External Factors in the Reorientation of Egypt's Economic Policy," in *Rich and Poor States in the Middle East,* ed. Malcolm H. Kerr and El Sayed Yassin (Boulder, Colo.: Westview Press, 1982), pp. 285–315.

2. Mancur Olson, *The Rise and Decline of Nations: Economic Growth, Stagflation and Social Rigidities* (New Haven: Yale University Press, 1982).

3. On the debate concerning a new social contract and social democracy, see Louis ʿAwad, *Aqniʿa al-Nasiriya al-Sabʿa* (Beirut: Dar al-Qadaya, 1975); Sufi Abu Talib, *al-Ishtirakiya al-Dimuqratiya* (Cairo, 1978).

4. Data for 1907 and 1917 include all manufacturing establishments; data for 1927–1980 include establishments with ten or more workers.

5. Data for all years include establishments with ten or more workers.

6. Similar tendencies of capital intensiveness are reported in John Waterbury, *The Egypt of Nasser and Sadat: The Political Economy of Two Regimes* (Princeton: Princeton University Press, 1983), chap. 9.

7. In 1980 Egypt's annual rate of population growth was estimated at 2.8 to 3.0 percent, resulting in an increase of about 1 million people every ten months. Büttner projects that under these conditions the economy must create between 350,000 and 500,000 new jobs each year merely to preserve current rates of employment. Friedemann Büttner, "A Country Scenario Analysis of Egypt," *Vierteljahresberichte* 96 (June 1984): 170.

8. Official estimates place the number of Egyptian workers abroad at about 3 million. Over 90 percent of these are believed to be located in five key oil-producing countries: 1,250,000 in Iraq; 800,000 in Saudi Arabia; 300,000 in Libya; 200,000 in Kuwait; and 150,000 in the United Arab Emirates. An additional 1 million workers are believed to have left the country illegally. Mustafa Amam and Jamal Zayadah, "al-Misriyun al-ʿAmalun fi al-Duwal al-ʿArabiya: al-Mustaqbal fi Sila al-Qalaq" [Egyptians working in the Arab states: The future in a basket of worries], *al-Ahram al-Iqtisadi,* May 9, 1983; "Tahrib 70 Sayyadan ʿala Dufʿatayn" [Seventy fishermen smuggled in two groups], *Ruz al-Yusuf,* October 25, 1982.

9. Büttner, "A Country Scenario Analysis of Egypt," p. 169; Chase Econometrics, *Economic Forecasts for Africa and the Middle East, 1985* (Philadelphia, 1985), p. 1.

10. Waterbury, *The Egypt of Nasser and Sadat,* p. 199; Büttner, "A Country Scenario Analysis of Egypt," p. 166; Chase Econometrics, *Economic Forecasts for Africa and the Middle East, 1985,* p. 1. During 1986 petroleum exports were slashed to $656 million and tourism receipts fell to only $309 million. Consequently, by 1987 Egypt's foreign debt had doubled once again, reaching nearly $40 billion. *Financial Times,* June 29, 1987.

11. The shifting class bases of successive regimes is summarized in Mahmoud Hussein, *Class Conflict in Egypt, 1945–1970* (New York: Monthly Review Press, 1973); Anouar Abdel-Malek, *Egypt: Military Society* (New York: Random House, 1968); Mark Cooper, *The Transformation of Egypt* (Baltimore: Johns Hopkins University Press, 1982).

12. John Waterbury, "Patterns of Urban Growth and Income Distribution in Egypt," in

The Political Economy of Income Distribution in Egypt, ed. Gouda Abdel-Khalek and Robert Tignor (New York: Holmes & Meier, 1982), pp. 307–50.

13. Heba Ahmad Handoussa, "Conflicting Objectives in the Egyptian-American Aid Relationship," in *The Impact of Development Assistance in Egypt,* ed. Earl L. Sullivan (Cairo: American University in Cairo Press, 1984); Karima Korayem, "The Agricultural Output Pricing Policy and the Implicit Taxation of Agricultural Income," in *The Political Economy of Income Distribution in Egypt,* ed. Gouda Abdel-Khalek and Robert Tignor (New York: Holmes & Meir, 1982), pp. 165–97.

14. Mahmud ʿAbd al-Fadil, *The Political Economy of Nasserism* (Cambridge: Cambridge University Press, 1980); Samir Radwan, *Agrarian Reform and Rural Poverty: Egypt, 1952–1975* (Geneva: I.L.O., 1977); Ahmed H. Ibrahim, "Impact of Agricultural Policies on Income Distribution," and Mohaya A. Zaytoun, "Income Distribution in Egyptian Agriculture and Its Main Determinants," in *The Political Economy of Income Distribution in Egypt,* ed. Gouda Abdel-Khalek and Robert Tignor (New York: Holmes & Meier, 1982), pp. 198–235, 268–306.

15. Saad Eddin Ibrahim, "Social Mobility and Income Distribution in Egypt, 1952–1977," in *The Political Economy of Income Distribution in Egypt,* ed. Gouda Abdel-Khalek and Robert Tignor (New York: Holmes & Meier, 1982), pp. 375–434; Georges Sabagh, "Migration and Social Mobility in Egypt," in *Rich and Poor States in the Middle East,* ed. Malcolm H. Kerr and El Sayed Yassin (Boulder, Colo.: Westview Press, 1982), pp. 71–95.

16. Saad Eddin Ibrahim, "Oil, Migration and the New Arab Social Order," in *Rich and Poor States in the Middle East,* ed. Malcolm H. Kerr and El Sayed Yassin (Boulder, Colo.: Westview Press, 1982), pp. 17–70.

17. David Hirst and Irene Beeson, *Sadat* (London: Faber & Faber, 1981), chap. 5.

18. The tone of the debate about "economic apartheid" was set by the editor of *al-Ahram al-Iqtisadi,* Lutfi ʿAbd al-ʿAzim, after the riots of January 1977. *al-Ahram al-Iqtisadi,* February 1, 1977.

19. This restrictive legislation, together with the series of plebiscites that ratified it, is described in Ghali Shukri, *Egypt: Portrait of a President, 1971–1981: The Counter-Revolution in Egypt, Sadat's Road to Jerusalem* (London: Zed Press, 1981).

20. The idea that current political conflicts are driven by a struggle between procapitalist and prosocialist constituencies is particularly pronounced in Cooper, *The Transformation of Egypt.*

21. See the text of President Mubarak's May Day address to union leaders in *al-Ahram,* May 2, 1983.

22. "Nadwa ʿal-ʿAmal' Hawl Mashruʿ Tatwir al-Qitaʿ al-ʿAmm" ['al-ʿAmal' roundtable on the proposed reform of the public sector], *al-ʿAmal,* December 1982; ʿAdal Hamam, "al-Qitaʿ al-ʿAmm fi Zil Qanun al-Tatwir" [The public sector in the shadow of the new reform law], *al-ʿAmal,* November 1983; Asama Mahran, "Khilafaat Hawl al-Muntakhibin fi Majalis al-Idaraat" [Disagreements about the elected representatives in management councils], *al-Ahram al-Iqtisadi,* April 12, 1982; ʿAdal al-Husayni Hamid, "Mazid min al-Ishtirakiya al-Faʿiliya fi al-Qitaʿ al-ʿAmm" [More effective socialism in the public sector], *al-Ahram al-Iqtisadi,* August 29, 1983.

23. Omar Saad el-Din, "The Role of State, Private, and Foreign Capital in Law 43 of 1974 Projects" (Master's thesis, Department of Economics and Political Science, American University in Cairo, 1984), p. 44; Kate Gillespie, *The Tripartite Relationship: Government, Foreign Investors, and Local Investors during Egypt's Economic Opening* (New York: Praeger,

1984), pp. 82, 109, 203. Gillespie notes that of twenty-seven wholly Egyptian joint ventures included in her survey, eighteen had less than 10 percent of their investment capital in foreign exchange and none had invested more than 25 percent in foreign exchange.

24. Forty-one percent of the state investment in joint venture firms went into industrial enterprises, as opposed to 27 percent of local private investment and 20 percent of foreign investment. Saad el-Din, "The Role of State, Private, and Foreign Capital," p. 29.

25. "Informal" sector refers primarily to the economy of personal services and "disguised unemployment" comprising urban squatters, street hawkers, day laborers, and domestics.

26. Mustafa al-Sa'id, "Haqiqat al-Rukud al-Iqtisadi Alladhi Yatahadith 'anhu al-Ba'd" [The truth about the alleged economic recession], al-Musawwar, November 5, 1982; "Egypt Lets Currency Float Down," New York Times, May 11, 1987.

27. "Najahna fi Tasni' Awwal Dababa Misriya Khalisa bi-Ism 'Ramsis Thani' " [We have succeeded in manufacturing the first completely Egyptian tank, named "Ramses the Second"], al-Ahram, April 29, 1987. The Financial Times has characterized the military enterprises as "an economic empire." Financial Times, June 29, 1987. The economic diversification of the military enterprises has been accompanied by new calls from General 'Abd al-Halim Abu Ghazala, the Egyptian chief of staff, for a unified military command among the Arab states. "al-'Aqida al-'Askariya al-'Arabiya Hiya al-Tariq al-Wahid ila al-Wahda" [An Arab military command is the sole path to unity], al-Hawadeth, April 4, 1987. On Abu Ghazala's rising influence, see Robert Springborg, "The President and the Field Marshal: Civil-Military Relations in Egypt Today," MERIP Reports 147 (July-August 1987): 5–16.

28. The enterprises of the engineers' syndicate are described in Nahed Dajani, "Corporatism in the Egyptian Context: A Profile of Business and Professional Politics in Egypt" (Master's thesis, Department of Economics and Political Science, American University in Cairo, 1982).

29. "Tanta: al-Jam'iya al-Ta'awuniya li-Naql al-Rukab Yara'saha Sahib Masna' Makaruna" [Tanta: The passengers' cooperative is being run by the owner of a macaroni factory], al-Ahali, January 18, 1984; "Mafia al-Tamwin fi al-Bahayra" [The supply Mafia in al-Bahayra], al-Sha'b, March 20, 1984; "Mukhalafaat Jadida bil-Jam'iya al-Istihlakiya fi Beni Swayf" [New violations in the consumer cooperative in Beni Swayf], al-Ahali, November 23, 1983.

30. Bank Faysal al-Islami, "al-Nadwa al-Uwla lil-Bunuk al-Islamiya wa Dawruha fi al-Tanmiya al-Iqtisadiya wa al-Ijtima'iya" [The first roundtable on Islamic banks and their role in economic and social development], al-Ahram al-Iqtisadi, December 5, 1983; Fu'ad al-Saraf, "Tamwil al-Tanmiya 'ala al-Tariqa al-Islamiya" [Financing development in the Islamic manner], al-Ahram al-Iqtisadi, September 19, 1983. The ties of the Muslim Brotherhood to the business community are discussed in Gilles Kepel, Muslim Extremism in Egypt: The Prophet and Pharaoh (Berkeley: University of California Press, 1986), chap. 4.

31. "al-'Iyadaat al-Islamiya bil-Masajid: al-Hal al-Wasat bayn Mustashfiyaat al-Hukuma wa Tib al-Istithmar" [The Islamic clinics in mosques: The compromise between state hospitals and medicine for profit], al-Wafd, April 12, 1987.

32. Martin French, "Clobbered by Cairo Irregulars," Euromoney, June 1987, pp. 81–87; Iliya Harik, "The Intractable Problems of the Patron State: The Roles of the Public and Private Sectors in Egypt" (Paper presented at the Social Science Research Council Conference on Retreating States and Expanding Societies, Aix-en-Provence, March 1988), pp. 18–21.

33. For an excellent summary of the debate over the political and economic ramifications of the Islamic investment companies, see the following articles in the July 18, 1988, issue of *Ruz al-Yusuf:* Tariq al-Bishri, "Asalib al-Sira' Hawl Tawzif al-Amwal" [The methods of the struggle over the investment companies]; Mahmud 'Abd al-Fadil, "al-Tawzif al-Siyasi li Sharikaat Tawzif al-Amwal" [The political exploitation of the Islamic investment companies]; Samir Tawbar, "Khalfiyat al-Sira'" [Behind the struggle].

Chapter 3

1. Statutes were coded in a binary fashion to distinguish those that merely regulated existing voluntary groups from those that established or strengthened monopolistic groups with semiofficial status, compulsory membership, and hierarchical organization. Once corporatist groups were created, subsequent legislation generally has tightened state controls by increasing organizational centralization and modifying formulas for leadership selection. When pluralist and corporatist groups have coexisted in the same sector, relevant portions of the graph have been evenly split between shaded and unshaded areas.

2. Gabriel Baer, *Egyptian Guilds in Modern Times* (Jerusalem: Israeli Oriental Society, 1964), chaps. 3, 4; Jacques Berque, *Egypt: Imperialism and Revolution* (New York: Praeger, 1972), pp. 328–31.

3. Gabriel Baer, *Studies in the Social History of Modern Egypt* (Chicago: University of Chicago Press, 1969), pp. 152–55.

4. Ibid., pp. 157–60.

5. Ra'uf 'Abbas, *al-Haraka al-'Ummaliya fi Misr, 1899–1952* (Cairo: Dar al-Katib al-'Arabi lil-Taba'a wa al-Nashr, 1967), p. 62; Ellis Goldberg, *Tinker, Tailor, and Textile Worker: Class and Politics in Egypt, 1939–1952* (Berkeley: University of California Press, 1986), chap. 5.

6. Donald M. Reid, "The Rise of the Professions and Professional Organizations in Modern Egypt," *Comparative Studies in Society and History* 16 (January 1974): 37–38.

7. 'Abbas, *al-Haraka al-'Ummaliya fi Misr*, pp. 58–59, 63–64; Arthur Goldschmidt, Jr., "The Egyptian Nationalist Party: 1892–1919," in *Political and Social Change in Modern Egypt*, ed. P. M. Holt (London: Oxford University Press, 1968), pp. 308–33.

8. Walid Kazziha, "The Evolution of the Egyptian Political Elite, 1907–1921: A Case Study of the Role of the Large Landowners in Politics" (Ph.D. diss., University of London, 1970).

9. Louis Joseph Cantori, "The Organizational Basis of an Elite Party: The Egyptian Wafd" (Ph.D. diss., Department of Political Science, University of Chicago, 1966).

10. Ibid.; Marius Deeb, "Labour and Politics in Egypt, 1919–1939," *International Journal of Middle East Studies* 10 (May 1979): 187–203.

11. Donald M. Reid, "The National Bar Association and Egyptian Politics, 1912–1954," *International Journal of African Historical Studies* 7 (1974): 608–46; Donald M. Reid, *Lawyers and Politics in the Arab World, 1880–1960* (Chicago: Bibliotheca Islamica, 1981), chaps. 1, 2, 5, 6.

12. Farhat J. Ziadeh, *Lawyers, the Rule of Law, and Liberalism in Modern Egypt* (Stanford: Stanford University Press, 1968); Reid, "The National Bar Association," pp. 632–35.

13. 'Abbas, *al-Haraka al-'Ummaliya fi Misr*, pp. 94–96; Deeb, "Labour and Politics," pp. 94–95.

14. Deeb, "Labour and Politics," pp. 197–99.

15. 'Abbas, *al-Haraka al-ʿUmmaliya fi Misr*, chaps. 5, 6, 7.

16. Berque, *Egypt*, pp. 405–9, 422, 448.

17. Samir Radwan, *Agrarian Reform and Rural Poverty: Egypt, 1952–1975* (Geneva: I.L.O., 1977), chap. 5.

18. Berque, *Egypt*, pp. 341–42; Eric Davis, *Challenging Colonialism: Bank Misr and Egyptian Industrialization, 1920–1941* (Princeton: Princeton University Press, 1983).

19. Ittihad al-Sanaʿaat al-Misriya, *al-Kitab al-Dhahabi lil-Ittihad al-Sanaʿaat al-Misriya* (Cairo: Schindler, 1947), pp. 33–39.

20. Whereas Robert Tignor emphasizes the extensive overseas links of the Belgian community in Egypt, Marius Deeb notes that European capital on the Continent was generally much more sympathetic to Egyptian industrial aspirations than were the British, who continued to regard Egypt as an essentially agricultural society. Deeb suggests that these inter-European rivalries help to explain the federation's early affinity for Belgian, French, and Italian, as opposed to British, investors. Robert Tignor, "The Economic Activities of Foreigners in Egypt, 1920–1950: From Millet to Haute Bourgeoisie," *Comparative Studies in Society and History* 22 (July 1980): 427–30; Marius Deeb, "The Socioeconomic Role of the Local Foreign Minorities in Modern Egypt, 1805–1961," *International Journal of Middle East Studies* 9 (1978): 19.

21. The state budget provided the federation with an early subsidy of £E 100,000, which was gradually increased to £E 300,000 and, by 1938, to £E 1,000,000. Berque, *Egypt*, p. 338.

22. Tignor, "Economic Activities," pp. 437–39.

23. Reassuring the French Chamber of Commerce of his friendly intentions toward foreign capital, Sidqi insisted, "I do not claim that it is necessary to industrialize Egypt overnight. On the contrary, I am of the opinion that the industrial movement must develop naturally and little by little. Mass industrialization would have disastrous social results, whereas by proceeding methodically we shall ensure for Egyptian industry a stability which it badly needs." Berque, *Egypt*, p. 339.

24. Tignor, "Economic Activities," p. 441. Concerning the growth of Italian influence in the royal court, see "Misr wa 'Alam al-Bahr al-Mutawassit" [Egypt and the Mediterranean world], *al-Ahram*, May 2, 1985.

25. 'Abd al-'Azim Ramadan, *Tatawwur al-Haraka al-Wataniya fi Misr Min Sanat 1937 ila Sanat 1948* (Beirut: Matbaʿa al-Watan al-'Arabi, n.d.), vol. 1, pts. 2, 3; Richard P. Mitchell, *The Society of Muslim Brothers* (London: Oxford University Press, 1969); James P. Jankowski, *Egypt's Young Rebels: "Young Egypt," 1933–1952* (Stanford: Hoover Institution, 1975).

26. P. J. Vatikiotis, *The Modern History of Egypt* (London: Weidenfeld & Nicolson, 1976), pp. 277–79.

27. Berque, *Egypt*, p. 441.

28. Note from Miles Lampson, the British Ambassador in Cairo, dated February 19, 1935. FO 371 (19069) 1935 J 703/110/16. I am grateful to Robert Vitalis for providing me with the text of this communication from the Foreign Office Archives.

29. Berque, *Egypt*, pp. 460–465.

30. Davis, *Challenging Colonialism*, pp. 96–97; Robert Tignor, *State, Private Enterprise, and Economic Change in Egypt, 1918–1952*, (Princeton: Princeton University Press, 1966), p. 67; Saʿid, pp. 28–31.

31. Debates among the Nasserists over the suitability of these foreign models are discussed by Anouar Abdel-Malek, *Egypt: Military Society* (New York: Random House, 1968),

chaps. 7, 8, and by Sa'id, ''Safahaat Majhula min Tarikh al-Haraka al-Niqabiya,'' *al-'Amal* 236 (January 1983), chap. 3.

32. Martin W. Wilmington, *The Middle East Supply Center* (Albany: State University of New York Press, 1971).

33. Niqabat al-Sahafiyin, *Niqabat al-Sahafiyin fi Arba'in 'Aman, 1941–1981* (Cairo: Matabi' al-Ahram al-Tijari, 1981); Berque, *Egypt,* p. 462.

34. Ittihad al-Sana'aat al-Misriya, *Tatawwur Ittihad al-Sana'aat al-Misriya fi Khamsin Sana, 1922–1972* (Cairo, 1972); 'Abbas, *al-Haraka al-'Ummaliya fi Misr,* pp. 131–33.

35. Subhi Wahida, *Fi Usul al-Mas'ala al-Misriya* (Beirut: Maktaba Madbuli, n.d.); Abdel-Malek, *Egypt,* pp. 42–43.

36. Radwan, *Agrarian Reform and Rural Poverty,* chap. 5; Iliya Harik, *The Political Mobilization of Peasants* (Bloomington: Indiana University Press, 1974), chap. 14.

37. 'Abd al-'Azim Ramadan, *al-Sira' al-Ijtima'i wa al-Siyasi fi Misr: 'Abd al-Nasir wa Azmat Maris* (Cairo: Ruz al-Yusef, 1975), chap. 11.

38. Sa'id, ''Safahaat Majhula min Tarikh al-Haraka al-Niqabiya,'' *al-'Amal* 236 (January 1983), pp. 14–23.

39. Abdel-Malek, *Egypt,* chap. 8; Kamal Rif'at, *Nasiriyun? Na'm* (Cairo: al-Qahira lil-Thaqafa wa al-'Arabiya, 1976).

40. Abdel-Malek, *Egypt,* chaps. 4, 10.

41. For a stinging attack on the syndical system, demanding its revolutionary reorganization, see ''al-Niqabaat al-Ha'ira'' [The confused syndicates], *Ruz al-Yusuf,* June 25, 1962. The key role of Kamal Rif'at in checking the A.S.U.'s campaign to control the unions is described in Sa'id, ''Safahaat Majhula min Tarikh al-Haraka al-Niqabiya,'' *al-'Amal* 236 (January 1983), chap. 3.

42. For an example of this ''contractual'' interpretation of Nasserism by one of Nasser's most prominent critics, see Louis 'Awad, *Aqni'a al-Nasiriya al-Sab'a* (Beirut: Dar al-Qadaya, 1975).

43. 'Ali Dessouki has argued that Nasser's unwillingness to devolve greater power to the interest groups created by the state left them incapable of protecting their revolutionary gains, thereby permitting Sadat to reinstate capitalist policies with surprisingly little resistance. 'Ali Dessouki, ''al-Mushkila al-Siyasiya fi Misr wa al-Tahawwul ila Ta'addud al-Ahzab'' [The political problem in Egypt and the transformation to party pluralism], in *Tajribat al-Dimuqratiya fi Misr, 1970–1981,* ed. 'Ali Dessouki et al. (Cairo: al-Markaz al-'Arabi lil-Buhuth wa al-Nashr, 1982); and ''The Politics of Income Distribution,'' in *The Political Economy of Income Distribution in Egypt,* ed. Gouda Abd al-Khalek and Robert Tignor (New York: Holmes & Meier, 1982), chap. 3.

44. Leonard Binder, *In a Moment of Enthusiasm: Political Power and the Second Stratum in Egypt* (Chicago: University of Chicago Press, 1978), chap. 14.

45. Salah al-Sayed, *Workers' Participation in Management: The Egyptian Experience* (Cairo: American University in Cairo Press, 1978), chap. 5; Raymond William Baker, *Egypt's Uncertain Revolution under Nasser and Sadat* (Cambridge: Harvard University Press, 1978), chap. 7.

46. On the deterioration of Sufi organizations before 1967, see M. D. Gilsenan, ''Some Factors in the Decline of the Sufi Orders in Modern Egypt,'' *Muslim World* 57 (January 1967): 11–18. Concerning the ideological and pedagogical role of the new Sufi federation, see Abu al-Wafa al-Ghanimi al-Taftazani, ''al-Tasawwuf fi Muwajahat Tahaddiyaat al-'Asr'' [Sufism confronting the challenges of the age], *al-Tasawwuf al-Islami* 59 (January 1984).

47. Iliya Harik, ''Continuity and Change in Local Development Politics in Rural Egypt:

From Nasser to Sadat,'' *International Journal of Middle East Studies* 16 (1984): 43–66; Huda Khalil, ''75 'Aman 'ala Nidal al-Fallahin al-Ta'awuniyin fi Misr'' [Seventy-five years of struggle of the cooperative peasants in Egypt], *al-Ahali,* December 14, 1983.

48. These conversations are recorded in the minutes of President Sadat's meetings with interest group leaders. al-Hay'a al-'Amma lil-'Istalamaat, *Misr wa Masirat al-Dimuqratiya: 'Alamaat 'ala al-Tariq* (Cairo: Matabi' al-Akhbar, 1980).

49. An edited text of Sadat's speech appeared in *al-Ahram,* September 6, 1981.

50. ''al-Mu'tamar al-Iqtisadi wa Da'waha lil-Hiwar wa Ibda' al-Ra'i'' [The economic conference and its invitation to dialogue and the expression of opinion], *al-Ahram,* February 8, 1982; ''al-Bayan al-Khatami lil-Mu'tamar al-Iqtisadi'' [The final statement of the economic conference], *al-Ahram,* February, 16, 1982.

51. ''Ijtima' li-Ru'asa' al-Qita'aat bil-Mu'tamar Misr al-Ghad'' [A meeting of the sectoral leaders in the Egypt of Tomorrow Conference], *al-Ahram,* May 5, 1982; ''Tarshih A'da' al-Hiwar lil-Mu'tamar Misr al-Ghad'' [Nomination of the conferees in the Egypt of Tomorrow Conference], *al-Ahram,* May 12, 1982.

52. Mubarak's ''discovery'' of pluralism and interest group politics was increasingly reflected in his speeches to parliament before and after the 1987 elections. As early as November 1986 he observed, ''The Arab Republic of Egypt is not only the presidency, or the legislative, executive, and judicial powers, or the majority party and the government press. The Egyptian state includes all of the parties, the party and government press together, as well as all groups and syndicates.'' For a summary of the opposition parties' responses to these overtures, see ''al-Mu'arada al-Misriya Tuhaddad Asas al-Hiwar'' [The Egyptian opposition determines the basis of dialogue], *al-Hawadeth,* December 19, 1986.

Chapter 4

1. Clement Henry Moore, ''Professional Syndicates in Contemporary Egypt,'' *American Journal of Arabic Studies* 3 (1975): 60–83; Robert Springborg, ''Professional Syndicates in Egyptian Politics, 1952–1979,'' *International Journal of Middle East Studies* 9 (1978): 275–95.

2. ''al-Niqabaat al-Ha'ira'' [The confused syndicates], *Ruz al-Yusuf,* June 25, 1962, pp. 12–15.

3. Springborg, ''Professional Syndicates in Egyptian Politics,'' pp. 286–87.

4. Ibid., p. 293; ''Hiwar al-Sha'b ma' Ahmad Baha' al-Din'' [al-Sha'b's dialogue with Ahmad Baha' al-Din], *al-Sha'b,* April 26, 1983.

5. Moore, ''Professional Syndicates in Contemporary Egypt,'' pp. 79–81.

6. After 1978 two additional syndicates were created for social workers and the fine arts.

7. See the party's weekly forum devoted to discussions of the freedom of association, ''Da'wa 'Amma li Munaqashat al-Hurriyaat al-Niqabiya'' [A public call to discuss syndical freedoms], *al-Sha'b,* May 10, 1983. See also the declaration of the group that eventually developed into the Egyptian Human Rights Association, ''8 Hulul li Muwasila al-Masira al-Dimuqratiya'' [Eight solutions to the continuation of the democratic journey], *al-Sha'b,* October 18, 1983.

8. Mushira al-Gaziri, ''The Role of the Bar Association in Egyptian Politics, 1952–1981'' (Master's thesis, Department of Economics and Political Science, American University in Cairo, 1982), pp. 99–105, 165; Kirk James Beattie, ''Egypt: The Struggle for He-

gemony, 1952–1981'' (Ph.D. diss., Department of Political Science, University of Michigan, 1985), pp. 351–56.

9. Mahmud Sami, ''Kul al-Munaqashaat Hawl al-Hizbiya wa al-Dimuqratiya'' [All of the debates about parties and democracy], *al-Ahram*, February 2, 1976.

10. al-Gaziri, ''Role of the Bar Association,'' pp. 105–7, 113; Beattie, ''Egypt,'' pp. 355–57; Muhammad ʿAsfur, ''Istiqlal al-Quda''' [The independence of the judiciary], *al-Sha'b*, March 20, 1984.

11. Mahmud Sami and Ahmad Mustafa, ''Intikhabaat Ghadan fi Niqabat al-Muhammiyin'' [Elections tomorrow in the lawyers' syndicate], *al-Ahram*, November 13, 1975.

12. ''Maʿrakat Intikhab Naqib al-Muhammiyin'' [The election battle for the presidency of the lawyers' syndicate], *al-Siyasa* (Kuwait), October 22, 1978; al-Gaziri, ''Role of the Bar Association,'' pp. 123–26, 175–76; Beattie, ''Egypt,'' pp. 545–48.

13. al-Gaziri, ''Role of the Bar Association,'' pp. 126–27.

14. Ibid., pp. 138–40.

15. The full text of Sadat's address was published in *al-Ahram*, May 18, 1981.

16. al-Gaziri, ''Role of the Bar Association,'' p. 148.

17. ''al-Tafasil al-Kamila li Waqa'iʿ al-Tahqiq maʿ Majlis Niqabat al-Muhammiyin'' [The complete details of the investigation into the council of the lawyers' syndicate], *al-Musawwar*, June 23, 1981.

18. ''al-Mu'tamar al-ʿAmm al-Thani lil-Muhammiyin'' [The second general congress of the lawyers], *al-Ahali*, April 6, 1983.

19. ''Limadha Yurfud al-Muhammun al-Qanun al-Jadid?'' [Why do the lawyers reject the new law?], *al-Ahali*, April 13, 1983.

20. ''Nadwa bi Niqabat al-Muhammiyin fi Dhikra ʿAbd al-Nasir'' [A roundtable in the lawyers' syndicate to commemorate ʿAbd al-Nasir], *al-Sha'b*, September 20, 1983; ''Ihtifal Qawmi bi ʿIyd Milad ʿAbd al-Nasir fi Niqabat al-Muhammiyin'' [A national celebration on the birthday of ʿAbd al-Nasir in the lawyers' syndicate], *al-Ahali*, January 11, 1984.

21. ʿAsam Hanafi, ''Majlis al-Niqaba Yuqarar al-Difaʿ ʿan al-Jundi al-Misri'' [The syndicate council decides to defend the Egyptian soldier], *al-Watan* (Kuwait), October 16, 1985.

22. Ahmad al-Khawaja, ''Niqabatna Qawmiya wa Laysat Hizbiya'' [Our syndicate is nationalist, not partisan], *al-Sharq al-Awsat*, May 7, 1985.

23. Hassan Badawi, Ahmad Mustafa, and Hashim ʿAbd al-Fatah, ''al-Sahafiyun Yiftah al-Nar ʿala Ru'asa' al-Muassassaat wa Majlis al-Shura'' [The journalists open fire on the heads of the publishing houses and the Majlis al-Shura], *al-Ahali*, March 2, 1983.

24. Niqabaṭ al-Sahafiyin, *Niqabat al-Sahafiyin fi Arbaʿin ʿAman, 1941–1981* (Cairo: Matabiʿ al-Ahram al-Tijari, 1981).

25. Springborg, ''Professional Syndicates in Egyptian Politics,'' pp. 290–91, 293; Beattie, ''Egypt,'' pp. 349–51.

26. Ghali Shukri, *Egypt: Portrait of a President, 1971–1981* (London: Zed Press, 1981), pp. 366–77.

27. Nasha't al-Taghlibi, ''Niqabat al-Sahafiyin fi Misr Tuʿalan al-Harb ʿala Majlis al-Shura'' [The journalists' syndicate in Egypt declares war on the Majlis al-Shura], *al-Hawadeth*, March 25, 1981.

28. ''al-Sahafiyun Madha Yuridun?'' [What do the journalists want?], *Ruz al-Yusuf*, March 30, 1981; ʿAdli Fahim, ''Mubaraza Fikriya bayn Ruz al-Yusuf wa Ra'is al-Majlis al-Aʿala lil-Sahafa'' [Intellectual dueling between *Ruz al-Yusuf* and the head of the Higher Council for the Press], *Ruz al-Yusuf*, May 10, 1981.

29. A lengthy joint declaration of the Socialist Party and the journalists' syndicate denouncing the new press laws appeared in *al-Sha'b*, February 3, 1981.

30. "Salah Jalal Naqiban lil-Sahafiyin ba'd Ma'raka Intikhabiya Sakhina" [Salah Jalal is president of the journalists after a heated election battle], *al-Ahram*, March 7, 1981. The text of Sadat's address to the journalists was published in *al-Akhbar*, April 1, 1981.

31. *al-Ahram*, March 5, 1983; *al-Akhbar*, March 6, 1983.

32. *al-Ahrar*, February 14, 1983.

33. "Mata Tuhamas Ru'asa' al-Tahrir?" [When did the editors become enthusiastic?], *al-Ahali*, March 9, 1983.

34. *al-Ahram*, March 4, 1983.

35. Several interviews with the new council members appeared in *al-Ahali*, March 2, 1983.

36. "Tajmid Mas'uliya Majlis Niqabat al-Sahafiyin bi Qarar Amriki" [The freezing of the responsibility of the journalists' syndicate council by American decision], *al-Ahali*, January 25, 1984.

37. See, for example, her article on the labor movement. Amina Shafiq, "al-Takamul fi 'Anasir al-Dimuqratiya al-Ijtima'iya" [Integrating the elements of social democracy], *al-Ahram al-Iqtisadi*, April 25, 1983.

38. Muhammad 'Abd al-Qaddus, "Limadha Difa' al-Mutadayyin 'an al-Shiyu'iyin?" [Why do the pious defend the communists?], *al-Ahali*, December 28, 1983; "Ahlan bil-Nasiriyin" [Greetings to the Nasserists], *al-Wafd*, April 12, 1984; "Huquq al-Insan fi al-Islam" [Human rights in Islam], *al-Sha'b*, November 2, 1982.

39. Clement Henry Moore, *Images of Development: Egyptian Engineers in Search of Industry* (Cambridge: M.I.T. Press, 1980), pp. 32, 34–35, 52–53, 60.

40. Ibid., pp. 175–78.

41. Nahed Dajani, "Corporatism in the Egyptian Context: A Profile of Business and Professional Politics in Egypt" (Master's thesis, Department of Economics and Political Science, American University in Cairo, 1982), pp. 54–56, 63, 69.

42. Ibid., pp. 56–60.

43. Ibid., pp. 64–69.

44. "Sharikaat 'Uthman La'bat Dawran Asasiyan fi Fawzihi bi Mansib al-Naqib" ['Uthman's companies played an essential role in his winning the office of president], *al-Sha'b*, March 15, 1983.

45. "Hal Yustahaq 'Uthman Ahmad 'Uthman An Yakun Naqiban lil-Muhandisin Mara Ukhra?" [Does 'Uthman Ahmad 'Uthman deserve to be the president of the engineers another time?], *al-Ahali*, December 29, 1982; "Niqabat al-Muhandisin Amam al-Mudda'i al-Ishtiraki" [The engineers' syndicate before the socialist prosecutor], *al-Ahali*, March 6, 1985.

46. "Ghayr al-Muhandisin Yumna'un al-Muhandisin min al-Kalam fi al-Jam'iya al-'Umumiya" [Nonengineers prevent engineers from speaking in the General Assembly], *al-Sha'b*, April 1, 1980; "Azma fi Niqabat al-Muhandisin" [Crisis in the engineers' syndicate], *al-Ahali*, March 7, 1984.

47. "'Uthman Ahmad 'Uthman Naqiban lil-Muhandisin" ['Uthman Ahmad 'Uthman is president of the engineers], *Akhbar al-Yawm*, March 5, 1983; *al-Ahali*, March 2, 1983.

48. Jamal Fadil, "al-Tanmiya al-Sha'biya: min 'Usiy Musa ila al-Intiqadaat" [Popular development: From Moses' staffs to criticisms], *al-Ahram al-Iqtisadi*, November 21, 1983.

49. "Tawfir al-Sila' li-A'da' al-Niqabaat al-Mihniya" [The provision of consumer commodities to the professional syndicates], *al-Ahram*, November 12, 1982.

50. *al-Ahram*, March 8, 1983; *al-Ahali*, November 2, 1983.

51. "Niqabat al-Tatbiqiyin: Iqama Mashru' al-Athath bi Musahama Shirka 'Alamiya" [The draftsmen's syndicate: Establishment of a furniture project with the participation of an international corporation], *al-Ahram,* November 19, 1982.

52. "Niqabat al-Zira'iyin bi Shimal Sina' " [The agronomists' syndicate in North Sinai], *al-Ahram,* March 4, 1983.

53. Nabil al-Mihi, "Intikhabaat Niqabat al-Sinima'yin" [Elections of the cinematographers' syndicate], *al-Ahali,* April 13, 1983.

54. "al-Duktur Hijazi Yuwasi Taqlil al-'Itimad 'ala Buyut al-Khibra al-Ajnabiya" [Doctor Hijazi recommends less reliance on foreign experts], *al-Ahali,* May 25, 1983.

55. "al-Duktur Hijazi Yutalib Fikr Jadid Yatawafiq al-Mutaghayyiraat Allati Yamurr biha Iqtisadna" [Doctor Hijazi demands new thinking compatible with the changes through which our economy is passing], *al-Sha'b,* April 29, 1980; "al-Duktur Hijazi Yutalib al-Hukuma An Tuhadid Siyasat al-Raqaba" [Doctor Hijazi demands that the government determine a policy of control], *al-Ahali,* May 25, 1983.

56. "al-Duktur Sa'id Yaqul 'an 'Abd al-Razaq 'Abd al-Majid . . ." [Doctor Sa'id says of 'Abd al-Razaq 'Abd al-Majid . . .], *al-Sha'b,* March 29, 1983; 'Abd al-Majid's self-defense in *al-Sha'b,* April 5, 1983.

57. "Haqiqa ma Jarrat fi Intikhabaat al-Tijariyin" [The truth about what happened in the commercial employees' elections], *al-Sha'b,* June 21, 1983.

58. "Musalsal Niqabat al-Tijariyin" [The soap opera of the commercial employees' syndicate], *al-Ahram,* March 6, 1984.

59. Ahmad Baha' al-Din, "Sarat Niqabat al-Tijariyin fi Misr Mithl Bayrut al-Gharbiya" [The commercial employees syndicate in Egypt has become like West Beirut], *al-Ahram,* March 6, 1984.

60. "Intikhabaat al-Tijariyin: Najah 10 min Murashshahi al-Mu'arada" [The commercial elections: Victory of ten opposition candidates], *al-Ahali,* June 1, 1983.

Chapter 5

1. The inherent tensions in authoritarian regimes that try to use corporatist associations to build variegated bases of social support are elaborated in O'Donnell's distinction between the "privatizing" and "statizing" aspects of corporatism, in Stepan's concepts of "inclusionary corporatism" versus "exclusionary corporatism"; and in the Colliers' notions of "inducements-oriented" and "constraints-oriented" varieties of corporatism. Guillermo O'Donnell, "Corporatism and the Question of the State," in *Authoritarianism and Corporatism in Latin America,* ed. James Malloy (Pittsburgh: University of Pittsburgh Press, 1977); Alfred Stepan, *State and Society: Peru in Comparative Perspective* (Princeton: Princeton University Press, 1978); David Collier and Ruth Berens Collier, "Inducements versus Constraints: Disaggregating 'Corporatism,' " *American Political Science Review* 73 (December 1979): 967–86.

2. Such criticisms are made by a wide range of observers, including historians of the labor movement, former Nasserists, public sector managers, and private businessmen. On the stifling impact of corporatist unionism, see Joel Beinen, "Class Conflict and National Struggle: Labor and Politics in Egypt, 1936–1954" (Ph.D. diss., Department of History, University of Michigan, 1982), especially chap. 9 and conclusion. On the "excessive" grants of privilege to the unions, see Ahmad Baha' al-Din, "Fi Yawm Awwal Mayo" [On May Day], *al-Ahram,* May 1, 1983; Fu'ad Abu Zaghla, "Mudat al-Mashru'aat al-Mushtaraka" [The fad of codetermination projects], *al-Sha'b,* December 28, 1982.

3. On the persistent political and organizational weaknesses of the cooperatives during the Nasser and Sadat eras, see Iliya Harik, *The Political Mobilization of Peasants* (Bloomington: Indiana University Press, 1974), chap. 14; Richard H. Adams, Jr., *Development and Social Change in Rural Egypt* (Syracuse: Syracuse University Press, 1986), chaps. 6, 7.

4. Law no. 85 for 1942, *al-Waqa'i' al-Misriya* 171 (September 10, 1942): 8–11; Law no. 319 for 1952, *al-Waqa'i' al-Misriya* 157 (December 8, 1952): 15–19; Law no. 91 for 1959, *al-Jarida al-Rasmiya*, n.d.; Ministry of Labour, Law no. 62 for 1964 Together with the Ministerial Executive Orders (May 1964); Law no. 35 for 1976, *al-Jarida al-Rasmiya* 22 (May 27, 1976); Law no. 1 for 1981, *al-Jarida al-Rasmiya* 2 (January 8, 1981).

5. Muhammad Muhammad 'Ali, "al-Qiyadaat al-Niqabiya li-'Ummal Misr" [Union leaders of the Egyptian workers], *al-'Amal* 247 (December 1983): 36–39, 248 (January 1984): 54–56.

6. 'Asam 'Abd al-Jawad, "al-Manahij al-Dirasiya li-Kulliyaat al-Jami'a al-'Ummaliya" [The curricula in the faculties of the Workers' University], *al-'Amal* 248 (January 1984).

7. These data are compiled from statistical yearbooks issued between 1948 and 1964 and from annual reports of the Ministry of Manpower and Vocational Training for 1976 and 1983. The most recent and comprehensive of these reports is Wizarat al-Quwa al'Amila wa al-Tadrib al-Mihani: al-Idara al-'Amma lil-Ihsa', *al-Nashra al-Sanawiya li-Ihsa'aat al-Niqabaat 'an 'Am 1983* (Cairo, December 1983).

8. Ibid., pp. 4–5.

9. Ra'uf 'Abbas, *al-Haraka al-'Ummaliya fi Misr, 1899–1952* (Cairo: Dar al-Katib al-'Arabi lil-Taba'a wa al-Nashr, 1967), pp. 118–120, 122–132.

10. 'Abd al-Mughni Sa'id, "Safahaat Majhula min Tarikh al-Haraka al-Niqabiya," *al-'Amal* 236 (January 1983): 11–13.

11. Ibid., pp. 24–25.

12. 'Abd al-'Azim Ramadan, *al-Sira' al-Ijtima'i wa al-Siyasi fi Misr* (Cairo: Ruz al-Yusuf, 1975), chap. 11, appendixes; Willard A. Beling, *Pan-Arabism and Labor* (Cambridge: Harvard University Press, 1961), chap. 2.

13. Sa'id, "Safahaat Majhula min Tarikh al-Haraka al-Niqabiya," pp. 14–23.

14. Ibid., pp. 24–38; Anouar Abdel-Malek, *Egypt: Military Society* (New York: Random House, 1968), pp. 294–96, 304.

15. Jamal al-Banna', *Buhuth fi al-Thaqafa al-'Ummaliya* (Cairo: Matba'a Hasan, 1977), chap. 8.

16. Muhammad Khalid, *al-Haraka al-Niqabiya bayna al-Madi wa al-Hadar* (Cairo: Akhbar al-Yum, 1975); Mahmoud Hussein, *Class Conflict in Egypt, 1945–1970* (New York: Monthly Review Press, 1973), chap. 8.

17. Salah al-Sayed, *Workers' Participation in Management: The Egyptian Experience* (Cairo: American University in Cairo Press, 1978), chap. 5; Raymond William Baker, *Egypt's Uncertain Revolution under Nasser and Sadat* (Cambridge: Harvard University Press, 1978), chap. 7.

18. *al-Ahram*, May 2, 1983.

19. The new minister of manpower is 'Asim 'Abd al-Haqq Salih of the textile workers' federation, and the new confederation president is Ahmad al-'Amawi of the chemical workers' federation.

20. "Niqabat 'Ummal al-Zira'a Tandam lil-Ittihad al-Hurr" [The agricultural workers' union joins the free confederation], *al-Ahali*, August 17, 1983; "Ba'da Khibrat Thalathin Sana ma' al-Ittihad al-Hurr" [After thirty years' experience with the free confederation], *al-Ahali*, February 23, 1983.

21. "Ittihad al-'Ummal Ya'tarid 'ala 'Ard Murashshahi al-Niqabaat 'ala al-Muda'i al-'Amm" [The labor confederation objects to the submission of union candidates to the socialist prosecutor], *al-Sha'b*, June 6, 1983.

22. "Sa'id Jum'a Yastaqil min Hizb al-Hukuma" [Sa'id Jum'a resigns from the government party], *al-Ahali*, May 18, 1983; "al-Hajj Muhammad Ahmad 'Umar: 'Istaqaltu min al-Hizb al-Watani' " [al-Hajj Muhammad Ahmad 'Umar: "I resigned from the national party"], *al-Sha'b*, May 1, 1984.

23. Final results of the 1984 elections appeared in *al-Ahram*, June 1, 1984. Also see Markaz al-Dirasaat al-Siyasiya wa al-Istratijiya, *Intikhabaat Majlis al-Sha'b, 1984: Dirasa wa Tahlil* (Cairo: Matabi' al-Ahram al-Tijariya, 1986).

24. Gamal-Eddine Heyworth-Dunne, *Egypt: The Cooperative Movement*, no. 6 of *Muslim World Series* (Cairo: Renaissance Bookshop, 1952), p. 47; *Statistical Yearbook* for 1955, 1960, 1966, 1980; al-Hay'a al-'Amma lil-Ta'awun al-Zira'i, *Bayan al-Jam'iyaat al-Ta'awuniya al-Zira'iya 'Am 1977* (Cairo, 1978).

25. Samir Radwan, *Agrarian Reform and Rural Poverty: Egypt, 1952–1975* (Geneva: I.L.O., 1977), chap. 5; Heyworth-Dunne, *Egypt: The Cooperative Movement*, pp. 6–7, 18.

26. Heyworth-Dunne, *Egypt: The Cooperative Movement*, pp. 27–31, 48.

27. Radwan, *Agrarian Reform and Rural Poverty*, chap. 5; Heyworth-Dunne, *Egypt: The Cooperative Movement*, pp. 25–26, 35–36.

28. Heyworth-Dunne, *Egypt: The Cooperative Movement*, pp. 13–17.

29. Ibid., pp. 23–26.

30. Harik, *The Political Mobilization of Peasants*, chap. 2; Radwan, *Agrarian Reform and Rural Poverty*, chap. 5; Baker, *Egypt's Uncertain Revolution*, chap. 8.

31. Radwan, *Agrarian Reform and Rural Poverty*, chap. 6.

32. Ibid.

33. Hamied Ansari, *Egypt: The Stalled Society* (Albany: State University of New York Press, 1986), chap. 1.

34. John Waterbury, *The Egypt of Nasser and Sadat: The Political Economy of Two Regimes* (Princeton: Princeton University Press, 1983), p. 326.

35. Leonard Binder, *In a Moment of Enthusiasm: Political Power and the Second Stratum* (Chicago: University of Chicago Press, 1978), chap. 14; Harik, *The Political Mobilization of Peasants*, chaps. 12, 14.

36. Huda Khalil, "75 'Aman 'ala Nidal al-Fallahin al-Ta'awuniyin fi Misr" [Seventy-five years of the struggle of the cooperative peasants in Egypt], *al-Ahali*, December 14, 1983.

37. Ibid.; Waterbury, *The Egypt of Nasser and Sadat*, pp. 294–95.

38. Khalil, "75 'Aman 'ala Nidal al-Fallahin al-Ta'awuniyin fi Misr."

39. Ibid.; Waterbury, *The Egypt of Nasser and Sadat*, p. 294.

40. *al-Akhbar*, July 2, 1976; *Akhbar al-Yawm*, July 28, 1976; *al-Akhbar*, August 20, 1976.

41. *Akhir Sa'a*, August 4, 1976.

42. Iliya Harik, "Continuity and Change in Local Development Policies in Egypt: From Nasser to Sadat," *International Journal of Middle East Studies* 16 (1984): 53–65; Huda Khalil, "Ra'is Bank al-Tanmiya wa al-I'timan al-Zira'i Yurad 'ala Intiqadaat al-Fallahin" [The president of the development and credit bank responds to the criticisms of the peasants], *al-Ahali*, December 28, 1983.

43. Harik, "Continuity and Change," pp. 53–65; Waterbury, *The Egypt of Nasser and Sadat*, pp. 295–96.

44. Samir Radwan and Eddy Lee, *Agrarian Change in Egypt: An Anatomy of Rural*

Poverty (London: Croom Helm, 1986); Adams, *Development and Social Change,* chaps. 3, 6.

45. "Fu'ad Muhi al-Din Yu'lan Bahth Tashkil Ittihad Ta'awuni 'Amm" [Fu'ad Muhi al-Din Announces an effort to establish a cooperative confederation], *al-Ahram,* November 2, 1982; Huda Tawfiq, "Hatta al-Ittihad al-Ta'awuni Hawwaluha ila Mu'assassa Taba' lil-Hizb al Watani" [They have turned even the cooperative confederation into an organization subordinate to the Nationalist Party], *al-Ahali,* December 21, 1983.

46. Tawfiq, "Hatta al-Ittihad al-Ta'awuni Hawwaluha ila Mu'assassa Taba' lil-Hizb al Watani."

47. Ibrahim Yunis, "Ba'd Bara'a al-Ittihad al-Ta'awuni wa Qiyadaatha Maratayn" [After the double acquittal of the cooperative confederation and its leaders], *al-Sha'b,* January 11, 1983; "Hawl Qidaya al-Ittihad al-Ta'awuni wa Bara'a Qiyadaatha Jami'an" [Concerning the case of the cooperative confederation and the acquittal of all of its leaders], *al-Sha'b,* May 4, 1982.

48. "I'lan Ta'sis Awwal Ittihad 'Amm lil-Fallahin al-Misriyin" [Announcement of the foundation of the first confederation of Egyptian peasants], *al-Ahali,* June 22, 1983.

49. "Ittihad al-Fallahin al-Misriyin: Bunuk al-Qarya la Takhdim al-Qadiya al-Zira'iya" [The confederation of Egyptian peasants: The village banks do not serve the cause of agriculture], *al-Ahali,* August 17, 1983.

Chapter 6

1. Yusuf al-Qa'id, "Misr: al-Nizam al-Masrafi fi Khatar" [Egypt: The banking system in danger], *al-Mustaqbal,* November 3, 1984.

2. Markaz al-Dirasaat al-Siyasiya wa al-Istratijiya bil-Ahram, *al-Taqrir al-Istratiji al-'Arabi, 1986* (Cairo: Matabi' al-Ahram al-Tijariya, 1987), p. 381.

3. Layla Muhammad Ibrahim, "Dirasa fi al-Ghuruf al-Tijariya" [A study of the chambers of commerce], report prepared for the Cairo Chamber of Commerce (1983).

4. "Tashri'aat al-Ghuruf al-Tijariya" [Legislation of the chambers of commerce], *Majalat al-Ghurfa al-Tijariya lil-Qahira,* January, 1977; al-Ghurfa al-Tijariya lil-Qahira, *al-Tanzim al-Idari lil-Ghurfa: al-Ahdaf wa al-Ikhtisasaat al-'Amma* (Cairo, 1979).

5. "Fi Intikhabaat al-Ghuruf al-Tijariya" [In the elections of the chambers of commerce], *al-Ahali,* June 1, 1983; "'Udw bil-Hizb al-Watani wa al-Ghurfa al-Tijariya Yataharab min al-Dara'ib" [A member of the National Party and the Chamber of Commerce evades taxes], *al-Sha'b,* February 22, 1983.

6. Nahed Dajani, "Corporatism in the Egyptian Context: A Profile of Business and Professional Politics in Egypt" (Master's thesis, Department of Economics and Political Science, American University in Cairo, 1982), pp. 85–86, 88, 90.

7. Amani Qandil, "al-Qarar 119 wa Humum San' al-Siyasa al-Iqtisadiya" [Proclamation 119 and the concerns of economic policy-making], *al-Ahram al-Iqtisadi,* April 14, 1986; "al-Ghurfa al-Tijariya Tu'abin Ra'isaha" [The Chamber of Commerce eulogizes its president], *al-Ahram al-Iqtisadi,* January 2, 1984.

8. Dajani, "Corporatism in the Egyptian Context," pp. 91–98; "Mashru' Qanun lil-Guruf al-Tijariya" [A draft law for the chambers of commerce], *al-Ahram,* February 17, 1981.

9. "Khitab Maftuh ila al-Sayyid 'Izzat Ghidan, Ra'is Ittihad al-Ghuruf al-Tijariya" [An open letter to Mr. 'Izzat Ghidan, president of the Confederation of Chambers of Commerce], *al-Sha'b,* March 22, 1983; "al-Ghurfa al-Tijariya: Ilgha' Brutukul al-Ta'awun ma'

al-Ittihad al-Sufyati Yu'athar 'ala Sadaraatna min al-Sajjad'' [The Chamber of Commerce: Abrogation of the protocol of cooperation with the Soviet Union affects our exports of carpets], *al-Ahram,* February 22, 1984; ''al-Ghurfa al-Tijariya: al-Qita' al-Khass Yurawwij Adawaat Manziliya Radi'a'' [The Chamber of Commerce: The private sector is marketing inferior household goods], *al-Ahali,* November 20, 1983.

10. Ittihad al-Sana'aat al-Misriya, *al-Tatawwur al-Tarikhi lil-Ittihad al-Sana'aat al-Misriya* (Cairo, 1978), pp. 1–3.

11. Ittihad al-Sana'aat al-Misriya, *Tatawwur Ittihad al-Sana'aat al-Misriya fi Khamsin Sana, 1922–1972* (Cairo, 1972).

12. Ittihad al-Sana'aat al-Misriya, *al-Tatawwur al-Tarikhi lil-Ittihad,* p. 10.

13. Ibid., pp. 3–9.

14. ''al-Hukuma Tatadakhal li Waqf Irtifa' As'ar al-Ahdhiya'' [The government intervenes to stop the rise in the price of shoes], *al-Ahram al-Iqtisadi,* December 5, 1983; ''Rudud Fi'l Hada fi Ghurfa Sana'a al-Julud'' [A sharp reaction in the chamber of the leather industry], *al-Ahali,* December 14, 1983.

15. In 1974 Sadat dismissed 37 chairmen and 104 board members from public sector industrial establishments; in 1975 he dismissed 10 chairmen and 99 board members; in 1977 he transferred or dismissed 21 chairmen and 76 board members. 'Adal Husayn, *al-Iqtisad al-Misri min al-Istiqlal ila al-Taba'iya, 1974–1979* (Beirut: Dar al-Wahda, 1981), vol. 2, pp. 490–91.

16. Sharif Shukri, ''al-Sina'a al-Radi'a La Tastahaqq al-Himaya'' [Bad industry doesn't deserve protection], *Ruz al-Yusuf,* May 5, 1983.

17. Ibid.; Isis Sulayman, ''al-Nuhud bil-Sana'aat al-Saghira . . . Kayf?'' [The revival of small industries . . . how?], *al-Ahram al-Iqtisadi,* April 16, 1984.

18. 'Abd al-Mun'im 'Uthman, ''150 min Rijal al-A'mal al-Amrikiyin wa al-Misriyin fi Liqa' al-Sanawi bil-Qahira'' [One hundred fifty American and Egyptian businessmen in an annual meeting in Cairo], *al-Ahram,* May 5, 1982; Usama Saraya, ''Wazira al-Iqtisad wa al-Istithmar fi Hiwar ma' Rijal al-A'mal'' [The ministers of economy and investment in a dialogue with businessmen], *al-Ahram,* October 12, 1982.

19. Jam'iyat Rijal al-A'mal al-Misriyin, *al-Taqrir al-Sanawi wa Dalil al-A'da' lil-Jam'iyat Rijal al-A'mal al-Misriyin* (Cairo: Dar al-'Alam al-'Arabi, 1983), pp. 32–33.

20. 'Imad Ghanim, ''Wazir al-Takhtit fi Liqa' Nadi al-Idara wa Jam'iyat Rijal al-A'mal'' [The minister of planning in a meeting with the Management Club and the Businessmen's Association], *al-Ahram al-Iqtisadi,* February 27, 1983.

21. Kamal Jab Allah, ''Shahr 'Asl Jadid bayna Wizarat al-Maliya wa Rijal al-A'mal'' [A new honeymoon between the Ministry of Finance and the businessmen], *al-Ahram al-Iqtisadi,* April 11, 1983.

22. 'Imad Ghanim, ''Musalaha bayna Wizarat al-Kahraba' wa Rijal al-A'mal'' [A compromise between the Ministry of Electricity and the businessmen], *al-Ahram al-Iqtisadi,* May 23, 1983.

23. ''Musaddiru al-Qita' al-Khass Yutalibun bi Hasilat al-Sadaraat'' [Private sector exporters demand the proceeds of exports], *al-Ahram al-Iqtisadi,* April 18, 1983; ''Rijal al-A'mal al-Misriyun fi Amrika li Bahth Ziyadat al-Sadaraat al-Misriya'' [Egyptian businessmen in America to discuss more Egyptian exports], *al-Ahram al-Iqtisadi,* May 16, 1983.

24. Jam'iyat Rijal al-A'mal al-Misriyin, *al-Taqrir al-Sanawi,* p. 6.

25. Markaz al-Dirasaat al-Siyasiya wa al-Istratijiya bil-Ahram, *al-Taqrir al-Istratiji al-'Arabi, 1986* (Cairo: Matabi' al-Ahram al-Tijariya, 1987), p. 381; Amani Qandil, ''Man Hum Rijal al-A'mal wa Ayna Jama'aat al-Masalih al-Ukhra?'' [Who are the businessmen and where are the other interest groups?], *al-Ahram al-Iqtisadi,* January 6, 1986.

26. Muhammad ʿAbd al-Fatah Rajab, "Rijal al-Aʿmal Laysu Jamaʿa Daght" [Businessmen are not a pressure group], al-Ahram, May 3, 1986.

27. Amani Qandil, "Ayna Ittihad Niqabaat al-ʿUmmal min Jamaʿaat al-Daght?" [Where is the Confederation of Labor among the pressure groups?], al-Ahram al-Iqtisadi, January 20, 1986.

28. Karam Badra, "al-Malyuniraat al-Misriyun fi Almanya" [The Egyptian millionaires in Germany], al-Ahram, August 9, 1987.

29. "Majala Jadida lil-Difaʿ ʿan Siyasat al-Infitah" [A new magazine to defend the open door policy], al-Ahali, March 28, 1984; Badra, "al-Malyuniraat al-Misriyun fi Almanya."

30. Lutfi al-Khuli, "al-Muwatin wa al-Azma al-Iqtisadiya" [The citizen and the economic crisis], al-Ahram, April 19, 1986; Amani Qandil, "Jamaʿaat al-Masalih wa al-Tawazun al-Mafqud" [Interest groups and the lost balance], al-Ahram, April 26, 1986.

31. "ʿUmmal Misr Yuʾakidun lil-Hizb al-Hakim Istiqlaliyat al-Haraka al-Niqabiya" [Egypt's workers reaffirm to the ruling party the independence of the union movement], al-Shaʿb, November 18, 1986.

32. One indication of the growing concern with interest groups rather than political parties is the work of the research team at the al-Ahram Center for Political and Strategic Studies. The 1985 edition of the center's "Strategic Arab Report" devoted eight pages to Egypt's party system and seven pages to "pressure groups." However, the 1986 edition devoted eleven pages to parties and twenty-nine pages to "interest groups," including several Islamic and Nasserist associations that were described as "forces denied legitimacy."

33. The history of al-Azhar's numerous reforms is presented in A. Chris Eccel, Egypt, Islam and Social Change: al-Azhar in Conflict and Accommodation (Berlin: Klaus Schwarz Verlag, 1984); Bayard Dodge, al-Azhar: A Millennium of Muslim Learning (Washington D.C.: Middle East Institute, 1961); Daniel Crecelius, "Nonideological Responses of the Egyptian Ulama to Modernization," in Scholars, Saints, and Sufis: Muslim Religious Institutions since 1500, ed. Nikki R. Keddie (Berkeley: University of California Press, 1972).

34. Eccel, Egypt, Islam and Social Change, pp. 23, 134; F. De Jong, Turuq and Turuq-Linked Institutions in Nineteenth Century Egypt: A Historical Study in Organizational Dimensions of Islamic Mysticism (Leiden: E.J. Brill: 1978), p. 105.

35. Eccel, Egypt, Islam and Social Change, chaps. 4, 6.

36. Ibid., chaps. 5, 7; Crecelius, "Nonideological Responses of the Egyptian Ulama," pp. 197, 201.

37. Eccel, Egypt, Islam and Social Change, pp. 167–71.

38. Crecelius, "Nonideological Responses of the Egyptian Ulama," pp. 198–204; Saʿid Ismaʿil ʿAli, al-Azhar ʿala Masrah al-Siyasa al-Misriya (Cairo: Dar al-Thaqafa, 1974), chaps. 9, 10.

39. Eccel, Egypt, Islam and Social Change, pp. 55–56, 114, 129, 314, 402, 420, 513–24.

40. Gilles Kepel, Muslim Extremism in Egypt: The Prophet and Pharaoh (Berkeley: University of California Press, 1986), pp. 97–100.

41. Muhammad ʿAbd al-Qaddus, "ʿUlama' al-Azhar Yantaqidun Anfusihim" [The 'Ulama' of al-Azhar criticize themselves], al-Shaʿb, October 26, 1982.

42. "al-Hiwar maʿ Jamaʿat al-Takfir wa al-Hijra" [The dialogue with the al-Takfir wa al-Hijra group], al-Liwa' al-Islami, June 17, 1982; "'Ulama' Misr Yudirun al-Hiwar maʿ al-Mutatarrifin fi Liman Tura" [Egypt's 'Ulama' conduct the dialogue with the extremists in Liman Tura Prison], al-Musawwar, June 4, 1982.

43. al-Tilmisani's prison memoirs assert that he already had been playing such a role for some time. ʿUmar al-Tilmisani, Ayyam maʿ al-Sadat (Cairo: Dar al-Iʿtisam, 1984).

44. Misbah Qutb, "al-Sadat Rafad Insha' Niqaba li-A'imma al-Masajid bi Sabab Ma-shakilihi ma' Rijal al-Din" [al-Sadat rejected the establishment of a syndicate for imams of mosques because of his problems with men of religion], *al-Ahali,* April 4, 1984.

45. 'Atif Husayn, "Fi al-Ihtifal bi al-'Id al-Alfi lil-Azhar" [On the celebration of the one thousandth anniversary of al-Azhar], *al-Sha'b,* March 22, 1983.

46. "al-Lawa'ih al-Sufiya al-Rasmiya al-Jadida" [The new official Sufi regulations], *al-Muslim,* special issue, 1978.

47. De Jong, *Turuq and Turuq-Linked Institutions,* chaps. 1, 2.

48. Ibid., chaps. 3, 4.

49. Ibid., chap. 4.

50. Michael Gilsenan, "Some Factors in the Decline of the Sufi Orders in Egypt," *Muslim World* 57 (1967): 11–18.

51. "al-Ra'is Husni Mubarak fi Liqa' ma' A'da' al-Majlis al-A'la lil-Turuq al-Sufiya" [President Husni Mubarak meets with the members of the Higher Sufi Council], Shaykh al-Azhar, Jad al-Haqq 'Ali Jad al-Haqq, "Taharu al-Thaqafa min al-Tashkik wa al-Mafahim al-Mustawrida" [Cleanse the culture of doubt and imported ideas], *al-Tasawwuf al-Islami,* April, 1983.

52. Johannes J. G. Jansen, *The Neglected Duty: The Creed of Sadat's Assassins and Islamic Resurgence in the Middle East* (New York: Macmillan, 1986), chap. 3.

53. Michael Gilsenan, *Saint and Sufi in Modern Egypt: An Essay in the Sociology of Religion* (Oxford: Clarendon Press, 1973), chaps. 3, 4.

54. Michael Gilsenan, *Recognizing Islam: Religion and Society in the Modern Arab World* (New York: Pantheon, 1982), chap. 10.

55. Ibid.

56. Nawal Hasan, *The Role of Voluntary Associations in Egypt* (Cairo: Center for Egyptian Civilization Studies, 1981).

57. Morroe Berger, *Islam in Egypt Today: Social and Political Aspects of Popular Religion* (Cambridge: Cambridge University Press, 1970).

58. The provincial distribution of Christian and Muslim associations was provided by the Ministry of Social Affairs.

59. Sectarian differences among Egyptian Christians are discussed in Robert Brenton Betts, *Christians in the Arab East* (Athens: Lycabettos Press, 1975), pp. 41–63. A useful overview of the Coptic community is Milad Hana, *Na'am Iqbat, Lakin Misriyun* (Cairo: Maktabat Madbuli, 1980). Links between the Copts of Cairo and Upper Egypt are described in L'Association Chretienne de la Haute Egypte, *A Profile of the Association Today* (Cairo, 1979).

60. On sectarian tensions between Copts and Muslims see Hamied Ansari, "Sectarian Conflict and the Political Expedience of Religion," *Middle East Journal* 38 (Summer 1984); Tariq al-Bishri, *al-Muslimun wa al-Iqbat fi Itar al-Jama'a al-Wataniya* (Beirut: Dar al-Wahda, 1982), and Mustafa al-Fiqi, *al-Iqbat fi al-Siyasa al-Misriya: Makram 'Ubayd wa Duwruhu fi al-Haraka al-Wataniya* (Cairo: Dar al-Shuruq, 1985).

61. The provincial distribution of government and private mosques from 1980 to 1982 was provided by the Ministry of Awqaf.

62. Fearing adverse public reaction to Sadat's disrespect toward a popular religious leader, government editors removed this phrase from the printed transcript of the speech. The early activities of the imams' associations in Alexandria and Suez were discussed in the following issues of *al-Sha'b:* March 18, 1980; April 1, 1980; March 13, 1984.

63. Berger, for example, speaks of "the associative injunction and propensity" in *Islam in Egypt Today,* chaps. 1, 5. On the diversity of voluntary collective action among Mus-

lims, also see James Heyworth-Dunne, *Religious and Political Trends in Modern Egypt* (Washington, D.C., 1950); Richard P. Mitchell, *The Society of Muslim Brothers* (London: Oxford University Press, 1969); Kepel, *Muslim Extremism in Egypt.*

64. Hamid Zaydan, "Hiwar al-Sha'b ma' al-Shabab al-Muslim" [al-Sha'b's dialogue with the Muslim youth], *al-Sha'b,* March 27, 1984.

65. Ibid.

66. Ibid.

67. Ahmad al-Suyufi, "al-Amn Yaft'al al-Mashakil li Tashwih Suratna fi al-Jami'a" [The security forces fabricate problems in order to distort our image at the university], *al-Sha'b,* April 24, 1984; Ahmed Abdalla, *The Student Movement and National Politics in Egypt, 1923–1973* (London: Zed Books, 1985), pp. 226– 28.

68. Ahmad al-Suyufi, "al-Amn Yaft'al al-Mashakil li Tashwih Suratna fi al-Jami'a" *al-Sha'b,* April 24, 1984.

69. Ibid.

70. "Tulab al-Jami'aat Yutalibun bil-'Awda ila La'iha Ittihadaatihim al-Qadima" [University students demand the return to the regulations of their old unions], *al-Sha'b,* November 23, 1982; Mustafa al-Safani, "al-Haraka al-Tulabiya Tuwasal Kifahiha li-Isqat al-La'iha al-Tulabiya" [The student movement continues its struggle to overthrow the student regulations], *al-Sha'b,* March 13, 1984; and Kepel, *Muslim Extremism in Egypt,* p. 150.

71. Hamid Zaydan and Ahmad al-Suyufi, "Ahdath al-Zawiya al-Hamra' Masnu'a" [The events of al-Zawiya al-Hamra' were fabricated], *al-Sha'b,* March 13, 1984.

72. One such incident concerned an alleged attack by association members on a man who was walking with his daughter in the town of Minya. Sadat cited the incident in one of his public attacks on the associations. But *jama'aat* leaders in Minya said that a local police officer who admitted that the story was untrue was quickly reposted to another province. Ahmad al-Suyufi, "Khatt Tilifun Sakhin bayna al-Nabawi Isma'il wa al-Duktur Hilmi al-Jazzar" [The hot line between Nabawi Isma'il and Dr. Hilmi al-Jazzar], *al-Sha'b,* March 20, 1984.

73. Ibid.

74. *al-Sha'b,* March 13, 1984; Ansari, "Sectarian Conflict and the Political Expedience of Religion."

75. Majdi Ahmad Husayn, "Saqatat Qa'imat al-Hizb al-Watani bi-Kamilihi fi Intikhabaat Nadi A'da' Hay'aat al-Tadris" [The entire list of the Democratic Party failed in the elections of the faculty clubs], *al-Sha'b,* April 3, 1984; "Islam in Egypt: Health Behind the Veil," *Economist,* December 5, 1987; Tom Masland, "Mosques See the Way to Egypt's Heart," *Chicago Tribune,* December 28, 1986.

76. Ahmad al-Suyufi, "Risalatna fi al-Hayah 'An Nahayya bil-Islam" [Our mission in life is to revitalize Islam], *al-Sha'b,* April 17, 1984.

77. "al-Tilmisani Yada'u lil-Ta'anni fi Tatbiq al-Shari'a al-Islamiya" [al-Tilmisani calls for deliberateness in the application of the Islamic law], *al-Sharq al-Awsat,* March 5, 1985.

78. Statement of Dr. Muhammad al-Badrawi, a leader of the Islamic associations in Cairo and a graduate of al-Azhar's medical school, quoted in Muhammad 'Abd al-Qaddus, "Nahnu Abriya' min Tuhmat al-Irhab" [We are innocent of the accusation of terrorism], *al-Sha'b,* May 18, 1982.

79. *al-Sha'b,* April 17, 1984.

80. Ibid.

81. Ansari, "Sectarian Conflict and the Political Expedience of Religion," pp. 406, 415.

82. Yusuf al-Qardawi, *al-Sahwa al-Islamiya bayna al-Juhud wa al-Tatarruf* (Cairo, 1984).

83. Saad Eddin Ibrahim, "Anatomy of Egypt's Militant Islamic Groups: Methodological

Note and Preliminary Findings,'' *International Journal of Middle East Studies* 12 (1980); and Hamied N. Ansari, "The Islamic Militants in Egyptian Politics," *International Journal of Middle East Studies* 16 (1984). For a summary and useful bibliography of recent studies of the revolutionary societies, see ʿAdal Hamuda, *al-Hijra ila al-ʿUnf: al-Tatarruf al-Dini min Hazimat Yuniya ila Ightiyal Oktobir* (Cairo, 1987).

84. The divisions within the Ikhwan are examined in Mitchell, *The Society of the Muslim Brothers,* chaps. 9, 10, and in Kepel, *Muslim Extremism in Egypt,* chap. 4.

85. For a discussion of the role of this tradition in the early debates of the Ikhwan, see Mitchell, *The Society of the Muslim Brothers,* pp. 18–19.

86. Ibid.

87. Muhammad Salim al-ʿAwwa, "Taghir al-Munkar . . . Man Yumlikhu wa Kayf Yakun?'' [Changing what is forbidden . . . who has the right and how should it be used?], *al-Hilal,* July 1987, pp. 19–20.

88. Ibid., pp. 20–21.

89. Ahmad Kamal Abu al-Majd, "al-Khaʾifun min al-Islam wa al-Khaʾifun ʿalayhi" [Those who are afraid of Islam and those who are afraid for it], *al-Hilal,* July 1987, p. 13. For leading examples of the debate over Islamic liberalism, see Muhammad ʿAmara, *al-Dawla al-Islamiya bayna al-ʿIlmaniya wa al-Sulta al-Diniya* (Cairo: Dar al-Shuruq, 1987), and *al-Islam wa Huquq al-Insan* (Kuwait: ʿAlam al-Maʿrifa, 1985); Shaykh Muhammad al-Ghazali, "Difaʿ ʿan al-Dimuqratiya wa Ahzab al-Muʿarada" [The defense of democracy and opposition parties], *al-Shaʿb,* April 10, 1983.

90. For similar arguments in the same issue of *al-Hilal* (July 1987), see Dr. Muhammad Ismaʿil, "Juzur al-Tatarruf al-Dini" [The roots of religious extremism]; Muhammad Nur Farhat, "Dawaʾir al-ʿUnf al-Thalath fi al-Mujtamaʿ al-Misri" [The three circles of violence in Egyptian society].

91. Mustafa Bakri, "Jeneralaat al-Din wa Mahakim al-Taftish fi al-Minya!" [Generals of religion and courts of inquiry in al-Minya!], *al-Musawwar,* September 25, 1987.

92. "Wazir al-Awqaf: Manʿ al-Aʾimma min Adaʾ Wajibihim fi Masajid Assyut Haram Sharʿan" [The Minister of Awqaf: Preventing imams from discharging their duty in the mosques of Assyut violates religious law], *al-Musawwar,* September 25, 1987.

Chapter 7

1. Alexis de Tocqueville, *Democracy in America,* vol. 2 (New York: Vintage Books, 1954), p. 126.

2. Ervand Abrahamian, *Iran between Two Revolutions* (Princeton: Princeton University Press, 1982), pp. 238–39, 244–45.

3. Ibid., p. 442.

4. Amir Taheri, "The Bazaar," *Kayhan International,* October 2, 1978, pp. 98–101; Sapehr Zabih, *Iran's Revolutionary Upheaval* (San Francisco: Alchemy Books, 1979), pp. 27–32.

5. Taheri, "The Bazaar," p. 99; Robert Graham, *Iran: The Illusion of Power* (London: Croom Helm, 1978).

6. Taheri, "The Bazaar," p. 98; Zabih, *Iran's Revolutionary Upheaval,* p. 28.

7. Leonard Binder, "The Proofs of Islam," in *Arabic and Islamic Studies in Honor of Hamilton A. R. Gibb,* ed. George Makdisi (Leiden: E.J. Brill, 1965), pp. 118–40; Hamid Algar, "The Oppositional Role of the Ulama in Twentieth-Century Iran," in *Scholars, Saints, and Sufis,* ed. Nikki R. Keddi (Berkeley: University of California Press, 1972), pp.

231–56; Shahrough Akhavi, *Religion and Politics in Contemporary Iran* (Albany: State University of New York Press, 1980).

8. Abrahamian, *Iran between Two Revolutions,* pp. 501–505.

9. Jerrold D. Green, *Revolution in Iran* (New York: Praeger, 1982), p. 154.

10. South Korea's industrialization policies are examined in two recent dissertations. Dal Joong Chang, "Japanese Corporations and the Political Economy of South Korean-Japanese Relations, 1965–1979" (Ph. D. diss., University of California, Berkeley, 1982); Hyun-Chin Lim, "Dependent Development in the World System: The Case of South Korea, 1963–1969" (Ph.D. diss., Harvard, 1982).

11. Jang Jip Choi, "Interest Conflict and Political Control in South Korea: A Study of the Labor Unions in Manufacturing Industries, 1961–1980" (Ph.D. diss., University of Chicago, 1983).

12. Chang, "Japanese Corporations," chap. 3.

13. Choi, "Interest Conflict and Political Control," chap. 8.

14. Ibid., chap. 3.

15. Ibid.

16. Ibid.

17. Ibid., chap. 4.

18. Ibid., chap. 6.

19. Chong-Sik Lee, "South Korea 1979: Confrontation, Assassination, and Transition," *Asian Survey* 20 (January 1980): 63–76.

20. Ibid., pp. 63–64, 69–70.

21. Lloyd I. Rudolph and Susanne Hoeber Rudolph, "To the Brink and Back: Representation and the State in India," *Asian Survey* 18 (April 1978): 379–400; W. H. Morris-Jones, "Creeping but Uneasy Authoritarianism: India, 1975–1976," *Government and Opposition* (Winter 1977): 20–41.

22. Rudolph and Rudolph, "To the Brink and Back," p. 382.

23. Morris-Jones, "Creeping but Uneasy Authoritarianism," p. 30.

24. Jyotirindra Das Gupta, "A Season of Ceasars: Emergency Regimes and Developmental Politics in Asia," *Asian Survey* 28 (April 1978): 315–49.

25. Morris-Jones, "Creeping but Uneasy Authoritarianism," pp. 31–33.

26. Rudolph and Rudolph, "To the Brink and Back," pp. 387–88; Stanley A. Kochanek, *Business and Politics in India* (Berkeley: University of California Press, 1974), chaps. 7, 8.

27. Rudolph and Rudolph, "To the Brink and Back," pp. 382, 389.

28. Ibid., pp. 389–90.

29. Ibid., p. 388.

30. Rakaharai Chattopadhyay, "The Political Role of Labor Unions in India: An Interstate Study of Labor Unions in West Bengal, Karnataka, and Rajasthan" (Ph.D. diss., University of Chicago, 1975), chap. 1.

31. Rudolph and Rudolph, "To the Brink and Back," pp. 390–91.

Bibliography

Books

ʿAbbas, Raʾuf. *al-Haraka al-ʿUmmaliya fi Misr, 1899–1952*. Cairo: Dar al-Katib al-ʿArabi lil-Tabaʿa wa al-Nashr, 1967.

ʿAbd al-Fadil, Mahmud. *Taʿammulaat fi al-Masʾala al-Iqtisadiya al-Misriya*. Cairo: Dar al-Mustaqbal al-ʿArabi, 1983.

———. *al-Iqtisad al-Misri bayna al-Takhtit al-Markazi wa al-Infitah al-Iqtisadi*. Beirut: Maʿhad al-Inmaʾ al-ʿArabi, 1980).

———. *The Political Economy of Nasserism*. Cambridge: Cambridge University Press, 1980.

———. *Development, Income Distribution, and Social Change in Rural Egypt, 1952–1970*. Cambridge: Cambridge University Press, 1975.

ʿAbd al-Fattah, Nabil. *al-Mushaf wa al-Sayf: Siraʿ al-Din wa al-Dawla fi Misr*. Cairo: Maktaba Madbuli, 1984.

Abd al-Khalek, Gouda, and Robert Tignor. *The Political Economy of Income Distribution in Egypt*. New York: Holmes and Meier, 1982.

ʿAbd al-Raziq, Husayn. *Misr fi 18 wa 19 Yanayir*. Beirut: Dar al-Kilma, 1979.

Abdalla, Ahmed. *The Student Movement and National Politics in Egypt, 1923–1973*. London: Zed Books, 1985.

Abdel-Malek, Anouar. *Egypt: Military Society*. New York: Random House, 1968.

Abrahamian, Ervand. *Iran between Two Revolutions*. Princeton: Princeton University Press, 1982.

Adams, Richard H., Jr. *Development and Social Change in Rural Egypt*. Syracuse: Syracuse University Press, 1986.

247

Ahmad, Muhammad Sid. *Mustaqbal al-Nizam al-Hizbi fi Misr.* Cairo: Dar al-Mustaqbal al-'Arabi, 1984.

Ajami, Fouad. "In the Pharaoh's Shadow: Religion and Authority in Egypt." In *Islam in the Political Process,* edited by James P. Piscatori. Cambridge: Cambridge University Press, 1983.

Akhavi, Shahrough. *Religion and Politics in Contemporary Iran.* Albany: State University of New York Press, 1980.

Alderman, Harold, and Joachim von Braun. *The Effects of the Egyptian Food Ration and Subsidy System on Income Distribution and Consumption.* Washington, D.C.: International Food Policy Research Institute, 1984.

Algar, Hamid. "The Oppositional Role of the Ulama in Twentieth-Century Iran." In *Scholars, Saints, and Sufis,* edited by Nikki R. Keddi. Berkeley: University of California Press, 1972.

'Ali, Sa'id Isma'il. *al-Azhar 'ala Masrah al-Siyasa al-Misriya.* Cairo: Dar al-Thaqafa, 1974.

'Amara, Muhammad. *al-Dawla al-Islamiya bayna al-'Ilmaniya wa al-Sulta al-Diniya.* Cairo: Dar al-Shuruq, 1987.

———. *al-Islam wa Huquq al-Insan.* Kuwait: 'Alam al-Ma'rifa, 1985.

Amin, Galal. *al-Tanmiya Am al-Taba'iya al-Iqtisadiya wa al-Thaqafiya?* Cairo: Matbu'at al-Qahira, 1983.

Amin, Mustafa. *Min 'Ali Amin ila Mustafa Amin.* Cairo: al-Maktab al-Misri al-Hadith, n.d.

Ansari, Hamied. *Egypt, the Stalled Society.* Albany: State University of New York Press, 1986.

'Awad, Louis. *Aqni'a al-Nasiriya al-Sab'a.* Beirut: Dar al-Qadaya, 1975.

Ayubi, Nazih. *Bureaucracy and Politics in Contemporary Egypt.* London: Ithaca Press, 1980.

Baer, Gabriel. *Egyptian Guilds in Modern Times.* Jerusalem: Israeli Oriental Society, 1964.

———. *Studies in the Social History of Modern Egypt.* Chicago: University of Chicago Press, 1969.

Baker, Raymond William. *Egypt's Uncertain Revolution under Nasser and Sadat.* Cambridge: Harvard University Press, 1978.

al-Banna', Jamal. *Azmat al-Niqabiya.* Cairo: al-Matba'a al-'Arabi al-Haditha, 1981.

———. *Buhuth fi al-Thaqafa al-'Ummaliya.* Cairo: Matba'a Hassan, 1977.

———. *al-Islam wa al-Haraka al-Niqabiya.* Cairo: Matba'at al-Nasir, 1981.

———. *al-Tanzim wa al-Bunyan al-Niqabi.* Cairo: Ruz al-Yusuf, 1976.

Barbour, K. M. *The Growth, Location, and Structure of Industry in Egypt.* New York: Praeger, 1972.

Beling, Willard A. *Pan-Arabism and Labor.* Cambridge: Harvard University Press, 1961.

Berger, Morroe. *Islam in Egypt Today: Social and Political Aspects of Popular Religion.* Cambridge: Cambridge University Press, 1970.

Berger, Suzanne D., ed. *Organizing Interests in Western Europe: Pluralism, Corporatism, and the Transformation of Politics.* Cambridge: Cambridge University Press, 1981.

Berque, Jacques. *Egypt: Imperialism and Revolution.* New York: Praeger, 1972.

Betts, Robert Brenton. *Christians in the Arab East.* Athens: Lycabettos Press, 1975.

Bianchi, Robert. *Interest Groups and Political Development in Turkey.* Princeton: Princeton University Press, 1984.

Binder, Leonard. *Islamic Liberalism: A Critique of Development Ideologies.* Chicago: University of Chicago Press, 1988.

————. *In a Moment of Enthusiasm: Political Power and the Second Stratum in Egypt.* Chicago: University of Chicago Press, 1978.

————. "The Proofs of Islam," In *Arabic and Islamic Studies in Honour of Hamilton A. R. Gibb,* edited by George Makdisi. Leiden: E. J. Brill, 1965.

al-Bishri, Tariq. *al-Haraka al-Siyasiya fi Misr, 1945–1952.* Cairo: al-Hay'a al-Misriya al-'Amma lil-Kuttab, 1972.

————. *al-Muslimun wa al-Iqbat fi Itar al-Jama'a al-Wataniya.* Beirut: Dar al-Wahda, 1982.

Cardoso, F. H., and Enzo Faletto. *Dependency and Development in Latin America.* Berkeley: University of California Press, 1979).

Collier, David, ed. *The New Authoritarianism in Latin America.* Princeton: Princeton University Press, 1979.

Cooper, Mark. *The Transformation of Egypt.* Baltimore: Johns Hopkins University Press, 1982.

Couland, Jacques. "Regards sur L'Histoire Syndicale et Ouvriere Egyptienne (1899–1952)." In *Mouvement Ouvrier, Communisme et Nationalismes dans le Monde Arabe,* edited by Rene Gallisot. Paris: Les Editions Ouvrieres, 1978.

Crecelius, Daniel. "Non-Ideological Responses of the Egyptian Ulama to Modernization." In *Scholars, Saints, and Sufis,* edited by Nikki R. Keddie. Berkeley: University of California Press, 1972.

Dassuqi, 'Ali al-Din Hilal. *al-Siyasa wa al-Hukm fi Misr: al-'Ahd al-Barlimani, 1923–1952.* Cairo: Matba'a Jami'at al-Qahira, 1977.

Dassuqi, 'Asam Ahmad. *Misr wa al-Harb al-'Alamiya al-Thaniya, 1939–1945.* Cairo: Ma'had al-Buhuth wa al-Dirasaat al-'Arabiya, 1976.

Davis, Eric. *Challenging Colonialism: Bank Misr and Egyptian Industrialization, 1920–1941.* Princeton: Princeton University Press, 1983.

Deeb, Marius. *Party Politics in Egypt: The Wafd and Its Rivals, 1919–1939.* London: Ithaca Press, 1979.

De Jong, F. *Turuq and Turuq-Linked Institutions in Nineteenth Century Egypt: A Historical Study in Organizational Dimensions of Islamic Mysticism.* Leiden: E. J. Brill, 1978.

Dessouki, Ali E. Hillal. "The Resurgence of Islamic Organizations in Egypt: An Interpretation," In *Islam and Power,* edited by Ali E. Hillal Dessouki and Alexander S. Cudsi. London: Croom Helm, 1981.

Dodge, Bayard. *al-Azhar: A Millennium of Muslim Learning.* Washington, D.C.: Middle East Institute, 1961.

Eccel, A. Chris. *Egypt, Islam and Social Change: al-Azhar in Conflict and Accommodation.* Berlin: Klaus Schwarz Verlag, 1984.

Evans, Peter. *Dependent Development: The Alliance of Multinational, State, and Local Capital in Brazil.* Princeton: Princeton University Press, 1979.

Farah, Nadia Ramsis. *Religious Strife in Egypt: Crisis and Ideological Conflict in the Seventies.* New York: Gordon and Breach, 1986.

al-Fiqi, Mustafa. *al-Iqbat fi al-Siyasa al-Misriya: Makram 'Ubayd wa Dawruhu fi al-Haraka al-Wataniya.* Cairo: Dar al-Shuruq, 1985.

al-Ghaytani, Jamal. *Mustafa Amin Yatadhakar.* Cairo: Maktabat Madbuli, 1983.

al-Ghurfa al-Tijariya lil-Qahira. *al-Tanzim al-Idari.* Cairo: 1969.

Gillespie, Kate. *The Tripartite Relationship: Government, Foreign Investors, and Local Investors during Egypt's Economic Opening.* New York: Praeger, 1984.

Gilsenan, Michael. *Recognizing Islam: Religion and Society in the Modern Arab World.* New York: Pantheon Books, 1983.

———. *Saint and Sufi in Modern Egypt: An Essay in the Sociology of Religion.* Oxford: Clarendon Press, 1973.

Goldberg, Ellis. *Tinker, Tailor, and Textile Worker: Class and Politics in Egypt, 1939–1952.* Berkeley: University of California Press, 1986.

Goldschmidt, Arthur, Jr. "The Egyptian Nationalist Party: 1892–1919." In *Political and Social Change in Modern Egypt,* edited by P. M. Holt. New York: Oxford University Press, 1968.

Graham, Robert. *Iran: The Illusion of Power.* London: Croom Helm, 1978.

Gran, Peter. *Islamic Roots of Capitalism: Egypt, 1760–1840.* Austin: University of Texas Press, 1979.

Green, Jerrold D. *Revolution in Iran: The Politics of Counter-Mobilization.* New York: Praeger, 1982.

Hana, Milad. *Na'm Iqbat, Lakin Misriyun.* Cairo: Maktabat Madbuli, 1980.

Handoussa, Heba Ahmad. "Conflicting Objectives in the Egyptian-American Aid Relationship." In *The Impact of Development Assistance in Egypt,* edited by Earl L. Sullivan. Cairo: American University in Cairo Press, 1984.

Harbison, Frederick, and Ibrahim Abdelkader Ibrahim. *Human Resources for Egyptian Enterprise.* New York: McGraw-Hill, 1958.

Harik, Iliya. *The Political Mobilization of Peasants.* Bloomington: Indiana University Press, 1974.

———, ed. *al-'Arab wa al-Nizam al-Iqtisadi al-Duwali al-Jadid.* Beirut: Dar al-Mashriq wa al-Maghrib, 1983.

al-Hay'a al-'Amma lil-'Istalamaat. *Misr wa Masirat al-Dimuqratiya: 'Alamaat 'ala al-Tariq.* Cairo: Matabi' al-Akhbar, 1980.

Heikal, Muhamed. *Autumn of Fury: The Assassination of Sadat.* New York: Random House, 1983.

Heyworth-Dunne, Gamal-Eddine. *Egypt: The Cooperative Movement.* Muslim World Series, no. 6. Cairo: Renaissance Bookshop, 1952.

Heyworth-Dunne, James. *Religious and Political Trends in Modern Egypt.* Washington, D.C.: The author, 1950.

Hilal, 'Ali al-Din, Mustafa Kamal Sayyid, and Akram Badr al-Din. *Tajribat al-Dimuqratiya fi Misr, 1970–1981.* Cairo: al-Markaz al-'Arabi lil-Buhuth wa al-Nashr, 1982.

Hinnebusch, Raymond. *Egyptian Politics under Sadat: The Post-Populist Development of an Authoritarian Modernizing State.* Cambridge: Cambridge University Press, 1985.

Hirst, David, and Irene Beeson. *Sadat.* London: Faber & Faber, 1981.

Holt, P. M., ed. *Political and Social Change in Modern Egypt.* London: Oxford University Press, 1968.

Husaini, Ishak Musa. *The Moslem Brethren: The Greatest of Modern Islamic Movements.* Beirut: Khayat, 1956.

Husayn, 'Adal. *al-Iqtisad al-Misri min al-Istiqlal ila al-Taba'iya, 1974–1979.* 2 vols. Beirut: Dar al-Wahda, 1981.

Hussein, Mahmoud. *Class Conflict in Egypt, 1945–1970.* New York: Monthly Review Press, 1973.

Ikram, Khalid. *Egypt: Economic Management in a Period of Transition.* Baltimore: Johns Hopkins University Press, 1980.

Imam, Samia Sa'id. *Man Yamluk Misr? Dirasa Tahliliya li Usul al-Ijtima'iya li Nukhbat al-Infitah al-Iqtisadi fi al-Mujtama' al-Misri, 1974–1980.* Cairo: Dar al-Mustaqbal al-'Arabi, 1986.

Istiphan, Isis. *Directory of Social Agencies.* Cairo: American University in Cairo Social Research Council, 1956.

al-Ittihad al-'Amm li Niqabaat 'Ummal Misr. *al-Ittihad al-'Amm li Niqabaat 'Ummal Misr fi 'Ishrina 'Aman.* Cairo: Matabi' al-Ahram al-Tijari, 1977.

———. *Injazaat al-Ittihad al-'Amm li-Niqabaat 'Ummal Misr: al-Dawra al-Sadisa, Julyu 1976–Nofambar 1979.* Cairo: Dar al-Sana, 1979.

Ittihad al-Sana'aat al-Misriya. *al-Kitab al-Dhahabi lil-Ittihad al-Sana'aat al-Misriya.* Cairo: Schindler, 1947.

———. *Tatawwur Ittihad al-Sana'aat al-Misriya fi Khamsin Sana, 1922–1972.* Cairo: 1972.

———. *al-Tatawwur al-Tarikhi lil-Ittihad al-Sana'aat al-Misriya.* Cairo: 1978.

'Izz al-Din, Amin. *Tarikh al-Tabaqa al-'Amila al-Misriya.* 3 vols. Cairo: Dar al-Katib al-'Arabi and Dar al-Sha'b, 1967, 1970, 1972.

al-Jam'iya al-Khairiya al-Islamiya. *al-Jam'iya al-Khairiya al-Islamiya.* Cairo: 1979.

al-Jam'iya al-Misriya lil-Iqtisad wa al-Siyasa wa al-Ihsa' wa al-Tashri'a. *Dur al-Dawla fi al-Nizam al-Iqtisadi al-Mukhtalat.* Cairo, 1983.

Jam'iyat Rijal al-A'mal al-Misriyin. *Al-Taqrir al-Sanawi wa Dalil al-A'da' lil-Jam'iyat Rijal al-A'mal al-Misriyin.* Cairo: Dar al-'Alam al-'Arabi, 1983.

Jankowski, James P. *Egypt's Young Rebels: "Young Egypt," 1933–1952*. Stanford: Hoover Institution, 1975.

Jansen, Johannes J. G. *The Neglected Duty: The Creed of Sadat's Assassins and the Islamic Resurgence in the Middle East*. New York: Macmillan, 1986.

Kepel, Gilles. *Muslim Extremism in Egypt: The Prophet and Pharaoh*. Berkeley: University of California Press, 1986.

Kerr, Malcolm H., and El-Sayed Yassin, eds. *Rich and Poor States in the Middle East: Egypt and the New Arab Order*. Boulder, Colo.: Westview Press, 1982.

Khalid, Muhammad. *al-Haraka al-Niqabiya bayna al-Madi wa al-Hadar*. Cairo: Akhbar al-Yawm, 1975.

Lehmbruch, Gerhard, and Philippe C. Schmitter, eds. *Patterns of Corporatist Policy-Making*. Beverly Hills: Sage, 1982.

Mabro, Robert. *The Egyptian Economy, 1952–1972*. Oxford: Clarendon Press, 1974.

Mabro, Robert, and Samir Radwan. *The Industrialization of Egypt, 1939–1973: Policy and Performance*. Oxford: Clarendon Press, 1976.

Markaz al-Dirasaat al-Siyasiya wa al-Istratijiya. *Intikhabaat Majlis al-Sha'b, 1984: Dirasa wa Tahlil*. Cairo: Matabi' al-Ahram al-Tijariya, 1986.

———. *al-Taqrir al-Istratijiya al-'Arabi, 1985*. Cairo: Matabi' al-Ahram al-Tijariya, 1986.

———. *al-Taqrir al-Istratijiya al-'Arabi, 1986*. Cairo: Matabi' al-Ahram al-Tijariya, 1987.

Mayfield, James. *Rural Politics in Nasser's Egypt*. Austin: University of Texas Press, 1971.

Mead, Donald C. *Growth and Structural Change in the Egyptian Economy*. Homewood, Ill.: R. D. Irwin, 1967.

Mitchell, Richard P. *The Society of the Muslim Brothers*. London: Oxford University Press, 1969.

Mohie el-Din, Amr. *Income Distribution and Basic Needs in Urban Egypt*. Cairo: American University in Cairo Press, 1982.

Moore, Clement Henry. *Images of Development: Egyptian Engineers In Search of Industry*. Cambridge: M.I.T. Press, 1980.

———. "Clientelistic Ideology and Political Change: Ficticious Networks in Egypt and Tunisia." In *Patrons and Clients in Mediterranean Societies*, edited by Ernest Gellner and John Waterbury. London: Gerald Duckworth, 1977.

Muna, Farid A. *The Arab Executive*. London: Macmillan, 1980.

Mursi, Fu'ad. *Hadha al-Infitah al-Iqtisadi*. Cairo: Dar al-Wahda, 1980.

Niqabat al-Sahafiyin. *Niqabat al-Sahafiyin fi Arba'in 'Aman, 1941–1981*. Cairo: Matabi' al-Ahram al-Tijari, 1981.

O'Brien, Patrick. *The Revolution in Egypt's Economic System: From Private Enterprise to Socialism, 1952–1965*. London: Oxford University Press, 1966.

O'Donnell, Guillermo. *Modernization and Bureaucratic-Authoritarianism: Stud-

ies in South American Politics. Berkeley: Institute of International Studies, University of California, 1973.

―――. "Corporatism and the Question of the State." In *Authoritarianism and Corporatism in Latin America,* edited by James Malloy. Pittsburgh: University of Pittsburgh Press, 1977.

Olson, Mancur. *The Rise and Decline of Nations: Economic Growth, Stagflation and Social Rigidities.* New Haven: Yale University Press, 1982.

Peroncel-Hugoz, Jean-Pierre. *Le Radeau de Mahomet.* Paris: Flammarion, 1984.

al-Qardawi, Yusuf. *al-Sahwa al-Islamiya bayna al-Juhud wa al-Tatarruf.* Cairo, 1984.

Qutb, Muhammad. *Jahiliya al-Qarn al-'Ashrin.* Cairo: Dar al-Shuruq, 1974.

Qutb, Sayyid. *al-Islam wa Mushkilaat al-Hadir.* Cairo: Dar al-Shuruq, n.d.

Radwan, Samir. *Agrarian Reform and Rural Poverty: Egypt, 1952–1975.* Geneva: I.L.O., 1977.

―――. *Capital Formation in Egyptian Industry and Agriculture: 1882–1967.* London: Ithaca Press, 1974.

Radwan, Samir, and Eddy Lee. *Agrarian Change in Egypt: An Anatomy of Rural Poverty.* London: Croom Helm, 1986.

Rajab, Mansur 'Ali. *al-Azhar bayna al-Madi wa al-Hadir.* Cairo: Matba'at al-Muqtataf wa al-Muqattam, 1946.

Ramadan, 'Abd al-'Azim. *Mudhakaraat al-Siyasiyin wa al-Zu'ama fi Misr, 1891–1981.* Beirut: Matba'a al-Watan al-'Arabi, 1984.

―――. *Al-Sira' al-Ijtima'i wa al-Siyasi fi Misr: 'Abd al-Nasir wa Azmat Maris.* Cairo: Ruz al-Yusuf, 1975.

―――. *Sira' al-Tabaqaat fi Misr, 1837–1952.* Beirut: al-Mu'assassa al-'Arabiya lil-Dirasaat wa al-Nashr, 1978.

―――. *Tatawar al-Haraka al-Wataniya fi Misr min Sanat 1937 ila Sanat 1948.* 2 vols. Beirut: Matba'a al-Watan al-'Arabi, n.d.

Ramadan, 'Abd al-'Azim, et al. *Misr wa al-Harb al-'Alamiya al-Thaniya.* Cairo: Matba'a al-Ahram al-Tijari, n.d.

Reid, Donald M. *Lawyers and Politics in the Arab World, 1880–1960.* Chicago: Bibliotheca Islamica, 1981.

Richards, Alan. *Egypt's Agricultural Development, 1800–1980.* Boulder, Colo.: Westview Press, 1982.

Rif'at, Kamal. *Nasiriyun? Na'm.* Cairo: al-Qahira lil-Thaqafa wa al-'Arabiya, 1976.

Rivlin, Paul. *The Dynamics of Economic Policymaking in Egypt.* New York: Praeger, 1985.

Rugh, Andrea, B. *Reveal and Conceal: Dress in Contemporary Egypt.* Syracuse: Syracuse University Press, 1986.

Saraj al-Din, Fu'ad. *Limadha al-Hizb al-Jadid?* Cairo: Dar al-Shuruq, 1977.

al-Sayed, Salah. *Workers' Participation in Management: The Egyptian Experience.* Cairo: American University in Cairo Press, 1978.

El Sayed, Mustapha K. "Professional Associations and National Integration in the Arab World with Special Reference to Lawyers' Associations." In *Beyond Coercion: The Durability of the Arab State,* edited by A. I. Dawisha and I. William Zartman. New York: Croom Helm, 1988.

Sayf al-Dawla, 'Ismat, *Hal Kana 'Abd al-Nasir Diktatura?* Beirut: Dar al-Masira, 1977.

Sayyid, Mustafa Kamal. *al-Mujtama' wa al-Siyasa fi Misr: Dawr Jama'aat al-Masalih fi al-Nizam al-Siyasi al-Misri, 1952–1981.* Cairo: Dar al-Mustaqbal al-'Arabi, 1983.

al-Sayyid-Marsot, Afaf Lutfi. *Egypt's Liberal Experiment, 1922–1936.* Berkeley: University of California Press, 1977.

Shabanah, Zaki Muhammad. *al-Iqtisad al-Ta'awuni al-Zira'i.* Alexandria: Dar al-Ma'arif, 1965.

al-Sha'rawi, Sheikh Muhammad Mutawali. *al-Insan: Musayyar aw Mukhayyar?* Cairo: Dar al-Muslim, n.d.

Schmitter, Philippe C. "Neo-Corporatism and the State." In *The Political Economy of Corporatism,* edited by Wyn Grant. London: Macmillan, 1986.

Shukri, Ghali. *Egypt: Portrait of a President, 1971–1981: The Counter-Revolution in Egypt, Sadat's Road to Jerusalem.* London: Zed Press, 1981.

Springborg, Robert. *Sayyid Mar'i: Family Power and Politics in Egypt.* Philadelphia: University of Pennsylvania Press, 1982.

———. "Patterns of Association in the Egyptian Political Elite." In *Political Elites in the Middle East,* edited by George Lenczowski. Washington, D.C.: American Enterprise Institute, 1975.

Stepan, Alfred. *State and Society: Peru in Comparative Perspective.* Princeton: Princeton University Press, 1978.

Streeck, Wolfgang, and Philippe C. Schmitter. "Community, Market, State—and Associations? The Prospective Contribution of Interest Governance to Social Order." In *Private Interest Government: Beyond Market and State,* edited by Woolfgang Streeck and Philippe C. Schmitter. Beverly Hills, Calif.: Sage, 1985.

Sullivan, Earl L. *Women in Egyptian Public Life.* Syracuse: Syracuse University Press, 1986.

Tignor, Robert. *Modernization and British Colonial Rule in Egypt, 1882–1914.* Princeton: Princeton University Press, 1966.

———. *State, Private Enterprise, and Economic Change in Egypt, 1918–1952.* Princeton: Princeton University Press, 1984.

al-Tilmisani, 'Umar. *Ayyam ma' al-Sadat.* Cairo: Dar al-I'tisam, 1984.

Trimingham, J. Spencer. *The Sufi Orders in Islam.* Oxford: Clarendon Press, 1971.

Turner, Frederick C., and José Enrique Miguens, eds. *Juan Peron and the Reshaping of Argentina.* Pittsburgh: University of Pittsburgh Press, 1983.

'Uthman, 'Uthman Ahmad. *Tajribaati.* Cairo: al-Maktab al-Misri al-Hadith, 1981.

'Uthman, Wa'il. *Asrar al-Haraka al-Tullabiya, 1968–1975.* Cairo: Matabi' Madkur, 1976.

United Arab Republic Information Administration. *The Charter.* Cairo, n.d.

Vatikiotis, P. J. *The Modern History of Egypt.* London: Weidenfeld & Nicolson, 1976.

———. *Nasser and His Generation.* New York: St. Martin's Press, 1978.

Wahida, Subhi. *Fi Usul al-Mas'ala al-Misriya.* Beirut: Maktabat Madbuli, n.d.

Wakin, Edward. *A Lonely Minority: The Modern Story of Egypt's Copts.* New York: Morrow, 1963.

Waterbury, John. *Egypt: Burdens of the Past, Options for the Future.* Bloomington: Indiana University Press, 1978.

———. *The Egypt of Nasser and Sadat: The Political Economy of Two Regimes.* Princeton: Princeton University Press, 1983.

———. "Egypt: The Wages of Dependency," In *The Middle East: Oil, Politics and Hope,* edited by L. Udovitch. Lexington, Mass.: Lexington Books, 1976.

———. *Hydropolitics of the Nile Valley.* Syracuse: Syracuse University Press, 1979.

Weinbaum, Marvin G. *Egypt and the Politics of U.S. Economic Aid.* Boulder, Colo.: Westview Press, 1986.

Wilmington, Martin W. *The Middle East Supply Center.* Albany: State University of New York Press, 1971.

Wizarat al-Shu'un al-Ijtima'iya. *Dalil al-Jam'iyaat fi al-Qahira.* Cairo, 1970.

———. *Taqwim al-Jam'iyaat wa al-Mu'assassaat al-Ijtima'iya.* Cairo, 1960.

———. *Taqwim al-Jam'iyaat wa al-Mu'assassaat al-Ijtima'iya.* Cairo, 1967.

Yusuf, Nahas Bak. *Juhud al-Niqabaat al-Zira'iya al-Misriya al-'Amma fi Thalathin 'Aman.* Cairo: Dar al-Nabil lil-Taba'aat, 1952.

Zabih, Sapehr. *Iran's Revolutionary Upheaval.* San Francisco: Alchemy Books, 1979.

al-Zawahiri, Fakr al-Din al-Ahmadi. *al-Siyasa wa al-Azhar.* Cairo: Maktabat al-Halabi, 1940.

Ziadeh, Farhat J. *Lawyers, the Rule of Law, and Liberalism in Modern Egypt.* Stanford: Stanford University Press, 1968.

Articles, Dissertations, and Unpublished Reports

Ahmad, Kamal Ibrahim. "The Impact of Nasser's Regime on Labor Relations in Egypt." Ph.D. diss., University of Michigan School of Business Administration, 1970.

Ansari, Hamied, "The Islamic Militants in Egyptian Politics." *International Journal of Middle East Studies* 16 (January 1984).

————. "Sectarian Conflict and the Political Expedience of Religion." *Middle East Journal* 38 (Summer 1984).

Beattie, Kirk James, "Egypt: The Struggle for Hegemony, 1952–1981." Ph.D. diss., Department of Political Science, University of Michigan, 1985.

Beinen, Joel. "Class Conflict and National Struggle: Labor and Politics in Egypt, 1936–1954." Ph.D. diss., Department of History, University of Michigan, 1982.

Bianchi, Robert. "Interest Group Politics in the Third World." *Third World Quarterly* 8 (April 1986).

————. "The Corporatization of the Egyptian Labor Movement." *Middle East Journal* 40 (Summer 1986).

Cantori, Louis Joseph. "The Organizational Basis of an Elite Political Party: The Egyptian Wafd." Ph.D. diss., Department of Political Science, University of Chicago, 1966.

Chang, Dal Joong. "Japanese Corporations and the Political Economy of South Korean-Japanese Relations, 1965–1979." Ph.D. diss., Department of Political Science, University of California, Berkeley, 1982.

Chattopadhyay, Rakaharai. "The Political Role of Labor Unions in India: An Interstate Study of Labor Unions in West Bengal, Karnataka, and Rajasthan." Ph.D. diss., Department of Political Science, University of Chicago, 1975.

Choi, Jang Jip. "Interest Conflict and Political Control in South Korea: A Study of the Labor Unions in Manufacturing Industries, 1961–1980." Ph.D. diss., Department of Political Science, University of Chicago, 1983.

Clark, Paul G. "Private Sector Industrial Development Strategy." Cairo: U.S. Agency for International Development, 1981.

Coronis, Susan Dee. "The Impact of Trade Unions in Egypt, 1952–1984." Ph.D. diss., Department of Political Science, Northwestern University, 1985.

Dajani, Nahed. "Corporatism in the Egyptian Context: A Profile of Business and Professional Politics in Egypt." Master's thesis, Department of Economics and Political Science, American University in Cairo, 1982.

Das Gupta, Jyotirindra. "A Season of Caesars: Emergency Regimes and Developmental Politics in Asia." *Asian Survey* 28 (April 1978).

Deeb, Marius. "Labour and Politics in Egypt, 1919–1939." *International Journal of Middle East Studies* 10 (May 1979).

————. "The Socioeconomic Role of the Local Foreign Minorities in Modern Egypt, 1805–1961." *International Journal of Middle East Studies* 9 (1978): 11–22.

al-Gaziri, Mushira. "The Role of the Bar Association in Egyptian Politics, 1952–1981." Master's thesis, Department of Economics and Political Science, American University in Cairo, 1982.

Gilsenan, Michael. "Some Factors in the Decline of the Sufi Orders in Modern Egypt." *Muslim World* 57 (1967): 11–18.

Gundi, Fadwa. "The Emerging Islamic Order: The Case of Egypt's Contemporary Islamic Movement." *Journal of Arab Affairs* 1 (April 1982).

Haddad, Yvonne Y. "Islamic 'Awakening' in Egypt." *Arab Studies Quarterly* 9 (Summer 1987): 234–59.

Harik, Iliya. "Continuity and Change in Local Development Policies in Egypt: From Nasser to Sadat." *International Journal of Middle East Studies* 16 (1984): 43–66.

———. "al-Sira´ al-Tabaqi wa al-Intaligansia al-´Arabi." Paper presented to the Arab Sociological Association conference on the Arab intelligensia, Cairo, March 1987.

Hasan, Nawal. "The Role of Voluntary Associations in Egypt." Cairo: Center for Egyptian Civilization Studies, 1981.

Homerin, Th. Emil. "Ibn Arabi in the People's Assembly: Religion, Press, and Politics in Sadat's Egypt." *Middle East Journal* 40 (Summer 1986).

Ibrahim, Saad Eddin. "Anatomy of Egypt's Militant Islamic Groups: Methodological Note and Preliminary Findings." *International Journal of Middle East Studies* 12 (December 1981).

Jones, Leroy, P. "Improving the Operational Efficiency of Public Industrial Enterprise in Egypt." Cairo: U.S. Agency for International Development, 1981.

Kassem, Layla. "The Opposition in Egypt: A Case Study of the Socialist Labor Party." Master's thesis, Department of Economics and Political Science, American University in Cairo, 1983.

Kazziha, Walid. "The Evolution of the Egyptian Political Elite, 1907–1921: A Case Study of the Role of the Large Landowners in Politics." Ph.D. diss., University of London, 1970.

Landau, Jacob M. "Prolegomena to the Study of Secret Societies in Modern Egypt." *Middle Eastern Studies* 1 (January 1965).

Lee, Chong-Sik. "South Korea 1979: Confrontation, Assassination, and Transition." *Asian Survey* 20 (January 1980).

Lim, Hyun-Chin. "Dependent Development in the World System: The Case of South Korea, 1963–1979." Ph.D. diss., Department of Sociology, Harvard University, 1982.

Lockman, Zackary. "Class and Nation: The Emergence of the Egyptian Workers' Movement." Ph.D. diss., Department of History, Harvard University, 1983.

Mansur, Muhammad, B. "The Development of the Industrial Relations System in Egypt." Ph.D. diss., Graduate School of Business Administration, New York University, 1972.

Moore, Clement Henry. "Authoritarian Politics in Unincorporated Society: The Case of Nasser's Egypt." *Comparative Politics* 6 (1974): 193–218.

———. "Professional Syndicates in Contemporary Egypt." *American Journal of Arabic Studies* 3 (1975): 60–82.

Morris-Jones, W. H. "Creeping but Uneasy Authoritarianism: India, 1975–1976." *Government and Opposition* 12 (Winter 1977).

Reid, Donald M. "The National Bar Association and Egyptian Politics, 1912–1954." *International Journal of African Historical Studies*. 7 (1974): 608–46.

———. "The Rise of the Professions and Professional Organizations in Modern Egypt." *Comparative Studies in Society and History* 16 (January 1974).

Rudolph, Lloyd I., and Susanne Hoeber Rudolph. "To the Brink and Back: Representation and the State in India." *Asian Survey* 18 (April 1978).

Saad el-Din, Omar. "The Role of State, Private, and Foreign Capital in Law 43 of 1974 Projects." Master's thesis, Department of Economics and Political Science, American University in Cairo, 1984.

Sa'id, 'Abd al-Mughni. "Safahaat Majhula min Tarikh al-Haraka al-Niqabiya." *al-'Amal* 236 (January 1983).

al-Sayyid-Marsot, Afaf Lutfi. "Religion or Opposition? Urban Protest Movements in Egypt." *International Journal of Middle East Studies* 16 (1984): 541–52.

Schmitter, Philippe C. "Still the Century of Corporatism?" *Review of Politics* 36 (January 1974).

Springborg, Robert, "Professional Syndicates in Egyptian Politics, 1952–1970." *International Journal of Middle East Studies* 9 (1978): 275–95.

———. "Sayed Bey Marei and Political Clientelism." *Comparative Political Studies* 12 (October 1979).

Tignor, Robert. "The Economic Activities of Foreigners in Egypt, 1920–1950: From Millet to Haute Bourgeoisie." *Comparative Studies in Society and History* 22 (July 1980).

Vermeulen, Bruce, and Gustav F. Papanek. "Labor Markets and Industry in Egypt: Analysis and Recommendations for Employment Oriented Growth." Cairo: U.S. Agency for International Development, 1982.

Waterbury, John. "The 'Soft State' and the Open Door." *Comparative Politics* 18 (October 1985).

Weinbaum, Marvin. "Egypt's Infitah and the Politics of U.S. Economic Assistance." *Middle Eastern Studies* 21 (April 1985).

———. "Politics and Development in Foreign Aid: U.S. Economic Assistance to Egypt, 1975–1982." *Middle East Journal* 37 (Autumn 1983).

Weinbaum, Marvin, and Rashid Naim. "Domestic and International Politics in Egypt's Economic Policy Reforms." *Journal of Arab Affairs* 3 (Fall 1984).

Periodicals

al-Ahali
al-Ahram
al-Ahram al-Iqtisadi
al-Ahrar
al-Akhbar

Akhbar al-Yawm
Akhir Sa'a
al-'Amal
al-Da'wa
al-Ghurfa al-Tijariya lil-Qahira
al-Hawadeth
al-Hilal
Huquq al-Insan
al-Jarida al-Rasmiya
al-Jumhuriya
al-Liwa' al-Islami
Mayo
al-Muhamma
al-Musawwar
al-Muslim
al-Mustaqbal
al-Nahar al-Duwali wa al-'Arabi
Oktobar
Sabah al-Khayr
al-Sha'b
al-Sharq al-Awsat
al-Tasawwuf al-Islami
al-'Ummal
al-Wafd
al-Waqa'i' al-Misriya
al-Watan al-'Arabi

Index